THE SMALLPOX WAR
IN NUXALK TERRITORY

THE SMALLPOX WAR
IN NUXALK TERRITORY

Tom Swanky, J.D.

Tom Swanky (signature)

DRAGON HEART
British Columbia

Published by Dragon Heart
British Columbia, Canada
2016

ISBN 978-1-365-41016-1

10 9 8 7 6 5 4 3 2

Visit our online store:
www.shawnswanky.com
sales@shawnswanky.com

Contents

Contents

Preface

This study extends the Nuxalk territory part of my work on the 1862/63 B.C. smallpox epidemics. These epidemics devastated the west coast indigenous population in one of the greatest tragedies of Canadian history. I first outlined the relevant Nuxalk experience in *The True Story of Canada's 'War' of Extermination on the Pacific.*

Since that book's publication, the Government of British Columbia has acknowledged for the official record that settlers under Governor James Douglas' watch spread smallpox intentionally in Tsilhqot'in territory during 1862.[1] Most of the settlers who committed those crimes took the disease there through Nuxalk territory.

This study's organizing thread is the origin of the constitutional relationship between Canada and the Nuxalk. The Nuxalk are one of the West Coast indigenous Peoples whose territory Canada occupies without a political treaty. This study explores the role of knowing disease distribution in the circumstances under which the indigenous sovereign authorities in Nuxalk territory were displaced by settler institutions. It covers the period from the British Crown's first indication of a desire to pursue some future political interest here in 1846, through the arrival of settlers beginning in Sept. 1860 and then to Jan. 2, 1865 when the British Crown effectively annexed this territory to British Columbia.

Of necessity, the point of departure for studying this political transition must be the record passed down by those who lived there. Since first invited to learn about the Chilcotin War as told in Tsilhqot'in communities, my preferred approach to oral records has been to listen for the generalized content and themes as shared within communities, especially in settings or on occasions where Elders or leaders take the initiative. Repeated hearings supply refinement. As it happens in this case, there is little mystery about the oral record's main elements or general themes for *Usqalits'txw*, the smallpox time.

An issue arising from this record affects the caution with which one must proceed. The indigenous authorities of that time believed that their

---

1. "Reconciliation with Tsilhqot'in Nation," Hon. Christy Clark. Third Session, 40th parliament, 2014. Hansard, Debates of the Legislative Assembly, Thursday Oct. 23, Vol. 16, Number 2, p. 4860. Or see: www.shawnswanky.com/articles/canadas-war/exoneration-of-the-chilcotin-chiefs/.

People became targets of a foreign policy that included a mass killing of innocents. If one allows that this may be true, then one must anticipate that the perpetrators also would have instituted a practice of denial and of erasing the victims from memory. Further, students in such cases will find many subtle opportunities and much social pressure to assist or indulge these evils. As a result, one must remain vigilant that one's own work does not come to serve the perpetrators or to begin new waves of distress for the targeted group.

Requiring of an official oral record the same precision, detail or elements as one can expect from a documentary record is already bad faith. To demand of this record more coherence, orderliness or share in the burden of proof than in similar such cases is also bad faith. Survivors or their descendants usually can be expected to have only the limited direct evidence of their local experience.[2] Meanwhile, the perpetrators and their subsequent apologists will have had custody of the bureaucratic record with a motive, opportunity and practice in manipulating it, continuing the original dehumanization through their authorized, accepted or "peer reviewed by others of the same ilk" histories of the relevant period. Succeeding beneficiaries of a mass killing also can be expected to have developed several socially acceptable means for protecting their self-regard. Good faith in retelling B.C. history demands a careful regard for these realities.

The purpose of an appropriate discipline is not to treat any oral record as closed to question, or as if in need of some concession from charity. This would be disrespectful. The principle that consistency is the cardinal virtue of truth must remain one's guide. The closest approximation to the truth, then, will be one where the evidence from each side is treated on its own terms and given the greatest weight where it tends to cross-verification. The best narrative will connect these points in a logical thread. For, when all is said and done, these records arise only from the same one set of events on the ground.

In this case, the documentary record not only supplements the original Nuxalk finding, the same finding follows independently from the evidence in that record alone. I concentrate on this second proof for three reasons: first, in our present circumstances, diverse indigenous leaders have supposed to me that an important need of their communities

---

2. For some issues in the comparative study of genocides see John-Paul Himka, "The Holodomor in the Ukrainian-Jewish Encounter Initiative." www.academia.edu/4999209/

is the spiritual healing that may come with shared historical narratives; second, the non-indigenous public most in need of understanding and help has been trained to see its own history in narratives that treat the documentary record as a form of gospel with little need for philology; third, while the effects of colonialism are comparatively well known, its beneficiaries seem all too willing to gloss over the process, a disservice to everyone.

No official agency of the Crown, which includes settler colonial universities, or of any First Nation provided funding or received any right of approval in this work. Nor has it been undertaken out of some desire for personal profit. I am cursed by a constant curiosity. My work has little motive but the joy of shining light in neglected caves. With some old illusions digested more in new lights perhaps we all can get on with choosing better paths and becoming more the elders for which future generations will hope.

I am grateful for the patience and trust of countless Elders, indigenous citizens and community leaders now over many years. Among the Nuxalk so many have gone out of their way to show me the kindness of family that I hesitate to try naming them, especially the South Bentinck contingent. This includes everyone down to the children who found me, after listing to Mr. Schooner's stories, admiring his public art at the Co-op and who then offered a bicycle tour and explanations of all the totems in town. The present Nuxalk generation seems to be giving the next a good start.

I owe a special debt of gratitude to Staltmc *Sixilaaxayc* Noel Pootlass of the Nuxalk Nation gathered at Q'umk'uts (Bella Coola.) Staltmc Pootlass heard my keynote address at the 150th anniversary of the martyrdom of the "Chilcotin Chiefs" and invited me to continue my study of smallpox in Nuxalk territory with another visit to some of the relevant spaces. At Q'umk'uts, Noel introduced my son, Shawn, and me to the *Smayusta* with a review of artifacts in the "House of *Smayusta.*" He also guided us through a petroglyph field connecting yesterday's "storytellers" with today and tomorrow, and it was our privilege to enjoy contact with the sacred waters.

Whatever assistance I may have had with this work, I am, alone, responsible for errors or its poverty of rhetorical skill. Please do other readers the kindness of bringing faults to my attention.

1

Introduction

During October 1864, a Nuxalk contingent from Bella Coola traveled for days and over 1000 km to honor the "Chilcotin Chiefs."[3] They would bear witness as the Colony of British Columbia martyred five Tsilhqot'in public servants, including the "Head War Chief."[4] The supervising official estimated the mostly indigenous crowd at 250.[5] It was one of the largest public executions in Canadian history.

The Nuxalk sent by Staltmc Pootlass may have covered the most ground to attend this mass hanging.[6] His people also had been more intimately involved than most in the preceding events. Indeed, in many respects, the trail leading to this scaffold began at Pootlass' village. Nevertheless, the prior events had moved all the surrounding indigenous Peoples to honor the Tsilhqot'in martyrs.[7]

This large showing on short notice was even more remarkable as the entire Pacific shelf indigenous population had just suffered a sudden, catastrophic decline. Seventy percent or more of all Nuxalk and Tsilhqot'in had died in one year or less.[8] Nor did local Dakelh swell the crowd's number artificially. Save one, they had died in just three

---

3. HBC Archives, B.5/a/a., *Fort Alexandria Journal*, Oct. 30, 1864 records their visit on the return. In the usual course, Bella Coola People did not visit Ft. Alexandria. This round trip is 1100 km by car today. On foot and gathering food, it may have taken a month in 1864.

4. The first 49 sections of *The True Story of Canada's 'War' of Extermination on the Pacific. Plus the Tsilhqot'in and Other First Nations Resistance* covers the background to the Chilcotin War and the hanging of the "Chilcotin Chiefs."

5. BCARS. Colonial Correspondence. GR-1372.104.1284. B01352. Peter O'Reilly to the Colonial Secretary, Oct. 28, 1864.

6. A Staltmc heads or speaks for an ancestral community. The duties and powers of a Staltmc may not coincide with those implied by the English word "chief" in its common political sense. The same is true of a Nits'il?in in Tsilhqot'in culture.

7. In the two weeks after the hanging, the *Fort Alexandria Journal* noted several large contingents gathering there for the apparent return of the Tsilhqot'in delegation.

8. The scale of destruction among the Nuxalk is documented here in later chapters.

months during the catastrophe.[9] Indeed, the supervising official placed the scaffold in a graveyard of these local victims, apparently to underline the Colony's implicit message.[10] However that may be, all the indigenous attendees had undertaken several days' travel to be there. This impressive tribute proves the importance of this event in the relationship between Canada's Pacific shelf founders and the long-established indigenous political entities.

When the Colony of B.C. martyred the "Chilcotin Chiefs" in 1864/65, it was still so new that its founding officials had not yet approached the Nuxalkmc or Tsilhqot'in for some constitutional right to act in those territories.[11] That is, like an unregistered corporation, the Colony had by-laws and officials but no license from the appropriate sovereign authorities to begin lawful operations. Without having extended the Colony's jurisdiction honorably or through the rule of law, the rogue officials conducting this execution were merely pretending to authority in an elaborate charade. In fact, they were using this unjust and unlawful execution to gain through intimidation and humiliation what they had refused to gain by civil means. It was a blood-soaked stain on the Crown's honor.

150 years later, in an historic unanimous statement on the floor of the Legislative Assembly, British Columbia acknowledged the wrong perpetrated by these dishonorable officials.[12] The Premier said the martyred Chiefs *were not criminals and they were not outlaws.* That is, they were not what these founding officials and what academics still serving colonial mythology at settler universities have painted them for 150 years.[13] They were public servants. In the actions for which Colonial officials condemned them, some had been defending the integrity of

9. The Dakelh experience at Quesnel is told in *Canada's 'War'* s. 114, pp. 402-410.

10. On the location of the hanging site see *Canada's 'War'* s. 2.

11. B.C. was created on paper in 1858. See Chapter 6 for a short description of its first official contact with the Tsilhqot'in, July 20, 1864. Chapter 14 contains an extended description of the first official contact from the Colony to the Nuxalk, July 3, 1862.

12. "Reconciliation with Tsilhqot'in Nation," Hon. Christy Clark. Third Session, 40th parliament, 2014. Hansard, Debates of the Legislative Assembly, Thursday Oct. 23, Vol. 16, Number 2, p. 4860. Or see: www.shawnswanky.com/articles/canadas-war/exoneration-of-the-chilcotin-chiefs/

13. See www.canadianmysteries.ca/sites/klatsassin/home/indexen.html for a University of Victoria website still describing the Tsilhqot'in as murderers and criminals throughout its self-generated material and seemingly putting the university in breach of the United Nations Declaration on the Rights of Indigenous Peoples, partly through colonial anti-indigenous-ism and partly through a tolerance for poor scholarship in regards to indigenous communities. This website is reviewed in Tom Swanky, *A Missing Genocide and The Demonization of its Heroes.* (www.shawnswanky.com: Dragon Heart, 2014.)

their homeland, like soldiers, and some had been administering the established law, like policemen.[14] That is, Colonial officials killed them for doing nothing more than properly performing common public duties on behalf of all the Tsilhqot'in.

Creating a dishonorable mythology casting these Tsilhqot'in heroes as outlaws or criminals was an integral part of the harm begun in 1864. This fraud goes to the core issue of which officials had the necessary legitimate authority to exercise sovereign power at the relevant time and place. Legitimate authority is power lent in trust by the resident citizenry to public servants acting in their name. Staltmc Pootlass and the Nits'il?in "Chilcotin Chiefs" had it. The rogue settler officials acting in the name of the Crown did not have it. Their dishonorable actions violated the sacred sense that usually accompanies lawful official behavior in normal settings. Without this aura of cleanliness while using force, officials wielding power and applying violence are no better than tyrannical brutes and bullies.

For the record, it should be noted that the Crown's own subjects with interests in Nuxalk or Tsilhqot'in territory were then hardly a dozen. Without exception these had been treated with justice under Tsilhqot'in or Nuxalk law, the legitimate law of the land.

Compounding their original harms, these rogue founders then sowed a pattern of dishonor. This pattern soon became embedded in the non-indigenous community's routine treatment of its hosts and has burdened that community's intellectual history with an insidious legacy of disrespect and denial ever since.

The Premier noted this legacy. She said the non-indigenous community had perpetrated "many wrongs" against the Tsilhqot'in. She acknowledged that this included intentionally spreading smallpox during 1862, eventually provoking the Chilcotin War in self-defense.

Yet these "many wrongs" often came through policies of general application and in teaching formulated at settler colonial universities. Such policies affected not only the Tsilhqot'in or Nuxalk but all other indigenous residents of the Pacific shelf as well. Many of these harms still need repair. In a tentative step toward reconciliation, on behalf of B.C.'s

---

14. Indigenous communities may have had less concrete job descriptions or more ad hoc responsibilities. Yet the functions were the same as described by these categories.

non-indigenous residents, the Premier expressed "profound sorrow" for these "many wrongs."

The B.C. government officially communicated its exoneration of the "Chilcotin Chiefs" to the Tsilhqot'in at Lhats'asʔin Memorial Day 2014, the 150th anniversary of this martyrdom. Named for the "Head War Chief" during the Chilcotin War, this is now an annual public holiday of remembrance for the Tsilhqot'in.

Meanwhile, the Government of Canada, which has an explicit constitutional duty to represent the non-indigenous community with honor, chose to snub this historic step by a studied absence. This gratuitous insult covered Canadians attending the ceremony with a blanket of shame. It hints at how difficult are the obstacles erected by denial, cultural arrogance or ignorance. It suggests how long is the journey from the heart of colonial darkness to the embrace of simple facts, let alone to milestones of restitution, reconciliation and justice.

The widespread indigenous attendance at the 2014 ceremony proves the contemporary importance of these events. Once again, a Nuxalk delegation travelled 1000 km to attend. Staltmc *Sixilaaxayc* Noel Pootlass led this delegation. He raised his hands to the "Chilcotin Chiefs" for their example on behalf of all those who value honor, the rule of law and resistance to the arbitrary use of power.

Martyrdom of the "Chilcotin Chiefs" by the Colony of British Columbia at Quesnel, October 26th, 1864 — Artwork by Shawn Swanky.

2

New Pathways of Respect and Healing

Since the best path became obscure, since Canada's Constitution Act of 1982 affirmed the prior rights of indigenous Peoples, since the 1996 Royal Commission on Aboriginal Peoples, since the 2015 Report of the Truth and Reconciliation Commission and since much Supreme Court parsing, spirits of good faith have begun rising from their resting places to resume the search for a New World. Only when less easily deceived explorers begin walking its trails will Canada escape the uncleanliness of its colonial legacy. What is to be done?

While expressing sorrow and delivering exoneration, the Premier also said that B.C.'s non-indigenous residents and their governments must begin steering toward a different future. Abandoning the prior course of ignorance guiding our unfinished founding, we must "begin a process of healing" and take "a new path of mutual respect."[15]

No willful change begins anywhere until those with power show a desire to retain their strength by searching out and mending their weaknesses or until circumstances bring the arrogant, complacent or decadent face to face with theirs. The first steps toward both goals identified by the Premier necessarily include developing a common narrative of the historical background. Until one knows how and why the previous course was set, one cannot be sure of any new tack.

Acknowledging the ongoing failure of educational institutions to prepare non-indigenous community leaders for setting this course or navigating such new paths, the Chief Justice of B.C.'s highest court as recently as 2012 has said that this imposes a special "duty to learn."[16] Since this systemic educational failure has its roots in the intellectual history and educational foundations prepared at settler universities still

15. "Reconciliation with Tsilhqot'in Nation." As cited above.
16. Lance Finch, "The Duty to Learn: Taking Account of Indigenous Legal Orders in Practice." (Paper presented at the Continuing Legal Education of B.C. Indigenous Legal Orders and the Common Law Conference, Vancouver, Nov. 15, 2012.)

today, the duty he identified necessarily extends beyond the judicial system to all those with position or authority.

This duty would seem to have two aspects: first, to acquire the information necessary to wield the non-indigenous community's power with wisdom, honor and justice where power cannot be restored in a timely way or by more effective means; and, second, a duty to unlearn the unhelpful or harmful mythologies still being taught in the authorized or "peer reviewed by others of the same ilk" narratives originated by settler colonial academics.

We are "all here to stay."[17] So Canada's Supreme Court has stated an immutable political reality. This is a diplomatic reminder that the strong do what they can while the weak do as they must.

Nurturing a more decorous community on the Pacific shelf, then, also involves recognizing several other equally immutable facts:

1) the prior political occupation here by many long-established, legitimate sovereign social entities, each with its own constitution;

2) that few of those still surviving entities have relinquished any of their original sovereign rights by law, treaty or free abandonment;

3) that, in the indigenous narrative of B.C.'s constitutional history, Elders and community leaders teach, therefore, that they retain most of their original *de jure* (legitimately acquired) sovereign features, losing only substantial *de facto* (effective) power;

4) that, again as Elders commonly teach it, the non-indigenous community originally displaced this *de facto* power through an extremely violent and dishonorable insurrection against the *de jure* authorities and then began a paramilitary occupation under which these authorities have been, and still are, routinely humiliated; and,

5) Canada's own constitution nevertheless confirms that these surviving social entities retain all their original rights until shared, given up, delegated or otherwise vacated by the rule of law.

Regardless, Canada has, can and will continue to mobilize its *de facto* power against the *de jure* authority of surviving indigenous social entities, with great violence if necessary, as far as it alone sees fit and as a public indoctrinated with colonial mythology will allow.

All this leaves Canada a flawed sovereign force. Its agents can find themselves employing force or threatening official violence

---

17. *Delgamuukw v. British Columbia*, [1997] 3 SCR 1010, p. 186.

against indigenous communities in situations where the Crown has an insufficient *de jure* authority and, therefore, an insufficient color of moral right for these actions. Down that road there is only injustice, perceptions of injustice, a necessity of self-deception, dishonor and attempts to co-opt innocents through fraud. A circumstance of flawed *de jure* authority is something more common to places with poor leadership, unlawful tyrannies, opportunistic occupations and wars of aggression than it is to places one would wish for anyone's children.

A sure signpost along any path to new destinations will be one with respect for indigenous narratives of B.C.'s history. Standing out from the list above as most in need of attention is the Elders' teaching concerning the degradation of their original *de facto* power. For any *de jure* authority without the *de facto* power to defend territory, cultivate order and see justice done is also a flawed institution.

As the Elders teach B.C.'s constitutional history, this degradation and the subversion of the original *de jure* authorities began through a settlers' insurrection against indigenous rule. As the broad teaching goes, it was only the extreme violence of this insurrection during 1862 that enabled non-indigenous authorities to displace the *de jure* authorities at their leisure and without treaties.

Studying the Nuxalk experience in this regard has a special advantage. The Nuxalk and their Ancestors were intimately involved in several events preceding the wrongful execution of the "Chilcotin Chiefs." Analyzing the initial degradation of *de facto* power in Nuxalk territory, then, can provide a bridge. On the near side of the Nuxalk experience is the violent displacement of the Tsilhqot'in authorities, one featuring the now-admitted weaponization of disease. On the other side is an opening to some understanding of the sudden, catastrophic political experience shared by most other Pacific shelf Peoples.

3

The Right of Sovereignty in Nuxalk Territory

From a rule of law perspective, a constitution giving form to an established governing system within any political territory remains in effect until some amendment, repeal or similar constitutional event intervenes.[18] The logical place to begin, then, is with the Ancestral constitution. This is where the original *de jure* authority and the law of the land had its root before any degradation of its *de facto* power.

I
Nuxalk claim to sovereign authority.

The Ancestors established a lawful right to exercise sovereign power within their territory through a sacred sense originating so long ago that the circumstances are unimportant. No serious person doubts that a legitimate sovereign authority came into being and was maintained continuously among the Ancestors since long before non-indigenous[19] visitors founded distant Canada in 1604, 1763, 1791, 1840, 1867, 1871, 1931 or 1982. It is enough to say that, as far as can be known, the citizens of this territory commonly acknowledged the same Ancestral authority.[20] And their neighbors respected the claim.

---

18. Sometimes expressed in international law as the "presumption of continuity."

19. This term includes both settlers (those who intend to impose a wholly new culture without consent from their hosts) and non-settlers or immigrants. Other terms to describe the succeeding social entity, such as European, White and so on, each have limitations. British Columbia's non-indigenous community has always had a large Asian component that does not identify with "European" or "white" and yet who were settlers. The non-indigenous community in most indigenous territories in British Columbia also includes people who may be indigenous elsewhere. A Mohawk living in a Coast Salish territory is not indigenous to Haida Gwaii. He or she may or may not be assimilated to settler culture. Indigenous communities are host authorities living in their homelands, with the values and perspectives formed by those surroundings. Everyone else is a non-indigenous guest sharing similar guest duties vis-à-vis the indigenous host communities.

20. More or less, in the form of commonly accepted origin stories through which each community derived its own essential autonomy. For a commonly cited source acknowledged at Bella Coola, see Thomas McIlwraith, *The Bella Coola Indians*. (Toronto: University of Toronto Press, 1948) Vol. 1, pp. 16-18.

The Ancestors enjoyed full *de jure* authority. That is, they had the same choice of rights, privileges, duties and law-making powers as any other sovereign social entity. This includes acceptance by the citizens who lent their public authority for a constitution, a system of governance, a set of rules or practices, enforcement, administering violence on the public's behalf, allocating resources, making treaties, defending territory with violence, protecting a preferred way of being and so on as this agenda may be adapted by any culture. That the result may not have resembled forms familiar to those from other cultures is neither here nor there. The locus of sovereign authority in Nuxalk territory is as conveyed through the *Smayusta,* and as those traditional ways might be amended or extended by leading figures recognized in the eyes of the citizen majority as so authorized.[21]

At the pertinent threshold in time as it emerges from a study of events, before Jan. 2, 1865, the Ancestral authority's official hands unquestionably held both *de jure* sovereign authority and legitimate *de facto* control. The law of the land was given shape by the table of values, rights, privileges and duties derived from the *Smayusta.*

II
Canadian sovereignty and the honor of the Crown.

What about Canada's current claim to sovereign authority in Nuxalk territory? For, where the Ancestral authorities once ruled with undisputed legitimacy, Canada now wields *de facto* sovereign power.

Whatever the case elsewhere, in founding Canada's claim to sovereign authority on the Pacific shelf, its Supreme Court commonly rejects the cultural narcissism of supposed discovery; the intolerance of Christian privilege; the racist doctrine of European exceptionalism; the false, and in the Nuxalk context absurd, doctrine of *Terra Nullius* (territory belonging to no collection of sovereign citizens); and the malicious doctrine that *de facto* power alone can create legitimacy.

Instead, the Court roots Canada's claim in a more general theory. It holds that, in their relations with indigenous communities, non-indigenous officials can be held to the standard of a disinterested process

---

21. See "Our Sovereignty" www.nuxalk.net/html/sovereignty.htm. "Smayusta" means something like the wisdom of the ancestors as conveyed in the traditional teachings.

and to results upholding the "Honor of the Crown."[22] This may not be the only theory now pertinent to this relationship but it is the only one that can be relevant to the earliest interactions.

In Canada, "The Crown" is no more than a convenient fiction. It is a mythological sacred institution where public authority delegated by the citizenry is unified for sovereign actions.

Honor, by its nature, requires that *de facto* control be exercised in the interest of what is right, lawful or *de jure* even when, indeed especially when, to do so would disadvantage the perceived interests of those with power or of one's own constituency. Canadian officials, then, are supposed as being able to act against the perceived interest of a non-indigenous public if necessary, which their office ordinarily requires them to advance, where that interest may conflict with, say, Nuxalk interest as defined by the Nuxalk citizenry or its authorities.

While this may seem demanding, it requires little more than some small appreciation of honor's civic value. No spiritually healthy person takes by dishonorable means what he or she can gain with honor and justice. A bear has the power to kill almost anything in its path but only one infected by some pathological weakness does more harm than necessary.

Those accustomed to the effective use of great power keep to the highest standard of honor. The privilege of power comes with a natural duty of care in its use for honor is also in the self-interest of the holders as a means of preserving their power.

Nevertheless, given our seemingly infinite human capacity for self-deception and our usual tendency to benefit our friends, one can forgive the indigenous public for its skepticism. The indigenous/non-indigenous relationship in Canada seems sometimes a case of the fox guarding a chicken house, sometimes of wolves in sheep's clothing and sometimes of a thief sitting in judgment on his or her own case.

Yet, what is the judicial system to do? Canadian officials trying to force present realities to match the preferred mythologies of its settler-colonial intellectual history consistently have failed to notice the universal principle that justice requires neutral institutions.

Would Canadians accept the justice of a circumstance in which all-American tribunals within an all-American system manned by

---

22. For example, see, *Haida Nation v. British Columbia*, [2004] 3 SCR 511, p. 16 -19.

all-American officials trained at American colleges where they chant "U.S.A! U.S.A! U.S.A!" resolved all of Canada's disputes with the United States? It seems hypocritical and against the rules of natural justice, then, to force indigenous sovereign entities always into Canadian courts populated only by people trained at settler-colonial institutions. Yet here we are.

How does the "Honor of the Crown" apply then? It implies that Canada can claim *de jure* sovereign authority to act in indigenous territories to the extent that its *de facto* power is deployed honorably.

As a corollary, the Supreme Court holds that Canada's historical circumstances as an occupying power also impose a duty to facilitate reconciliation with non-indigenous communities. Underlining this duty, the Chief Justice said, *(T)he Crown's duty of honorable dealing toward aboriginal peoples...arises from the Crown's assertion of sovereignty over an Aboriginal people and [its] de facto control of land and resources that were formerly in the control of that people.*[23]

The root of this legal theory is in an ordinary principle of equity as understood by English common law judges. These judges could overturn grossly unfair results as being offensive to the public good, even if these might have met the strict letter of written law.

Experience also teaches that little undermines official legitimacy faster than behavior that ordinary citizens perceive as an unprincipled use of power or as the abuse of authority in its administration. It will always harm the public good for those with disproportionate power or knowledge to rely on this alone for self-enrichment in dealings with those who have less of this good fortune or privilege, but over whose interests the powerful might have *de facto* control.

Protecting the "Honor of the Crown," then, is neither charity nor a duty owed especially to benefit indigenous Peoples. It is one owed to Canada's citizens. It is always in the general public interest to have a society in which people shame officials who abuse authority and a culture in which those with power do not tolerate its unprincipled use by their equals. This standard benefits, first of all, Canada's public self-interest and the self-interest of its citizens.

Canada holds disproportionate power over the interests, rights, assets and lives of indigenous citizens. Yet these citizens owe their first

---

23. *Haida Nation v. British Columbia (Minister of Forests)*, [2004] 3 S.C.R. 511, p. 32.

or primary political obligation to other social entities, entities where Canada may be seen as an occupying foreign power. As a point of departure in these circumstances, the Court holds that honor requires officials, as a first benchmark, to act as if the Crown has a trustee-like fiduciary duty to the beneficiaries of indigenous interests and rights, regardless of their disposition toward Canada.

This is no more than what would be owed to the citizens of, say, Korea if Canada suddenly found itself in control of Korea's public accounts. Justice actually requires that the standard of honor applied should be that of the culture at risk, again entailing a duty to learn.

It goes without saying that, in this example, control should be returned to Korea's citizens as soon as suitable means emerge. Canadians would be embarrassed if their representatives retained control of Korea's public accounts longer than necessary or took advantage of the occasion for Canada's unjust enrichment.

Good faith holds the same with Canada's control of indigenous lives. Since indigenous interests are no more Canadian in origin than those of Korea, neither the officials nor the courts can discover the appropriate standards of honor or the interests needing protection by referring to Canadian cultural values alone, as they might for ordinary fiduciary duties.

The protected interests can be discovered only from consulting the relevant local values: that is, by discharging the duty to learn. In this way, standards of official performance arising under the "Honor of the Crown" doctrine deliver only basic justice to indigenous citizens. No more, and no less, than is owed to everyone.

III
Nuxalk relations with Canada: origins.

At what threshold in time, then, did the duty imposed on officials to uphold the "Honor of the Crown" begin in Nuxalk territory?

Recent Supreme Court decisions place the origin of Canada's interest in Nuxalk territory at the Oregon Treaty of June 15, 1846.[24] Yet the Ancestors were not a party to this Treaty. It was an agreement

---

24. Like the rest of the Pacific shelf. See *Tsilhqot'in Nation v. British Columbia*, [2014] 2 SCR 257 at p. 60. And *Delgamuukw v. British Columbia* [1997] 3 SCR 1010, p. 145. The issue there was agreed between those litigants rather than argued. It is difficult to see how that can affect, say, Nuxalk rights. Some issues around this "assertion" are canvassed briefly in Michael Doherty, "Recent Developments in Aboriginal Rights and

between the United States and Canada's stepparent, the British Empire. The Ancestors did not have notice or consent to its terms. Since agreements between two parties cannot diminish the rights of a third, the Ancestors cannot have lost any of their own long-standing sovereign rights or radical title to land through this event. How, then, did it come to affect the status of sovereignty in Nuxalk territory?

The Treaty's preamble refers to some uncertainty "respecting the sovereignty and government of the territory." By "territory" here the Treaty means everything north of California and south of Russian America, now mostly Alaska. Yet no one supposes there was any uncertainty about the status of sovereignty in the Nuxalk Ancestors' territory. So this uncertainty can only refer to the signatories feeling a need to resolve some political issues between themselves.

Namely: 1) which of them might govern relations among the small but growing non-indigenous population of the Pacific shelf, so far as those relations might be insufficiently covered by the rules of their host sovereign authorities; and 2) which of them, before the other, might begin approaching the relevant indigenous authorities for closer relationships. It would be a strange world if mere indications of interest in pursuing a relationship could affect a third party's rights before any approach is made to that party.

Article III contemplates "future appropriation of territory" within the agreement's boundaries. Here the signatories are simply clarifying who between them would have the privilege of approaching the many indigenous occupiers for closer associations and access to resources.

In the process, this implicitly acknowledges the underlying "unappropriated" nature of the territory as a quality only between each other. Two parties acknowledging their lack of any claim to a thing vis-a-vis each other cannot affect the rights of a third party, the one actually in legal possession of the thing for which the first two hope to bargain. Legal and logical minds the world over would laugh.

The Oregon Treaty, then, did not give Great Britain, and in its wake Canada, any increment of legitimate sovereign right to rule, or any color of sovereign claim to manage resources, anywhere on the Pacific shelf. The British Crown earned nothing here but an exclusive

---

Title cases," Aboriginal Law Conference 2009, paper 3.1 at 3.1.5/6. And see Vickers J. in *Tsilhqot'in Nation v. British Columbia*, 2007 BCSC 1700, p. 595 and 596.

right to approach the relevant indigenous Peoples vis-a-vis the United States. Interpreting this agreement otherwise would see in it an implicit declaration of an unjust war of aggression. This would be inconsistent with the Supreme Court finding here the origins of a just, legal and honorable foundation for Canada, one that might include the Nuxalk as free, willing and grateful partners.

Notice that the origin of Great Britain's opportunity to make the Oregon Treaty did not come about through "discovery" or the grace of gods. It came about through the disproportionate political power that always accompanies great technical ability when combined with the resources and willingness to organize and use great violence. The British Empire always could have crushed Nuxalk or Tsilhqot'in authorities at will, if the true conservators of that power had deemed it wise or necessary. The true conservators, however, always knew that it was never either of these things and that the disciplined use of power is one of the fundamental secrets to its preservation: hence the doctrine of the "Honor of the Crown" as always more a matter of self-respect, self-interest and self-preservation than protection of the weak.

The mere fact or bare existence of great political power by itself cannot produce any constitutional change for citizens who have not authorized its exercise. Canada's constitution has not changed simply by virtue of China's recent rise as a world power. China now could crush us at will. Like the British of that day, it also has an interest in our resources. For that matter, it easily could have some undisclosed arrangement already, just like the Oregon Treaty, with Russia or the United States. Most probably, one supposes, the Supreme Court of Canada would not accept any such *ex parte* treaty, like the Oregon Treaty, as changing Canada's constitution today.

In sum, the Oregon Treaty did not produce any constitutional change in the Ancestors' territory. It would be a strange and chaotic world if two sovereigns agreeing with each other could be taken as having made a legitimate assertion of sovereignty over a third People. Any such theory of law could not have any more *de jure* validity in a congress of Peoples than, say, if some Ayatollah attempted to divide the whole world in two through a unilateral religious decree.

By the ordinary operation of the rule of law, then, the Ancestors retained all their usual *de jure* and *de facto* rights of sovereignty as much the day after the signing of the Oregon Treaty as they did the day before. From a constitutional perspective, nothing had changed.

IV
From "asserting an interest" to "asserting control."

The Oregon Treaty, however, did reveal the Crown's interest in approaching the various indigenous citizen majorities in the relevant geographic area for some association or constitutional innovation. This included the Nuxalk Ancestors.

The mere assertion of an interest in pursuing a relationship does not give anyone rights to control or actual power over someone. An "assertion of sovereignty" requires more. An authority needs to have a physical presence and to take responsibility for: 1) defending a citizenry's control of its territory or resources; 2) delivering the benefits of having a sovereign power; and 3) administering the legal relations governing the behavior of people within a territory. And it must stand ready to prevail through the application of official violence if necessary. It is a factual certainty that the Crown made no such efforts in Nuxalk territory before the time covered here.

Yet somehow between the Oregon Treaty in 1846 and the Chief Justice's statement of current Canadian law as given above, the Crown has gone from revealing an interest in approaching indigenous sovereign powers to "asserting sovereignty over Aboriginal people" vis-a-vis the Pacific shelf Peoples themselves without treaties. Not having made the good faith approaches contemplated by the Oregon Treaty, or having its unimaginative offers rejected, Canada nevertheless "asserts sovereignty" as an ongoing colonial power on the Pacific shelf. It governs here, including in Nuxalk territory, as a power willing to prevail by organized violence when and where it sees fit, and against the legacy *de jure* authorities or their citizenry at will.

In 1995, the assembled Staltmc reaffirmed that, *Our nation is not interested in treaties...[that concede] our Nuxalk Nation hereditary rights and title.*[25] That is, the Nuxalk citizenry is not interested in an association where it must abandon its underlying sovereign rights.

25. Nuxalk Nation Government, "Nuxalk Nation Position," House of *Smayusta*, Bella Coola, B.C. Sept. 10, 1995, p. 2.

In cases such as Nuxalk territory, where Canada governs without treaties, the Supreme Court implicitly acknowledges that, on the ground, its circumstances remain those of a paramilitary occupation with colonial roots. It is because of the resentment, dysfunction, hurt and violent resistance often generated by such occupations that the Court finds the national self-interest in a duty of reconciliation.

However all that may be, officials have been seized with this legal duty of honor toward the Nuxalk and their Ancestors since June 15, 1846, when the Crown first asserted an active interest in pursuing relations by signing the Oregon Treaty. From that day, this required officials to protect the Crown's honor in approaches and relations with the Ancestors, and in overseeing interactions between the Ancestors and any future non-indigenous guests where the territorial indigenous *de facto* power may have been an insufficient control.

This is not something seen only in retrospect or out of time. It merely reflects the Crown's North American policy as set out in the Royal Proclamation of 1763. Where applicable to Canada, this policy was already wound into the law governing non-indigenous behavior on the Pacific shelf before 1846. The Canada Jurisdiction Act of 1803 extended the laws of Lower Canada to British subjects in the west. When the Crown consolidated the Northwest Company and the Hudson's Bay Company (H.B.C.) in 1821, it substituted the laws of Upper Canada for the west. But this was all just one garment vis-a-vis indigenous relations.

4

The Colony of British Columbia

The next possible moment of constitutional change in the Nuxalk Ancestors' territory came with Great Britain's creation of the Colony of British Columbia in distant London on Aug. 2, 1858.

Notice that British Columbia did not come into being as a sacred expression of moral will by the 100,000 citizens or so then resident within its prospective boundaries. It came about instead through the fretting of pallid clerks in the political back rooms of a foreign and strange culture. These clerks had only a narrow mandate to protect some comparatively minor commercial interests and to shelter a few British subjects from American exceptionalism. Nothing more. They had no legal or moral mandate for broad constitutional change rooted in some expression of communal political will by the indigenous citizen majorities then resident on the grounds in question.

The first agents of the Crown appointed to represent this prospective new political entity then publicly announced themselves Nov. 19, 1858. They did not give any notice to the Ancestors. They made this announcement as guests in yet another foreign territory two or three weeks' travel away among a Hul'qumi'num speaking People hosting some European settlements on the lower Fraser River.

To put this in perspective, imagine if today China proposed a new regime for Manitoba and then introduced its representatives with a ceremony before some Chinese businessmen living in Quebec. Such an absurd event rightly would be given short shrift everywhere, except perhaps in some Chinese propaganda. It would have been only right and lawful for every indigenous legal authority to disregard B.C.'s creation in 1858 in much the same way as today every Canadian authority would disregard a similar event.

When eventually hearing "the Colony" referenced, the Ancestors may have imagined the two existing British Pacific Colonies: Queen

Charlotte Islands or Vancouver Island. Neither touched their territory. Even when they discovered otherwise, the Ancestors would have had little reason to believe anything but that this new entity would operate along the lower Fraser River where its officials remained as guests and where a few British subjects had some financial interests. Indeed, Lord Lytton, British Columbia's formal colonial founder was still referring to British Columbia as the "Fraser River settlements" in late 1861.[26] In any case, no British subject had economic interests of any kind within the Ancestors' territory as of 1858. None. British subjects only visited occasionally for trade or tourism. As, today, Canadians might visit France or Algeria without making claims of a sovereign right to interfere in the constitutions of those territories.

When Parliament created British Columbia, it could empower the new Colony with no more color of sovereign right or share of title to resources than the Crown itself might already have acquired. This is simple logic. You cannot give what you do not have. It is a factual certainty that the Crown had acquired no sovereign right of any kind from the Ancestral authority under the law of the land before 1858. And, therefore, neither did the Colony have any such rights.

So, at first, the Colony of B.C. had only the two sovereign rights noted: an exclusive right vis-a-vis the United States to make laws governing the small non-indigenous community north of the 49th parallel, so far as these did not diminish the rights and privileges of the resident indigenous citizens as overseen by their own sovereign authorities; and an exclusive right vis-a-vis the United States to approach the relevant indigenous authorities for new arrangements or associations and access to resources. Protecting the "Honor of the Crown," where the rule of law is a bare minimum standard, colonial officials had a legal obligation to begin their work from there.

Although B.C.'s prospective boundaries may have included the Ancestors' territory, these were no more than mere lines on a map. When drawn, these lines lacked the necessary force of law that can be gained only through the appropriate sovereign authority's approval. Without this, these lines had nothing but prospective value. Officials in Alberta, for example, might create maps with pipelines running through

---

26. "The British North America Question," *Victoria Daily Press,* Dec. 12, 1861, p. 3.

Montana but those lines have no legal value or import on the ground until the appropriate U.S. government approves them.

B.C.'s projected boundaries indicated only where it was that the Crown had authorized its officials to approach indigenous authorities on its behalf. As it happened, no Colonial representative visited the Ancestors before July 3, 1862. It is impossible for any constitutional innovation to have taken place, or for these maps to have gained any legal significance, before then, if then: for they had not been ratified within the established system of governance. This is ordinary legal logic. Whatever geography the Colony of B. C. might have included at its inception in 1858, the Ancestors' territory cannot have been part of it. Colonial rules did not govern any legal relations among the citizenry, nor did the Colony post any magistrates here before 1865.

Two clauses in B.C.s founding document bear on this topic.[27] First, its preamble references this as a place where British subjects have *resorted to and settled on certain wild and unoccupied territories...for mining and other purposes*. Yet, as of 1858, no British subject had "resorted to" or "settled on" the Ancestors' territory for mining or any other purpose. None. So even the document's framing explicitly excluded this territory at the outset.

To suppose that this description might have been intended to include the Ancestors' territory because of some activity by British interests in other foreign territories, or because of some other maps showing a foreign business entity's sales districts (the Hudson's Bay Company,) is a disingenuous adventure in fantasy. Logical and legal minds would dismiss the notion instantly if applied to European territories. British laws applying in Spain on account of Gibraltar are not held to change the constitution of Portugal, even though British companies also have maps of their commercial districts in Portugal.

Nor was any square centimeter of the Ancestors' territory "wild" or "unoccupied" in any legal sense. "Wild" is a parochial European conceit with little parallel in Pacific shelf ontologies. It is doubtful that the term covers anything other than things not under the care of particular individuals. Yet these "wild" things, whether ground, field, forest, water or sky, or the things on and in them, are still "owned" in common by the community. There may have been things like this among the Ancestors

---

27. The Act of Parliament can be quickly accessed now online, for example, at https://en.wikisource.org/wiki/Proclamation_of_the_Colony_of_British_Columbia.

but the "Honor of the Crown" required that these remain as defined by indigenous practice and not by English custom. In any case, Norway cannot give itself any right to govern parts of Canada merely because of how Norwegian law might define "wild."

As for "unoccupied," it remains a curious mystery of Canadian mythology why its legal theorists can suppose that, say, the highest point of land touched by *Ista*[28] as she descended to the Ancestors' territory should be taken as unoccupied by the Ancestors in 1858 for the lack of permanent camps while, nevertheless, this very same land should be considered as fully occupied by Canada today despite this same lack. The rule of law, first of all, implies consistency.

More ominously, one might interpret "wild" to mean inhabited only by indigenous residents: people who the Colonial founders in their ignorance or cultural arrogance considered more like nuisance animals; or as an inferior class lacking the capability for a properly cultivated civility; or as primitive beings lacking the provident good fortune of superior cross-breeding.[29]

By "unoccupied," the document might be thought perhaps to describe territory unclaimed or ungoverned by any other Christian or Euro-cultural sovereign. This interpretation sometimes may have seemed the more likely as the Governor had an explicit mandate for crusade-like policies to spread Christianity.

If these interpretations might be supposed as reflecting the document's true implication, then they would clothe an implicit declaration of an unjust war of aggression against the existing sovereign social entities and their citizens. Such actions are repugnant to political civility and offensive to honor. People of good faith universally condemn them. Any attempt to found legitimacy for Canada there would be so torturous as to be worthy only of scorn. Honor may rise over dishonor but it does not rest on it.

The Ancestors knew their bounds, even if these bounds may not have had the same discrete edges sometimes found elsewhere. They had permanent villages. They had a political system supported by citizens

28. "*Ista* is the name of the first woman and of the place that relates her to Tatau, the Creator, the land and the people who descend from her." See Jacinda Mack, "Remembering Ista: Nuxalk Perspectives on Sovereignty and Social Change," Project paper in partial fulfillment for the degree of Master of Arts, York University, p. 2.

29. On supposed Anglo-Saxon superior breeding see Dr. John Sebastian Helmcken, *Reminiscences*, ed. Dorothy Blakey Smith. (Vancouver: UBC Press, 1975) p. 329.

with a sense of political obligation common to lasting regimes. They had a system for allocating resources, a thriving trade economy with goods processed for export, land under agricultural cultivation[30] and a vibrant cultural calendar. Hearing this preamble, they would have been well justified in concluding that, whatever the Colony of British Columbia might be, it had nothing to do with them.

Second, while the document does not explicitly address the laws of any indigenous nation, it does repeal the laws of Upper Canada as they had applied within the Pacific shelf non-indigenous community since 1821, now substituting the laws of England in their place. This proves: 1) that Parliament had considered the issue of laws already in effect; 2) that it had no intention of making this document an implicit declaration of war by pretending a right to touch anything but laws of its own jurisdiction; and 3) that, since Parliament does not create legal vacuums, the document implicitly directs its officials upholding the "Honor of the Crown" to use any residual *de facto* power of the British Empire to support the existing indigenous laws and public institutions until the appropriate sovereign authorities might be approached for other arrangements. Good faith required no less.

The formal creation of the Colony of British Columbia, then, did not bring about any constitutional change, repeal or otherwise alter the laws in effect throughout the Ancestors' territory. How could it? It would be a strange and chaotic world if a foreign power could change the constitution of another People, repeal laws or impose laws where its officials had never visited, never contacted the local government, never secured consent or a mandate from the citizen majority, and where its own citizens had no presence of any kind. Only frauds and tricksters would ever pretend otherwise. Actual "assertions of sovereignty" require the exhibition of a will to public action backed by a real presence on the ground to defend territory, administer law or enforce the public will, with violence if necessary.

Once again, the Ancestors retained their long-held sovereign rights as much the day after British Columbia's creation as they did the day before. No constitutional event had taken place within their territory. The Crown only had identified its agents for making the honorable approaches foreseen in the Oregon Treaty. Nothing more.

---

30. See BCARS, Map of Cavendish Venables, Sept. 1861, CM/B91

Nevertheless, British Columbia's creation did reflect the way in which the Oregon Treaty channeled certain underlying cultural, economic and political forces after 1846. It was these that provided the main impetus for B.C.'s creation in 1858 and then favored the choice of an insurrection as the means of constitutional reform.

An insurrection is an unlawful uprising against an established authority or system of governance. Where the resident citizenry has not lent its support and where, if successful, a new constitution is then imposed against the will of the citizen majority, the result is an immoral insurrection. So British Columbia's constitutional history vis-à-vis its indigenous residents seems best described. As Nuxalk and other Elders from diverse Pacific shelf communities teach it: *Our laws have been subverted, not extinguished.*[31]

This Settlers' Insurrection incurred massive indigenous death tolls. In the Ancestors' territory, the Insurrection's first manifestation through the actual application of violence to the indigenous residents, as documented here at length in later chapters, can be dated to early June 1862. Perhaps seventy percent, or more, of all the Ancestors then died over just the next nine months.

On the Pacific shelf as a whole, these violent events transformed the settler community's political circumstance. From three ephemeral political entities with one regime controlling few people and little land, its officials finally could begin filling out the hopeful maps sanctified only in a foreign country by a strange government with no political connection to the resident citizenry. What were the cultural, economic and political forces shaping British interests following the Oregon Treaty that would see the advent of a Settlers' Insurrection in Nuxalk and Tsilhqot'in territory?

---

31. Nuxalk Nation website, nuxalknation.ca/government/Nuxalk-rights/

5

The Evolution of British Interests Before
The Settlers' Insurrection, 1846 – 1862

At the time of the Oregon Treaty in 1846, three foreign entities had significant commercial operations in the Pacific Northwest.[32] Only the two British concerns affected British Columbia's formation. Those associated with these two entities in 1846 constituted almost the whole non-indigenous community in the relevant geography.

The Oregon Treaty dramatically affected the operation, interests and plans of both concerns. It also refocused the political ambitions of an important non-indigenous faction. It was these that eventually determined the first course in relations between the non-indigenous guest community and the Ancestors as host social entities.

(A detailed outline of the sequence of events that began with the Oregon Treaty and ended with the British Crown's unilateral assertion of a right to sovereign control in Nuxalk territory in 1865 has been made available in the Timeline section p. 193-208.)

I
The Rule of Law and The Hudson's Bay Company.

Since 1821, the British Crown had licensed the H.B.C. for a monopoly on European trade with the indigenous population of what is now B.C. The Crown also delegated to the H.B.C. some jurisdiction over the administration of law among the non-indigenous community. The Company was to apply the laws of distant Upper Canada to those of the non-indigenous community living within its Pacific Northwest commercial districts.

---

32. The Russian-American Company had abandoned its California franchise in 1842 but retained a prominent presence in the area north of the Hudson's Bay Company's regional sales districts until selling its operations to the Alaska Commercial Company in 1867.

It should go without saying that the Crown could not exempt the non-indigenous community from, in addition, the ordinary duty of obeying the law of the land as administered by the local authorities. While Canadians remained dependent on their hosts, this remained straightforward. When an H.B.C. manager violated the laws on credit and fraud, the Tsilhqot'in authorities banished him.[33] Or, when the H.B.C. brought in illegal immigrants as employees, the Tsilhqot'in authorities expelled them.[34]

Notice that, by sourcing the laws of Upper Canada, the Crown explicitly had not delegated any law-making authority to the H.B.C. The H.B.C.'s presence was for trade not for constitutional change. Nor does the Supreme Court date Great Britain's assertion of a desire for some future sovereign interest here to the H.B.C.'s founding in 1670; to the 1803 Canada Jurisdiction Act extending the laws of Lower Canada to Canadians operating in western "Indian" territories; or to the commercial reorganization giving the H.B.C. its Pacific presence in 1821.

The H.B.C. had no presence in Nuxalk territory before 1862. The Ancestors travelled to the H.B.C.'s Fort McLoughlin in Heiltsuk territory or received boat-based, door-to-door salesmen. The H.B.C. did operate briefly in central Tsilhqot'in territory. It abandoned this franchise before 1846; in part, because the Ancestors would outbid them for Tsilhqot'in furs.[35] In short, it would be absurd to suppose that British concerns influenced the Ancestors in any way before the first official approach was made to them July 3, 1862. The H.B.C. itself was not the source of any agitation for constitutional reform.

Then, about 1840, a subset of H.B.C. associates created a new entity, the Puget's Sound Agricultural Company (P.S.A.C.) Since all P.S.A.C. shareholders and associates were also all H.B.C. associates, outside observers could not always distinguish their activities. Yet the P.S.A.C. had different objectives. While the H.B.C. was confined to plying the indigenous market, the P.S.A.C. was to grow through increasing non-indigenous trade. As an ancillary political objective, it also would promote British over American interests in the Pacific

---

33. HBCA. B.37/a/1 *Fort Chilcotin Journal,* Letter to William McBean, Nov. 2. 1837, concerning McIntosh.

34. *Fort Chilcotin Journal,* Feb. 29, 1840, on the rejection of three "Atnah" employees.

35. By 1862, the Tsilhqot'in normally delivered their furs into the coastal trade: see *Fort Alexandria Journal,* Nov. 17, 1862. The Ancestors also visited Tsilhqot'in territory as the H.B.C.'s pricing structure created opportunities for indigenous middlemen. On the Ancestors trading in Tsilhqot'in territory see, George Barnston, "A Trip from Alexandria to the Coast," *The British Colonist,* August 16, 1861, p. 2.

Northwest, especially at Puget's Sound, up the Columbia River and down the Willamette Valley. This accretion of a political objective was inspired in part by the H.B.C. operated Gaelic-speaking refugee colony imposed on the distant Red River Valley. In 1841, the H.B.C./P.S.A.C. imported 200 foreign settlers from Red River to the Pacific. This was a first sign of the implicit promise of constitutional innovation through colonialism that was integral to this development.

The different political spirit animating this new form of guest sparked the constitutional crisis that would envelope Nuxalk territory. Guests arriving only for trade retain their sense of political obligation to their own nations while obeying the local laws. Japanese salesmen assigned to the United States retain their sense of political obligation to Japan even if they might make strategic local marriages. From the host community's perspective, to use American concepts, one might say the first non-indigenous guests here had business visas rather than "green cards." These second guests wanted something different. Having gained access for trade, the H.B.C/P.S.A.C. and its associates became a stalking horse for The Settlers' Insurrection.

II
The side effects of failed political policies elsewhere.

Many P.S.A.C. founders were exiles from genocidal policies in Scotland or Ireland, or their direct descendants. These had lost their homeland. Yet they came to the Pacific shelf with the knowledge or experience of replacement homelands promised elsewhere in North America since 1770, like Nova Scotia or Red River.

The presence of these politically homeless people eventually attracted refugees from other ill-considered or inopportune policies around the world.[36] These had abandoned their homelands voluntarily for new enfranchisements. Ordinarily, when such people arrive with good faith amidst a new community, they become immigrants: guests who have given up their homeland for citizenship with new neighbors and new political obligations. The founders of the P.S.A.C. and their fellow travellers, instead, had thoughts of founding new regimes. They imagined increasing the size of the non-indigenous community with

---

36. An outline of non-indigenous developments in Oregon territory and the evolution of relations with the indigenous population in regard to American, as opposed to British, imperialism there can be found in Gray H. Whaley, *Oregon and the Collapse of Ullahee*, (University of North Carolina Press, 2010.)

the promise that people could leave their homeland without also losing a familiar culture and British institutions. In other words, they imagined that they could move their homes to a new political territory without the ordinary good faith of arriving as immigrants undertaking or sharing the common duties of citizenship in new neighborhoods.

In addition, rather than becoming joined to a community through the land, the promise was that these guests would be able to imagine themselves as individuals separate from the land and the People. Even to imagine the surrounding environment itself as something somehow separate from the community occupying it, or vice versa. And to think of land as disposable real estate: a mere commodity with distinct conceptual borders capable of being transformed into small islands of European private property on foreign soil rather than as something ineffable wound up with the great mystery of life.

Immigrants and guests often have interesting and useful ideas. Yet, without first approaching the local authorities, every step was bad faith. No Canadian today would imagine moving to, say, Russia with the intent of reordering the allocation of resources there without first consulting the local authorities. And, if anyone did, he or she soon would be deported, imprisoned for theft or sent to a Gulag.

After the Insurrection, later immigrants intending good faith then, unwittingly, took up their new sense of political obligation to the illegal and dishonorable Colonial regime rather than to the true *de jure* sovereign powers, of which they usually were kept in ignorance through the complicity of settler-colonial academics.

In any case, upholding the "Honor of the Crown" in the midst of these shifting interests, it was the responsibility of Colonial officials to prevent actions being taken under this politically rebellious spirit. Except, that is, for making their own formal approaches in good faith to the indigenous authorities or citizen majorities. Indeed, this was the only course consistent with the Crown's own stated policy as laid down in the Royal Proclamation of 1763.

Insurrections sometimes have popular support. Those benefit the public interest. The resident citizenry soon ratifies these, lending *de jure* authority to the new regime. However, overthrowing regimes that retain support from the resident citizenry frequently sees a breakdown of order, an institution of counterinsurgencies and the long-lingering resentment that can lead to incidents of terrorism or protracted civil wars. The

Chilcotin War of 1864, for example, was just such a counterinsurgency authorized by the resident citizenry.

It is for this reason that those contemplating an insurrection must always consider how to deal with the previous regime and the citizens who may continue to honor it. Sometimes assassinating or exiling the royal family is enough. However, when an insurrection calls for replacing not only the previous regime but also displacing the resident citizenry itself, then something more dramatic, like "ethnic cleansing," may seem necessary. It is the claim of Elders throughout the Pacific shelf that something of this order happened in their case.

III
The Oregon Treaty's effect on the Ancestors' territory.

The Oregon Treaty delivered both victory and defeat to the P.S.A.C. and its associates or political allies. Their political ambitions received encouragement as the Crown upgraded its regional interest. The Crown went from simply keeping a watch for its subjects' economic interests to expressing a will toward some undefined future power sharing with the existing sovereign authorities. Those seeking constitutional innovations were the greatest potential beneficiaries of this new political direction.

The Treaty also dealt the P.S.A.C. a profound economic defeat. The new boundary separating American and British interests was to follow the artificial barrier of the 49th parallel rather than the natural border of the Columbia River. Ultimately, it was the adoption of this unnatural border that shaped the course of events in Nuxalk and Tsilhqot'in territories. This came about through two developments.

First, since Puget Sound had been the P.S.A.C.'s focus and since this was lost to American control in 1846, the Company would spend years refocusing its efforts. The H.B.C. and the P.S.A.C. both began relocating to Fort Victoria on Vancouver Island. Parliament then created the Colony of Vancouver Island as its first attempt at expressing the desire for a sovereign presence on the Pacific shelf.

Ominously, the second Governor of this new political entity, James Douglas, was also a key agent for the P.S.A.C., the locus of insurrectionist sentiment. Douglas routinely violated the "Honor of the Crown." His Regime would act as if the Colony's mere creation, rather than authorizing approaches to the indigenous authorities, somehow had supplanted this politically necessary step. His Regime suffered from the colonial delusion that the mere stroke of a pen could create a magical constitutional change affecting the political rights and obligations of the whole indigenous citizenry without even its knowledge; that, somehow, his office had been authorized to assert control over citizens and resources without considerations of consent.

In place of approaches in good faith, when the opportunity arose, Douglas would humiliate the local indigenous authorities to prove their powerlessness in the face of the British Empire: as if "might created right" *vis-a-vis* indigenous residents. His practice was to gain by force and fraud what his Regime could not bring itself to gain through law or honor. The only limit that his Regime recognized was the practical prudence of not over-reaching its political power base as governed by growth in the settler presence. Subsequently, Douglas became Governor of the Colonies of Queen Charlotte Islands and British Columbia, and administrator of the Stikine Territories. It was under Douglas' leadership that the non-indigenous community would begin the most violent phase of its Insurrection against the Nuxalk Ancestors and Tsilhqot'in authorities.

Second, the new border profoundly affected the prospective distribution of benefits from a Pacific terminus for a Northwest Passage by land. In the absence of a viable Northwest Passage by sea, the H.B.C. already was operating such a route. Connecting H.B.C. establishments east of the Rockies, it crossed the Mountains through the Assiniboine Pass and followed the Columbia River to the Ocean at Fort Vancouver, now Portland, Oregon. After the Oregon Treaty, most of the Pacific shelf part of this route was in American hands. For British interests to retain their economic position the route would have to be reconsidered and a new terminus targeted. But where?

Experience had taught the H.B.C. that the Fraser River did not provide a viable transportation corridor from the interior to the ocean. Fierce rapids and intrusive rocks rendered it impassable for boats, and the surrounding banks were too steep and high for packers to portage. The Fraser had frustrated attempts to master it in the 1790s, 1800s and 1820s. This was the main reason that the H.B.C. accessed the whole interior from the Columbia. Forced to reconsider after the Oregon Treaty, the H.B.C. began searching means of bypassing Fraser Canyon, especially through the meandering Harrison River system to

Fort Langley on the Lower Fraser. Langley was, however, still part of the Puget Sound economic region. Given occasion and the common disregard Americans show to other regimes, thoughtful people could anticipate that those interests one day might rudely re-fashion the border to fit the geography. This second destination, too, then would be lost to American control. Canada everywhere is a flight from American jurisdiction and B.C. was no different.

A gold rush created primarily by associates of the P.S.A.C. so as to increase trade in the non-indigenous market eventually flooded this area with American miners. This brought into focus the very risk presented by an artificial border. These miners little troubled to gain a proper license from the indigenous authorities. A war soon broke out. Experienced at organizing the application of violence to over-power indigenous communities one-by-one, miner militias soon pacified the Lower Fraser for creation of the "Fraser River settlements."

This sudden non-indigenous activity forced Parliament to create the Colony of British Columbia as a means of preserving the Oregon Treaty status quo. It thwarted the eventuality of an American led change in the border by providing British officials to maintain order among a swollen non-indigenous community that no longer fit under the H.B.C.'s umbrella. Yet none of this new authority to control the non-indigenous population changed the legal obligation of these officials to approach indigenous sovereign authorities in good faith for the privilege of operating in their territories.

Political change creates its own momentum. The new entity required a Capital. The H.B.C. wanted Ft. Langley. Inaccessible by ocean-going vessels, a settlement here would remain an economic captive of Victoria where the H.B.C. and P.S.A.C. had relocated. However, under his separate military authority, the Colony's new Lieutenant Governor, Colonel Richard Moody, immediately moved the new Capital downriver and created New Westminster. Here the British Navy and steam-powered ocean vessels could serve it directly. Now, instead of becoming just another stop along a Northwest Passage served by a terminus at Victoria, the new capital was a threat to replace it. Undeterred by the H.B.C.'s experience, the new Lieutenant Governor, who also commanded a detachment of Royal Engineers, had his forces reconsider routes to the interior, including especially the Fraser Canyon where the gold rush had created a chain of settlements that might need military protection.

All this seemingly diminished Victoria's prospects. In reaction, important Victoria interests began considering alternate routes inland to by-pass New Westminster. H.B.C. associates knew that, in the 1790s, a Canadian business traveller had been shown an indigenous trade route from the interior to the coast. Westbound from the Fraser River in Dakelh territory, it went via the Blackwater and Bella Coola Rivers to North Bentinck Arm in the Ancestors' territory.

This route was also on a straight line to the H.B.C.'s Fort Edmonton, a sure stop on any future transcontinental crossing. In April 1827, the Fort Alexandria post manager had crossed from the Fraser eastbound from the edge of Tsilhqot'in territory on this indigenous trail via the Yellowhead Pass.[37] So this alternative to the Columbia and Fraser Canyon for a Northwest Passage by land was already known. Only its development to include a coastal leg from North Bentinck Arm to Victoria remained.

Developers pursing Victoria's interests in promoting this route arrived among the Ancestors in Sept. 1860.[38] They would identify the best access points via the river valleys and stake claims to the most strategic land for a harbor city. Mostly Scots-originated associates of the H.B.C., they planned to call this harbor city "New Aberdeen."[39]

Led by Attorney General George Cary, the Crown's third highest official in the colonies, the arrival of these land speculators was also the first harbinger of the coming Insurrection. The Ancestors and Tsilhqot'in had just become primary targets for those most impatient for constitutional innovation without good faith approaches.

---

37. The Valemont Historic Society published part of his Journal in *Yellowhead Pass and its People*, (D.W. Frieson and Sons, 1984) pp. 2-3.

38. Documented in detail throughout later chapters.

39. For example see, "More Indian Murders," *The British Colonist*, June 27, 1864, p. 3.

6

The Settlers' Insurrection in Tsilhqot'in Territory

Since the two Peoples suffered together in 1862, reviewing the Insurrection's more admitted course in Tsilhqot'in territory can serve well as an introduction to the Ancestors' experience.

The violent Insurrection through which settlers would begin overthrowing the legitimate authorities in Tsilhqot'in territory began in late June 1862. Here, as elsewhere, this Insurrection marks the dividing line in time between the non-indigenous community merely asserting an interest in some sovereign relationship and the beginning of an assertion of *de facto* control over land and people. Within just nine months disinterested eyewitnesses were already estimating that two-thirds of all the Tsilhqot'in were dead.[40] And the dying went on.

Tsilhqot'in Elders and community leaders have always taught that this Insurrection included episodes of ethnic cleansing, genocide, a "war" of extermination or however one may wish to describe the intentional mass killing of innocents as a social policy. By any name, the allegation is that the settler community used the greatest possible violence that one community can inflict on another.[41]

In the Tsilhqot'in case, there can be no doubt that it was only this intentionally produced, rapid, catastrophic loss of life and its inherent accompanying decline in political presence that subsequently allowed Colonial officials to institute a paramilitary occupation against the will of the resident citizenry and with flagrant violations of the Crown's honor. This was first in degree among the "many wrongs" for which the Premier of B.C. has now expressed profound sorrow.

While expressing this sorrow, the Premier acknowledged that, during the governorship of James Douglas, settlers had intentionally

---

40. For example, "Latest from Bentinck Arm," *The British Colonist*, Jan. 15, 1863, p. 5.

41. For example, see the 2003 restatement by the Tsilhqot'in National Government reprinted in *Missing Genocide*, p. 89.

created artificial smallpox epidemics to kill the Tsilhqot'in *en masse*. That is, settlers deployed smallpox as a weapon of mass destruction to further the goals of The Settlers' Insurrection on the Pacific shelf.

I

The outbreak of settler violence in Tsilhqot'in territory.

Francis Poole participated in the Insurrection's first overt action in both Nuxalk and Tsilhqot'in territories. Recalling his passage from North Bentinck Arm in the Ancestors' territory across Tsilhqot'in territory in June 1862, Poole's memoir said,

> *(F)or five or six days we were in hourly dread of attack from hostile savages...we left a sorrowful trail of blood behind us, nay, even the body of one of our companions.*[42]

Poole's report of being in "hourly dread of attack" marks the first documented Tsilhqot'in reaction to the institution of settler hostilities. Leaving Bella Coola at North Bentinck Arm June 15, 1862, Poole arrived at Ft. Alexandria on the Fraser River late July 4.[43] If his dread of attack began five or six days earlier, as his memoir implies, this reaction began near Chilcotin Lake. A bench on the Lake's north shore provides a spectacular setting for a settlement. In 1861, the first prospective settlers noted a large Tsilhqot'in community here.[44]

This lake also falls on the most direct line between Bella Coola and the Fraser River, a most desirable route for a road. Marking the trail for Poole's party a few days before, J.B. Pearson and Ranald McDonald of Attorney General George Cary's Bentinck Arm Company had stopped at Chilcotin Lake. McDonald was a company Director. He and others had gained both indigenous and colonial approval for a road passing here during summer 1861.[45] As a promotional gimmick for the 1862 season, the Company guaranteed passage for 40 men. Divided into two groups of 20, it had hired Pearson and Poole to lead them.[46]

---

42. Francis Poole, *Queen Charlotte Islands*, (Vancouver: J.J. Douglas, 1972) p. 65.

43. "Important from the Coast Route – Destitution and Suffering," *The British Colonist*, July 22, 1862, p. 3.

44. "Route from Alexandria to North Bentinck Arm," *The British Colonist*, Oct. 18, 1861, p. 2.

45. Documented at length in later chapters covering the Nuxalk experience.

46. Documented in later chapters covering the Nuxalk experience.

With 3000 acres suited for pasturing livestock, Chilcotin Lake was a prime roadhouse location. Pearson and McDonald paused to survey 480 acres on the north side for Pearson to claim under a land redistribution scheme newly proclaimed by the Douglas Regime. He would file this claim on returning from Tsilhqot'in territory.[47]

The fee simple titles promised to settlers under this redistribution scheme were radically incompatible with the established systems. This scheme also provided that prospective owners could not receive "title" unless they claimed that the desired land was vacant. Yet, as Colonial officials all well knew, there was, in point of fact, no vacant land suitable for European-style agriculture anywhere on the Pacific shelf. It is absurd to pretend that the Peoples occupying this space for thousands of years had left the most fertile ground vacant for an eventual free occupation by European colonists. There was only occupied land that might be redeployed in new ways. Without treaties, settlers had no means of knowing which land the indigenous residents might be pleased to allow them to share, and a powerful motive to remove any indigenous residents who might object to their taking possession of the most fertile land and most strategic locations.

Having been invited to invest time, capital and labor through the Douglas Regime's fraudulent promise of vacant land, what were prospective settlers to do when they arrived to find all the best land occupied? The Regime's highest officials knew that this was the common cause of every "Indian war" and a thing for which they needed to plan.[48] It bears repeating that, as of 1862, the Douglas Regime had made no approaches of any kind to the Nuxalk Ancestors or the Tsilhqot'in. By any rule of law, British Columbia's boundaries cannot have included any part of either territory at this time. The Regime also had no future plans for diplomacy, negotiations, treaties or compensation. Since the need to anticipate self-defensive counter measures by indigenous residents was obvious, in the alternative, then, what was the Douglas' Regime's plan? Whatever the plan, it is a certainty that Attorney General Cary was privy to its details.

---

47. BCARS. GR-1182, B.C. Dept. of Lands and Works, Cariboo, Lytton and Lillooet Pre-emption Records, taken by P. Nind and T Elwyn, Alexandria District 1860 to 1863, Folder 1. Claim of J.B. Pearson, et al.

48. See the extended discussion in Chapter 11.

In this very case, the prime location that Pearson wanted was visibly within a Tsilhqot'in community's precinct. An April 1862 Bentinck Arm Company advertisement had even noted Chilcotin Lake as the site of "a large Indian village."[49] It was a prominent feature for which the promoters had the time and opportunity to prepare. Following the company's route as marked for him by Pearson and McDonald, Poole arrived here within a few days of Pearson's staking activity. Since the purpose of "staking land" was to alert other non-indigenous interests to prior claims, it is a certainty that Pearson and McDonald marked this claim beside the road. It is equally as certain that, when Poole's party arrived here, it knew precisely the plot their colleagues intended to claim and instantly appreciated that it was not vacant as required.

On his return to the British colonies from these two still foreign territories, Poole described his arrival among the large Tsilhqot'in community at Chilcotin Lake this way,

> *(A)t [Chilcotin Lake] there is an Indian fishing station and a tract of excellent grass land probably 3000 acres.... At Chilcoaten Lake, two more Canadians...fell sick of the same complaint* [smallpox – the same complaint as two other Canadians previously left in the upper Bella Coola Valley and two others left at Fort Rupert on Vancouver Island] *and were left with the Chilcoaten Indians. These gave evidence of the disease in its worst or confluent form.*[50]

So it seems Poole's party became "in hourly dread of attack from hostile savages" immediately after it knowingly introduced smallpox among them. Moreover, it introduced the disease at a prime location that their colleagues seeking a Colonial title needed to be vacant.

Just three weeks behind Poole, another Bentinck Arm Company party led by John Morris provided this report: *A train of packhorses was at Chilcotin Lake. Smallpox had taken a terrible hold of the Indians of the vicinity and numbers were dying daily.*[51]

For the disease to have "a terrible hold" and for "numbers" to be dying daily, this community was large enough, then, not to have been evicted easily for the vacant possession required in a fee simple title. Moreover,

49. "Nearest and Cheapest way to the Cariboo Mines," *Daily Press*, April 15, 1862, p. 1.

50. "A Trip to Cariboo via Bentinck," *The British Columbian*, July 23, 1862, p. 3. "Important from the Coast Route..." *The British Colonist*, July 22, 1862, p. 3.

51. *Victoria Daily Press*, Aug. 6, 1862, p. 3. Morris arrived at Alexandria July 21, just 17 days behind Poole.

dispossessing these villagers would have been illegal under Tsilhqot'in law, the law actually in effect on the ground. Few people will stand by anywhere as land developers attempt their illegal dispossession. Some reactive violence was guaranteed. The smallpox epidemic knowingly created here by Poole's party pre-empted the risk of such an "Indian war."

II
Picturing the event at Chilcotin Lake.

Since Poole's party also introduced smallpox in Nuxalk territory, it will be insightful to analyze its activity at Chilcotin Lake. Poole's description that these men "fell sick" may be taken as implying that the resulting calamity happened naturally. Then, by "were left with" perhaps he expected observers to believe that these Tsilhqot'in had accepted the risk of nursing them. Yet, consider the following:

1) Under English law, the law governing settler activities, "incautiously exposing people with contagious diseases to the public" was a criminal act.[52] In the leading case, a mother carrying an infected child along a public road was held guilty of a crime even though others then died only inadvertently.[53] Poole's party did much worse than just act "incautiously." By Poole's own account, it knowingly sent diseased people into a healthy population. Whether Poole's party committed a crime at Chilcotin Lake cannot be of any real issue. The issue is which crime: mass murder or genocide?

2) Then, under English law, public hosts, such as the Tsilhqot'in village authorities here, had a legal right to refuse guests with deadly diseases.[54] This arises from an authority's higher legal obligation to keep the healthy population under its care safe. People of good faith do not then play on any unsuspecting or compassionate prospective hosts to risk the death of their charges. As in due course we learn more about the activities of Poole in Nuxalk territory, the more that all of his activities will reek of dishonor and murderous intent.

---

52. R. v. Burnett (1815) 4 Maule and Selwyn 75; 105 ER 762. R. v. Henson (1852) 1 Dears 24; 169 ER 621; cited as recently as R. V. Rimmington [2005] UKHL 63. [2006] 1 AC 459. Discussed in Richard Hyde, *Regulating Food-borne Illness*. (Hart Publishing: Oxford, 2015) p. 145.

53. R. v. Vantandillo (1815) 4 M&S 73; 105 ER 762: the leading case in 1862.

54. "Innkeeper's Right to Exclude or Eject Guests," 7 *Fordham Law Review* 417 (1938.)

3) Elsewhere, when a smallpox-infected man similarly was left near an indigenous community, Poole described the consequences as "certain."[55] In English law, when the consequences of any action are certain, the actor is held to have intended those consequences.[56] No objective auditor aware of the facts recited by Poole could have had any doubt that the consequence would be many deaths at this village. By the common standards of English law, Poole's own admissions show an intention to kill the Tsilhqot'in residents at Chilcotin Lake in accord with the various objectives of the Bentinck Arm Company.

4) Is it credible that, acting with good faith in the normal course, Poole's party would willingly abandon its diseased companions to the care of "hostile savages?"[57] No one would do this unless both these conditions applied: a) that the sick were beyond compassion; and b) that one intended to harm those same "hostile savages." Given the circumstances, the greater probability is that Poole's employers took these villagers as hostile to their purposes prior to this contact.

5) Suppose Poole did approach the Tsilhqot'in in good faith, as settler colonial historians have always pretended. How is one to imagine this conversation? Poole, "Hello, very pleased to meet you. Two of us have smallpox. This is most inconvenient as we are in a big rush to make money. Though it is certain that most of your community will die, we would like to leave them in your midst." Indigenous answer, "You Canadians, always in a big rush to make money. If it helps you out, of course we would be happy to risk our annihilation." Or does it seem more likely that, when this community suddenly discovered evidence of bad faith, its citizens then had no choice but to put Poole's party "in hourly dread of attack?"

6) It is open country at Chilcotin Lake. Poole noted 3000 acres of grass. Another settler said it was "chiefly prairie."[58] Avoiding the close contact necessary to spread smallpox, then, would have been exceptionally easy. Carriers must approach potential new victims close

---

55. Poole, *Queen Charlotte Islands*, p. 195.

56. For this widely used standard in relation to genocide, see, Paul Behrens, "The *mens rea* of genocide," in Eds. Paul Behrens and Ralph Henham, *Elements of Genocide*. (Routlege: New York, 2013) pp. 70 to 97.

57. "A Trip to Cariboo via Bentinck," *The British Columbian*, July 23, 1862, p. 3. "Important from the Coast Route…" *The British Colonist*, July 22, 1862, p. 3.

58. While making his pre-emption claim for agricultural land: see his note in the folder, BCARS. GR-1182. British Columbia Dept. of Lands and Works, Cariboo, Lytton and Lillooet pre-emption records, Folder 1, Claim of Denis Cain, records taken by P. Nind and T. Elwyn, Alexandria District, 1860-1863.

enough for skin-to-skin contact or an exchange of breath; little more than handshaking range. 3000 acres is almost five square miles, over 12 km squared. Walk it one day. Then imagine whether it would be a hard task to keep a mere two people quarantined in that space.

7) Suppose circumstances somehow did make it necessary to abandon these sick men. Poole's party did not have to leave them in Tsilhqot'in care. The Bentinck Arm Company party behind Poole, led by John Morris, included a French doctor.[59] Since Morris was making cost estimates for the Company and since McDonald was a Company director, the probability is that Poole's party knew the plan of how its activity fit within what went before and what was coming behind.

8) Smallpox did not appear unexpectedly among Poole's party. Or only after it had left behind sources of vaccine, doctors and help for containing the disease. As noted above, before Chilcotin Lake, Poole said that his party already had left two diseased men at Fort Rupert and two more at Nautlieff in the Upper Valley. Later chapters will show Poole also admitted responsibility at Bella Coola and South Bentinck Arm. A newspaper said his party previously left diseased men already at Nanaimo.[60] People acting in good faith would have vaccinated the rest there.[61] Chilcotin Lake was only the very last stop along what Poole, himself, described as "a sorrowful trail of blood."[62] Are mere accidents usually said to leave trails of blood in this sense?

9) Motive is relevant to a crime's proof. Poole had no personal motive anywhere along his route. However, as the agent of others, his party had several motives, both private and public. The Bentinck Arm Company sponsored Poole's party. Governor Douglas' formal legal adviser, Attorney General George Cary controlled this Company. The Attorney General is sure to have had a good command of the issues created by the colonial land scheme and of the necessity to anticipate conflict.[63] Especially where he had large private interests. There was no shortage of motive on many levels.

59. Trip to the head of Bentinck Arm..." *The British Colonist*, August 28, 1862, p. 3. Morris' party was delayed but Poole's party would not have known that.

60. "From Bentinck Arm, Fort Rupert and Nanaimo," *The British Colonist*, June 21, 1862, p. 3.

61. As another party did immediately on discovering a diseased man in their midst. See the discussion of Speight and his party in the article cited above.

62. Poole, *Queen Charlotte Islands*, p. 65.

63. For that matter, Cary was present in the Vancouver Island Assembly when this very issue was discussed, "House of Assembly," *The British Colonist*, Jan 22, 1861 p. 3 and again Jan 28, 1861, p. 3.

In short, the evidence is such that objective auditors would be justified in concluding beyond a reasonable doubt that Poole's party intentionally created an artificial epidemic to kill the Tsilhqot'in at Chilcotin Lake. This was a mass murder, at least. Was it genocide?

III
A widespread weaponization of smallpox.

The Poole/Pearson parties were remarkable as the first to create artificial epidemics in Tsilhqot'in territory. But they were not the last.

Puntzi Lake also had a desirable roadhouse location. Here some non-indigenous developers gained access by having one marry a female relative of the area leader.[64] Having gained a proper foothold, they then staked "all the land around," intending to operate under the Colonial system. They extorted exclusive possession by threatening their Tsilhqot'in co-occupants with smallpox.[65] Shortly afterward, according to a Tsilhqot'in survivor[66] and to a statement by the "Head War Chief," these settlers then created an artificial epidemic.[67] An eyewitness estimated 500 dead at Puntzi.[68]

In May 1864, the Tsilhqot'in removed these murderous guests. The "Head War Leader" advised them to abandon their possessions and leave or be killed.[69] Apparently expecting that the Tsilhqot'in were bluffing, or that the Colony would help them escape justice, the developers refused. The Tsilhqot'in authorities then executed them. Four of the six "Chilcotin Chiefs" later hanged were martyred on the pretext that their actions in dealing with these Puntzi mass-murderers somehow had been an offense under the colonial system.

Elsewhere, along a proposed Bute Inlet road, the developers had designs on the Tatla Valley, a prime location for an agricultural town.

---

64. For smallpox at Puntzi, see *Canada's 'War'* s. 61, p. 173.

65. At the time these were the only fixed settlers in Tsilhqot'in territory. On the threat see, Judge Begbie's, "Notes on the Trial of Six Indians," for the analogy of this occasion with the subsequent threat to use smallpox as a punishment at Bute Inlet, and also R.C. Lundin Brown, *Klatsassan*. (London: Gilbert and Rivington, 1873) pp. 10-11.

66. *Nemiah: The Unconquered Country*, (New Star Books: Vancouver, 1992) pp. 82-88.

67. BCARS. H.P.P. Crease Legal Papers, 1863 – 1895. Add Mss. 54, Box 3 File 12, Supreme Court of New Westminster, Testimony of Ach-pic-er-mous, May 31, 1865.

68. Alfred Waddington, "The Bute Inlet Massacre and its causes," *The British Colonist*, June 13, 1964, p. 3.

69. See testimony of Ach-pic-er-mous cited above. And Great Britain Public Records Office, Colonial Office Records, CO 60/19 p. 149 10601 Frederick Seymour to Cardwell, No. 37, para. 6 and 7.

Less than a month after this road manager first visited here in 1862, an admittedly artificial epidemic killed the Tsilhqot'in residents.[70] Only one resident survived.[71] This community chased its killers, just as those at Chilcotin Lake had chased Poole. John McLain later described how he had left a smallpox blanket here with some food *to accomplish my purpose for they all died of smallpox.*[72] Like Poole, he had no personal motive. So he was paid to do this. His confession shows that the intent here was to kill. Subsequently, a Bute Inlet Company *Prospectus* would note the Colony's readiness to grant it the whole Tatla Valley as increasing the Company's value.[73] Like Chilcotin Lake and Puntzi, Tatla Lake was another case of smallpox used as a weapon over control of land.

At Tatla, the perpetrators had rationalized the creation of an artificial epidemic as "punishment."[74] In spring 1864, again as a punishment, Bute Inlet agents threatened a new epidemic. Company agents here also: disputed a tax for access to Tsilhqot'in territory, violated common labor customs, disrespected the people, raped the War Chief's daughter, prostituted starving women for food and sexually or otherwise abused children.

After this new threat and after discovering evidence of a plan for "weaponizing" smallpox in the early stages, the necessity of pre-emptive action became urgent. A Leaders' Council then approved a plan to counter the non-indigenous community's ongoing Insurrection against the long established *de jure* constitution. It delegated a "Head War Chief" to pursue what became revealed as a four part plan: to end this smallpox threat with a formal act of war, to deal with the offending Puntzi developers, to expel all non-indigenous guests and to await an approach in good faith from the Colonial authorities.

In the battle to prevent smallpox at Bute Inlet, concluding on April 30, 1864, 14 non-indigenous community members died, four more died when the offending Puntzi developers were executed. The remaining non-indigenous guests, but one, were expelled from Tsilhqot'in and Nuxalk territory in June 1864 for evacuation from Bella Coola. The Tsilhqot'in

70. Waddington crossed his proposed route first in Sept. 1862. His Company's interest in Tatla Lake is expressed in the Company Charter and its *Prospectus* dated Dec. 7, 1863.

71. For smallpox at Tatla see *Canada's 'War'* s. 63, p. 176.

72. Franklin memoir as reported in Maurine Goodenough, *Only in Nazko*, 2008, p. 19.

73. Alfred Waddington, *Bute Inlet Wagon Road Company*, CIHM, 216921, p. 2.

74. See McLain's statement in Goodenough, reproduced in *Canada's 'War'* s. 63, where he refers to "the guilty ones."

then waited for the Colonial response to their *de facto* assertion of *de jure* constitutional sovereign authority.

IV

Assertion of British sovereignty in Tsilhqot'in territory.

Tsilhqot'in and non-indigenous scholars alike describe these last events collectively as the Chilcotin War, a counter-insurgent measure against The Settlers' Insurrection. The Tsilhqot'in understood that the intentional introduction of smallpox was from a desire to overthrow their authority. For this reason, whenever he would discuss the War's cause, the "Head War Leader" referred to these artificial epidemics.[75]

For its part, transitioning from "germ warfare" to conventional warfare, the non-indigenous community raised several militias "to invade" Tsilhqot'in territory.[76] Considering the Tsilhqot'in political presence before over 70 percent had died in smallpox attacks, the Colonial Governor still feared that they could "muster several hundred warriors."[77] Militias raised at settler outposts in Northern Secwepemc and Southern Dakelh territories invaded from the east. The Governor led a further militia through Nuxalk territory.[78]

While advising his superiors in London, the Governor explained that the militia would *proceed to the headquarters of Alexis, the great Chief of the Chilcoaten tribe, show [its] warrant and explain that the Queen's law must have its course.*[79] But why? No official had ever approached Tsilhqot'in citizens before then for consent to so favor "The Queen." So, the Governor dishonorably misrepresented the locus of constitutional legitimacy. Rather than administering law, he was undertaking a war of aggression against an indigenous authority that had been defending its public from genocide.

---

75. Collected in *Canada's 'War,'* s. 24 and 25, beginning p. 70.

76. The Colonial Governor used "to invade" and his description of Tsilhqot'in territory tends to confirm that this cannot have been considered then, in any "rule of law" sense, a part of B. C. See p. 3 to 5, Great Britain Public Records Office, Colonial Office Records, CO 60/19, p. 149 10601, Frederick Seymour, Letter to Cardwell, no. 37, Sept. 9, 1864. No official "invades" his own jurisdiction.

77. Great Britain Public Records Office, Colonial Office Records, CO 60/19, p. 149 10601, Frederick Seymour, Letter to Cardwell, no. 37, Sept. 9, 1864, p. 5.

78. Nuxalk participation in the Chilcotin War is described here in Chapter 17.

79. Great Britain Public Records Office, Colonial Office Records, CO 60/19, p. 273 6959, Frederick Seymour, Letter to Newcastle, no.8, May 20, 1864, p. 13.

Unfamiliar with this foreign ground, the Colonial forces could not capture any of the Tsilhqot'in public servants in question. The militia also failed to intimidate the citizens into betrayals.

The Governor was about to withdraw in defeat when the Tsilhqot'in began a diplomatic initiative. Using this opportunity, the Crown's agents held out: 1) that the Colony would absolve of blame any Tsilhqot'in for enforcing the law or defending the People; and 2) that the Governor would recognize Tsilhqot'in officials as the sovereign authority in their territory.[80] Following the usual diplomatic custom, Colonial officials sent a gift of tobacco to the "Head War Chief" and invited Tsilhqot'in officials to a peace conference with the Governor. Instead of the promised conference, Colonial officials ambushed the Tsilhqot'in party. It then martyred five of them.

Officials "surprised" still other Tsilhqot'in public servants at a second dishonorable ambush in Nuxalk territory during spring 1865. The Colony martyred a sixth Tsilhqot'in official that July. The Governor wrote to his superiors that, *[This] apprehension makes the assertion of the law complete over every Indian* who took part in resisting The Settlers' Insurrection.[81] Notice the Governor's explicit expression of an "assertion of law over" the Tsilhqot'in. The same phrase and description from 1864 as the Supreme Court of Canada now uses in indigenous rights cases from British Columbia.

At the sixth Tsilhqot'in martyr's trial, the Colonial judge noted that natives then "universally" believed settlers had spread smallpox intentionally.[82] From an apparent fear of reprisals, he cautioned the non-indigenous community "not to do or say" anything to confirm this belief. Apparently from a seeming need to sanctify B.C.'s founding, settler colonial academics have participated in this denial ever since...some willingly, some unwittingly.

In contrast, the official statement prepared by the Tsilhqot'in National Government for Lhats'as?in Memorial Day 2003 notes "the genocidal introduction of smallpox."[83] In *Tsilhqot'in Nation v. British Columbia (2007)*, Mr. Justice David Vickers noted the evidence of

80. These terms are documented at length in *Canada's 'War'* and in *Missing Genocide.*

81. Great Britain Public Record Office, Colonial Office Records, CO 60/22, p. 83, 8243, Frederick Seymour, Letter to Cardwell, No. 81, June 8, 1865. p. 2.

82. "The Special Assize," *The British Columbian,* July 4, 1865, p. 3.

83. Reprinted in Swanky, *Missing Genocide,* p. 89.

Tsilhqot'in Tribal Chairman, Ervin Charleyboy, concerning "germ warfare."[84] Referring to the 1862 policies carried out under the Douglas Regime's auspices, Charleyboy testified, *germ warfare was used on us, trying to do away with us.*[85] Explaining the 1864 engagements during the Chilcotin War, Elder and Nits'il?in Thomas Billyboy testified that the experience of seeing the non-indigenous community using "infested blankets" had "scared the hell" out of the Tsilhqot'in from the "toll it took on our people."[86] The 2016 *Nenqay Deni Accord* between the Tsilhqot'in and the Province of British Columbia refers to *the intentional spread of smallpox eradicating entire families and villages.*[87]

So it is that Elders and the legacy authorities in Tsilhqot'in territory have always described the degradation of their own *de facto* power for the eventual substitution of, as the Tsilhqot'in citizenry usually sees it, Canada's illegitimate *de facto* power, a regime upheld through a paramilitary occupation.

What happened, then, in Nuxalk territory? (For Nuxalk territory see map p. 178-179.)

---

84. *Tsilhqot'in Nation v. British Columbia*, 2007 BCSC 1700, para. 282, p. 88.

85. *Tsilhqot'in Nation v. British Columbia*, Evidence of Ervin Charleyboy, Proceedings at Trial, April 21, 2005 (Day 221) p. 24.

86. *Tsilhqot'in Nation v. British Columbia*, Evidence of Thomas Billyboy, Proceedings at Trial, June 1, 2005 (Day 237) p. 48.

87. *Nenqay Deni Accord: the People's Accord.* Between the Province of British Columbia and the Tsilhqot'in Nation. Feb. 11, 2016. B.C. Gov. Aboriginal Relations.

7

The Attorney General and the Ancestors

The Ancestors suffered a similar, sudden, catastrophic decline in population and *de facto* political presence as the Tsilhqot'in. Several thousands died in less than one year. The proportion of all the People suffering this sudden death was so great as to be an epochal marker. The name "Nuxalk" refers to the act of drawing together survivors of this very catastrophe to found a new community.

Was this sudden catastrophe in Nuxalk territory also an instance of genocide, ethnic cleansing or the like as the Elders teach it?[88] Or was all this now, instead, only a natural disaster, as settler academics teach it at colonial universities?

Analyzing any death for evidence of culpable homicide follows a well-known framework: 1) time, place and cause of death; 2) if the circumstances seem suspicious, identifying those with opportunity and access to the means of death; 3) finding the motives of plausible suspects; 4) uncovering evidence of plausible suspects applying the means and identifying their intentions. Then, if one finds homicide on a sufficient scale, one can go on to inquire whether this was also the mass murder of innocents for a *de facto* social policy.

Time, place and cause of death are not in doubt here. The alleged smallpox genocide in Nuxalk territory took place in the months after June 6, 1862. But were these deaths culpable homicides: deaths caused by criminally negligent acts, intentional acts or the actions of depraved minds. And, further, part of an ethnic cleansing-like policy?

On the direct evidence available to them, the authorities at that time found that some force within the settler community had begun an extermination policy. Analyzing this case today requires the

---

88. In the author's every conversation with senior members of the Pootlass family at Bella Coola, Aug. 2 to 8, 2015, it was said that Elders discussed these smallpox epidemics extensively and that it was common knowledge in their community that the disease had been introduced intentionally to kill them as a People; that is, in acts of genocide.

assimilation of that original finding with other evidence unavailable to those authorities: settler memoirs, colonial government documents, a developer's correspondence, maps and so on.

I

Bentinck Arm Co. and Edward Green v. Hood (1864).

The testimony heard under oath during *Bentinck Arm and Fraser River Road Co. Ltd. and Edward Green v. Hood (1864)* is among the key non-indigenous sources in this case.[89] One of the longest lawsuits in B.C.'s colonial period, this civil suit wholly concerned settler plans for the Ancestors' territory leading to the 1862 epidemics.

The issues in this case stemmed from two things: claims to non-indigenous interests in land occupied by the Ancestors and the disposition of revenue from tolls collected on their trails. All those with interests tied to the Bentinck Arm Company or its associated endeavors as described below may have had private or public motives for reducing the Ancestors' hold of their territory. Moreover, this was also the only non-indigenous organization operating here at the time.

Bentinck Arm Co. and Edward Green v. Hood named only three parties. However, the interests actually represented by each plaintiff were much more complex than it appears from this.

The Bentinck Arm Company's objective was a toll road between the Ancestors' territory and the Fraser River. Attorney General George Cary, Governor Douglas' formal legal adviser, created this Company. He controlled its executive decisions through powers of attorney from the other directors.[90] The Douglas Regime's highest legal official, Cary was M.L.A. for Victoria and first minister in the Colony of Vancouver Island Assembly (i.e. its Premier.)[91] While not named as a plaintiff, Cary had a large personal stake in the outcome. The jury awarded him a sixth

---

89. This case was extensively reported in *The British Colonist*, and the *Daily Chronicle*, Feb. 12, though Feb. 24, 1864. Since nothing turns on the various iterations that this entity went through, all variations here are identified as The Bentinck Arm Company. George Cary controlled every version. The case is referred to here simply as *Bentinck Arm Co. v. Hood.*

90. Testimony of George Cary, *Bentinck Arm Co. v. Hood,* Third Day, Feb. 15, 1864, *The British Colonist,* Feb. 17, 1864, p. 3.

91. On Cary as the leader of the government party in the Assembly and, therefore, the Prime Minister see the Speaker's memoir, Dr. John Sebastian Helmcken, *Reminiscences.* Ed. Dorothy Blakely Smith. (Vancouver: UBC Press, 1975) p. 178.

of the damages. Cary did not argue this case for the Company. Instead, he testified at length as a key witness.

The Bentinck Arm Company and Cary's other endeavor in the Ancestors' territory also had an unmistakable public aspect as policy instruments for officials in the Island Assembly. This shone through in the course of the trial. It took two weeks at a time when trials seldom exceeded a day or two. Appeals went for months. The case filled as many newspaper column-inches as the Chilcotin War. The trial saw some astonishing events, an apparent reflection of its public interest aspect. Jurors drawn from Victoria's business community intervened spontaneously with evidence from their own knowledge.[92] The court heard that the Attorney General had made a reckless or calculated claim outside the courtroom that the defendant, a wealthy California businessman, had sought an improper influence by buying up the judge's overdue promissory notes.[93] These exotic features only hint at the broad public aspect of these endeavors.

William Hood, the defendant, had contracted to complete certain work on the Company's road. Finding that he had failed to perform, the jury awarded damages, say today, of $840,000. It divided these on a finding that what began as a revenue assigning agreement actually gave Hood two-thirds ownership of the Company. So he owed most of the damages only to himself. Technically, Hood lost the case. Yet he won control of the company when it had no assets except his debt.

Neither side liked this strange result. On appeal, the judge set aside the verdict for "excess damages" and granted a new trial.[94] Now in control, Hood liquidated the Company before the appeal process had taken its course. Instead of a trial, Cary sought the court's leave to argue the case before a superior court of appeal in England.[95] The judge then made an obscure recalculation of the potential damages. Alas, these were now of a

---

92. See the re-examination of William Hood by Mr. Wood, *Bentinck Arm Company v. Hood,* Seventh Day, Feb. 19, 1864, *The British Colonist,* Feb. 20, 1864, p. 3.

93. Letter written by John Morris after his re-examination the previous day. See the proceedings beginning the defendant's case, *Bentinck Arm Company v. Hood,* Sixth Day, Feb. 18, 1864, *The British Colonist,* Feb. 19, 1864, p.3. The allegation is explained better in the Chronicle's transcript, "The Coast Muddle," *Daily Chronicle,* Feb. 19, 1864, p.3.

94. "Supreme Court of Civil Justice," March 29, 1864, *Daily Chronicle,* March 30, 1864, p.3. Notice the sidebar "The Coast Route Muddle," reporting the suggestion, apparently originating immediately with Cary, that he already had decided to appeal for a hearing in an English court before he would go the new trial route.

95. "Supreme Court," *The British Colonist,* July 15, 1864, p.3.

small claims order and so did not meet the threshold for such an appeal. Leave was denied. In the end, Hood prevailed and this Company came to the end of its unhappy road.

Hood had no prior knowledge of British Columbia before undertaking this contract. Under a time pressure created by Cary, he had signed it without study, trusting that Cary had represented their negotiations faithfully. To his surprise, the contract gave him until the end of July, less than 40 days, to open the first 110 of the road's 300 km. It was an impossible condition. No reasonable person would have agreed to it. Hood said he had agreed only to do his best as he might find the circumstances. The contract also failed to add Hood to the syndicate described below as promised.[96] Hood testified that, because Cary was a high official, he believed that he was among gentlemen; that is, men of honor who do not take "mean advantage." Instead, as Hood's lawyer put it, Cary *looked upon Hood as a sheep ready for shearing, and Mr. Cary seems to have thought his position entitled him to be the shearer.*[97] So Hood's two allegations were that Cary had used sharp business practice and that he had abused his public position.

Since the jury found against Hood, one might say it rejected his claims. More likely, it was only affirming that the better policy is for a signed contract to be held as containing all terms of an agreement negotiated between equals. Yet these jurors were Cary's constituents. Each one who had shared Cary's perspective on Victoria's future also had suffered a loss when this road failed. While they punished Hood for failing Victoria's perceived public interest, the tortured result also punished Cary by withholding the fruits. Probably, it was the credibility of Hood's allegations that left Cary at the end of this legal process with nothing. Both judge and jury came in with knowledge of his reputation. Nor do judges like calculated efforts to bully them.

In any case, this is our first character evidence of those behind the colonial movement in the Ancestors' territory. Cary and Co. left a trail of people feeling victimized by unscrupulous men seizing every possible advantage. Hood was neither first nor last in this line. M.L.A. Dr. John Sebastian Helmcken said of his friend Cary that the Attorney

96. Testimony of William Hood, *Bentinck Arm Co, v. Hood.* Seventh Day, Feb. 19, 1864, *The British Colonist,* Feb. 20, 1864, p. 3.
97. Wood's address to the jury, *Bentinck Arm Co, v. Hood,* Sixth Day, Feb. 18, 1864, *The British Colonist,* Feb. 19, 1864, p. 3.

General was *not overburdened with the ordinary ideas or right and wrong.*[98] This seems a strange testimonial for the Colony's highest legal official. Shortly after these events, in 1865, Cary was certified as insane and he died the following year.[99]

The other plaintiff was Edward Green. The Attorney General's friend and business partner, Green was the Bentinck Arm Company's secretary and operations manager. Yet he was not named here in that capacity. Instead, Green represented the purchasers on an 1860 deed to land as their trustee. Through this deed, the Crown supposedly had conveyed all the land for two miles upstream along the Bella Coola River to a syndicate of Victoria speculators.[100] Cary and Green had shares, variously said between five and eight percent each. Once the land became susceptible to corporate ownership, Cary planned to make this "The Bella Whoala Company."[101] In its pre-incorporative condition, this association can be called "the New Aberdeen land syndicate."[102] These speculators suffered the greatest monetary harm when the road failed. This entity had a clear motive for an extermination policy to remove the Ancestors from its claim.

Who were these adventurers? Edward Green owned one share.[103] He was married to the daughter of William Murray, a former H.B.C. manager. Murray owned one share. Green had come to Victoria as a clerk for Samuel Price and Co., a San Francisco shipping concern.

98. Helmcken, *Reminiscences*, pp. 176-77.

99. The ecology of his insanity seems uncertain but one could make a good case that his behavior in the colonies from the first showed signs of an already increasing sociopathy.

100. Without the documents, the precise nature of this association cannot be determined. Rather than a trust, it probably was intended from the beginning as a private joint-stock company that Cary hesitated to register until it became clear whether the Proclamation concerning supposed agricultural land allowed corporate claimants. Once the claimants of a pre-emption had title, there was nothing to prevent them from reselling to a corporation.

101. See Venables' map, BCARS CM/B91.

102. It cannot now be determined whether the syndicate was or was not also a party to Hood's contract. Naming Green as a plaintiff and Hood's belief that he had become a member suggests it may have been. Though the contract primarily was made to benefit the syndicate, third party beneficiaries had a difficult time recovering damages under the law of that time. In 1863, Green attempted to assign an interest in New Aberdeen to the Company. If effective, an exchange of rights may have given New Aberdeen an interest in the contract, and entitled the syndicate to be named as a plaintiff. By the appeal hearing in July, the defendant was arguing that Green's only interest was a personal one, as a Bentinck Arm Company shareholder. However, if the plaintiff's lawsuit had been conceived that way, given the final outcome, Cary also would/should have been co-named as a plaintiff. See also the judge's discussion confining Green's role to that of secretary in "Supreme Court of Civil Justice," March 29, 1864, *Daily Chronicle*, March 30, 1864, p.3.

103. This list and the further list below are compiled from BCARS. GR-1182, B.C. Dept. of Lands and Works, Cariboo, Lytton and Lillooet Pre-emption Records taken by P. Nind and T. Elwyn, Alexandria District, 1860 to 1863, Folder 1.

Samuel Price owned one share. Green's relation, Frederick P. Green, was Victoria agent for the London Life Insurance Co. He owned one share. Attorney General Cary owned one share. That makes five.

Green indicated 12 other interests, including those named below. Later, Cary would say they were about 20.[104] There is no way now of knowing who may have held multiple or fractional shares or to whom interests may have been transferred.[105] John Miles, for example, had died before 1862. Cary refused this disclosure to his replacement as attorney general for B.C. even in the penultimate hour of protecting their value. From this, one can infer that some unnamed holders might have found it embarrassing. In addition to the names above, those disclosed to the land office were, John Swanson, Herbert Lewis, Robert Miles (2 shares), John Miles, Duncan and Pat McKay. All these were H.B.C. managers, servants or associates. The H.B.C. eventually came into ownership of this land. It, or the P.S.A.C., may have been a large undisclosed beneficial owner all along.

In any case, the relevant fact is that important figures among the Governor's closest circles drove this syndicate's activity. With direct access to political power, they were at the ideological center of the settler-colonial movement, endorsing, shaping or acting in accord with its table of values.

II
The New Aberdeen adventurers among the Ancestors.

Representing the New Aberdeen land syndicate, then, Edward Green visited the Ancestors' territory in Sept. 1860. This was the first contact made by settlers seeking financial interests or property in the Nuxalk Ancestor's territory.

Green's testimony compared with the harbor record shows that he and an employee, James Kenny, came with Captain McKay, an experienced coastal fur trader. McKay brought to this endeavor his prior knowledge of the coastal inlets and their residents. The McKays holding New Aberdeen shares seem his relations. Afterward, McKay built a cabin here and acted as though he had a proprietary interest.

104. "The Coast Route Muddle," *Bentinck Arm v. Hood,* First Day, *The Daily Chronicle,* Feb. 12, 1864, p.3.

105. BCARS. GR-1372. British Columbia. Colonial Correspondence. B01313. F275. No. 94. A.G. Henry Crease to Colonel Moody, Commissioner of Lands, June 19, 1862.

Notice that this Sept. 1860 expedition clearly pre-dates the winter 1860/61 gold discoveries in the Cariboo Mountains. Not until 1862 did Cary add Quesnelle Forks as a possible destination for better access to the Cariboo mines.[106] The original impetus, then, had little to do with supplying a Cariboo gold rush that had not yet begun.

In turning the colonial movement's attention to the Ancestors' territory, George Cary's leading objective as M.L.A. and the Colony of Vancouver Island's prime minister was a "Coastal Route" to access B.C.'s interior hinterland generally. Such a route would bypass New Westminster and preserve for Victoria the benefit of direct access to the interior and of a Northwest Passage by land. In 1860, it was still unknown whether the Fraser Canyon would remain impractical for commercial purposes. The Harrison River bypass, known as the Douglas Road, was inefficient. So pursuing a coastal route was more reasonable than it might seem in the light of later knowledge that better engineering and much public capital could tame the Canyon.

Cary testified that he and Edward Green "devoted a great portion of their time" to planning for this project.[107] Dedication of time and money intensifies motive. As the Governor's legal adviser and as Attorney General for both colonies until Oct. 15, 1861, Governor Douglas said that he "constantly required" Cary's presence.[108] There is no reasonable prospect, then, that the Governor might have been unaware of Cary's plans on any front, especially not those publicly to benefit Victoria and Vancouver Island or those privately for himself and the Governor's former H.B.C./P.S.A.C. colleagues.

This endeavor's first major task was to settle on the best location for a harbor city. The expedition staked land at three potential landings for a road. Green testified, *We fixed upon the middle arm as the most desirable.... [However,] we took 960 acres at each arm, the north, south and middle; we paid $2,000* [say $80,000 today]*...to the Government, that's all we did that year....*[109] As solicitor for the syndicate, George Cary would have

---

106. BCARS. GR-1372. British Columbia. Colonial Correspondence. BO1313. F275/4, George Cary to B.C. Attorney General Henry Crease, Feb. 5, 1862.

107. Testimony of George Cary, *Bentinck Arm Co. v. Hood*, Third Day, Feb. 15, 1864, *The British Colonist*, Feb. 17, 1864, p. 3.

108. *The British Columbian*, Jan. 23, 1862, p. 3.

109. Testimony of Edward Green, *Bentinck Arm Co. v. Hood*, Day One, Feb. 11, 1864, *The British Colonist*, Feb. 12, 1864. Notice that by "middle" he means North Bentinck Arm. The original claim according to Green's map was for 1600 acres, see Chapter 11.

delivered this $2000 to Attorney General George Cary. The receipt returned to George Cary, solicitor for the syndicate, created an equitable interest more "perfect" than any other kind, pending only registration in the land office and the formal issue of a legal title. Or so Cary later would argue.[110]

No one noted the representations that Green and McKay surely made to the local authorities. Yet each of these locations was under the control of various indigenous communities: Kimsquit on the Dean Channel; Q'umk'uts and Soonochlim/Snxlhh at North Bentinck Arm; and Tallyu at South Bentinck Arm. 5000 to 10,000 permanent residents, or more, had interests here.[111] It was impossible to have taken control for the purposes intended without dispossessing them. For this reason, the Crown's policy as set out in the 1763 Royal Proclamation now required Colonial officials to intervene. Given Cary's official status, it is impossible that colonial officials simply had no knowledge of this imperative having arisen. To suppose otherwise one must argue that the Governor's legal adviser, Attorney General George Cary, had no knowledge of the interests being pursued by George Cary, private businessman. This would be absurd.

Three days later, mentioning McKay by name and using information that could only have come through him or Green's party, *The British Colonist* encouraged entrepreneurs to begin pursuing trade up the coast. It cited the "enormous profits" of the H.B.C.'s no longer protected monopoly.[112] In other words, with the best land now quietly locked up, the syndicate had begun making efforts calculated to increase its value. This shows that these men had an accomplished ability of foresight and planning. And, therefore, were certain to have anticipated also the challenges presented by indigenous occupation.

Indeed, this editorial discussed the indigenous population. Since the writer had no personal knowledge and since the piece otherwise depended on information supplied by those who had just visited the Ancestors, we can assume that this especially included them. And that it reflected the developers' mindset. It said,

---

110. BCARS. GR-1372. British Columbia. Colonial Correspondence. BO1313. F275, George Hunter Cary, solicitor, to B.C. Attorney-General Henry Crease, June 4, 1862.

111. Eyewitness estimates of the lower Bella Coola Valley population are discussed in detail during Chapter 12. These figures assume that population and, for the other centers, a range of more modest to the same size.

112. "Trade of the North-west Coast," *The British Colonist*, Sept. 25, 1860, p. 2.

It is very certain that, so far as civilizing the Indians is concerned, the [H.B.C.] has done little; and were they to remain sole traders on the northwest coast for the next century, they would never elevate the race to a higher position in the social scale than that they now occupy. Like the American slaves, they would be used only in the most degrading employment to provide for feudal masters. To catch fur-bearing animals and pull off the skin is the height of Hudson Bay civilization among the Indians. The advantage, then, of a huge trading monopoly, to the red man, [is] very little; certainly so long as they have no competition, the coast will never be settled, nor perhaps even frequented, by a higher race.... On the whole, the trade of the north-west coast deserves the attention of the enterprising.[113]

Disparaging others as "uncivilized" is a common feature in cultural contexts conducive to genocide. Every citizen of good faith holds those who imagine others inferior as dishonorably prejudiced. One imagines that it should go without saying that protecting the "Honor of the Crown" has always required non-indigenous officials to prevent such attitudes from leading to racial disadvantage or to the mass murders typical of genocide. Colonial apologists often imply that their favorite founders should be excused because, supposedly, the times were different then. Yet thefts of land, extortion, fraud, murder and mass murder were all crimes under English law in 1862. Indeed, these acts have been outlawed in every civil society. Decent people never excuse them. Nor do they accept subtle invitations to empathize with officials pushing through roads or having the trains run on time while engaging in dishonorable or genocidal acts.

Read constructively, this editorial supposes that the economic relations fostered by the H.B.C. interfered with the free flow of knowledge to the detriment of indigenous Peoples. This may or may not have been true. Indigenous citizens frequently acquired non-indigenous knowledge and then chose to reject its application as not worth the cost. Judge Mathew Begbie so observed this phenomenon among those natives most informed about "civilization" in 1872.[114]

---

113. "Trade of the North-west Coast," *The British Colonist*, Sept. 25, 1860, p. 2.

114. "Memorandum by Chief Justice Begbie," *British Columbia: Report of the Hon. H.L. Langevin*, Ottawa, Queen's Printer, p. 27.

More ominously, this editorial may be read to suppose that "civilizing" developments, such as New Aberdeen, would benefit the indigenous residents inherently: either in the same way as they might benefit a non-indigenous community through improved efficiencies or in some unique way as supposed by the arrogance of those who imagine themselves superior. In either case, the development would be assumed as in the interest of others with or without their consent, and then expropriated under doctrines like eminent domain; and, in the second case, the self-interested proponents might encourage the assumption that their supposed inferiors did not have the knowledge necessary for informed consent about their own interests.

The "Honor of the Crown," though, requires informed consent and just compensation. Where citizens of a foreign country are involved, as here, it requires approaches to official representatives to identify affected interests. The Royal Proclamation expressly provided that only the Crown could approach indigenous communities over land. It expressly forbids the activity contemplated by the New Aberdeen syndicate. Nor were the syndicate's members simply naïve. On the contrary, they were drawn from the most informed of the colonial elite, including H.B.C. officers from the time of its administration of Canadian laws that included the Proclamation. So, without a political treaty and without the Crown also purchasing some color of title as a legal means of appropriating resources, these developers were outlaws to their own community. This notwithstanding that foremost among them was the Governor's legal adviser, who was also then attorney general for both British Columbia and Vancouver Island.[115]

III
Gaining access with consent under the law of the land.

However things might have stood within the nascent British Colonies to the south, the Ancestors were perfectly capable of giving the only legal permission necessary for these investors to proceed so long as they respected the laws and paid their taxes. Permission that all the available evidence shows the Ancestors as having granted.

---

115. George Cary served as attorney general for both colonies from his appointment in 1859 until, given his choice, he resigned from the office in British Columbia effective Oct. 15, 1861. Douglas' successor forced Cary from his Vancouver Island office in August 1864.

The issue here was whether those who imagined themselves as racially superior, and who were guided by a colonial ideology, could operate with good faith under native authorities pending formal approaches from the Colony. If not, this provides another motive for an extermination policy.

Would Attorney General Cary have continued even if he had to advise his clients that the non-indigenous community might never see true "old world" fee simple titles here, only "new world" titles encumbered by prior aboriginal rights? That they could be expected to share revenues with local indigenous communities as a customary cost of access to territorial benefits and that these communities very reasonably might refuse political change if approached honorably? At best, one can assume these developers discussed supposed economic benefits and kept silent about their politics.

In March 1862, a newspaper correspondent arriving at Bella Coola provided this insight into the Ancestors' seeming expectations:

> *The natives here are rather poor, but civil, obliging and willing to work for almost anything you choose to give them, and desire nothing better than that the whites will come among them, for they say they will pack all the goods sent this road across to Cariboo for a few blankets.*[116]

This observer may have mistaken for poverty the choice of a virtuous and rich spiritual life lived with noble simplicity.

In any case, the Ancestors consistently showed themselves as welcoming and with a will to accommodate their guest's economic objectives. What they may have been led to expect from these private entrepreneurs, when "the whites came among them," seems a dock, warehousing and services for travelers. That is, for merely private concerns, not political objectives. One can understand approval for this. Yet nothing in that agenda requires a complete concession of land, policy or sovereignty to outsiders.

No constitutional change can have taken place simply on account of settlers arriving here to declare an interest in pursuing economic objectives. The existing sovereign authority continued to hold both *de jure* and *de facto* control throughout these private approaches.

The evidence seems that, while anticipating that the law of the land would be respected, the Ancestors expected settlers to regulate their own

---

116. "From Bentinck Arm and the Coast Route," *The British Colonist*, Mar 31, 1862.

behavior according, say, to their own laws of contract, rather than, say, to adopt the Potlatch system. Of course, once settlers had become better informed, it could be assumed that they would integrate themselves into the established norms as immigrants. And that, one day, inter-marriage would complete the work of integration.

On this 1860 groundwork, Cary and his cohorts were now in position to begin executing what they imagined as the best plans to drive up the value of their holdings. Personal enrichment and colonial expansion ran together in this.

8

A Coastal Route to Canada, 1861

Having secured the Ancestors' permission for access and having marked out the most strategic land to prevent non-indigenous claim jumping, Cary and the syndicate's agents now turned to the task of increasing its value within their various objectives.

I

The steamship subsidy committee.

Through a March 1861 public meeting of those most urgently concerned with Victoria's future, M.L.A.s George Cary and Robert Burnaby oversaw creation of a "Steamship Committee."[117] Sharing the platform with these government officials were "representatives of all the leading mercantile houses."[118]

This steamship committee was created in connection with and in part as an instrument for the public policy of opening a coastal route inland. (See map p. 182.) This event confirms that the desire for a coastal route was an expression of Victoria's public interest as seen by some of its most influential citizens. One newspaper explicitly described the resulting committee as "appointed by the citizens of Victoria."[119]

Victoria's leading newspaper also editorialized,

> *As a matter of general government policy...we deem it advisable to give every encouragement to the speedy exploration of the Bentinck Arm route.... Every man who is interested in the prosperity of this town cannot but feel a direct interest in a coast route as everything that tends*

117. "The Steamship Meeting," *The British Colonist*, March 18, 1862, p. 3.
118. "Direct Steam Communication with San Francisco," *The Daily Press*, March 19, 1861, p. 3.
119. "The Steamship Question," *The Daily Press*, March 22, 1861, p. 3.

to give permanence and adds to our facility to supply the surrounding trade adds to our importance....[120]

This underscores the quasi-public nature of the Bentinck Arm enterprises. It does not, of course, imply a constant unanimity. By year end, while again noting the project's wide public appeal, the first newspaper called attention to the ignoble character of those driving this policy, *It would be really laughable did the public know who the parties are and their [less than noble] aims...[in] striving so energetically to have a Northern coast route to the mines.*[121]

The steamship committee was to lobby the Governor for a subsidy encouraging a direct San Francisco to Victoria passenger service. The subsidy would be paid by both colonies. Nominally, the effect would be to thwart competition from Portland or Puget Sound. In reality, it would favor Victoria at New Westminster's expense.

Then, in *Bentinck Arm Co. v. Hood,* Cary disclosed that he also had negotiated a second leg: Victoria direct to New Aberdeen.[122] Not only would Victoria benefit from funds paid by New Westminster, George Cary and the New Aberdeen investors would have been the greatest beneficiaries of all. New Westminster's citizens, too, now learned about being "sheep ready for shearing" by George Cary.

With the subsidy authorized by the end of Dec. 1861, and with a budget to the end of July, the committee went to San Francisco to arrange a shipping company. Several, including Cary, signed large personal guarantees that the Colony would pay.[123] This intensified the motive to succeed. For Cary's second leg, the shipping company only wanted a road inland opened before committing a vessel. With all this in place for the 1862 mining season, one could expect the value of harbor land at Bella Coola to be stratospheric by, say, early June.

The committee returned to Victoria triumphantly on the first subsidized sailing, the *Brother Jonathan* arriving March 12, 1862. On this same sailing were two smallpox carriers. With only a few cases under quarantine in its hospitals, the disease was not then epidemic in San

---

120. "Northern Coast Route to Cariboo," *The British Colonist,* April 8, 1861, p. 2.

121. "The Coast Route Excitement," *The Daily Press,* Dec. 23, 1861, p. 2.

122. Testimony of George Cary, *Bentinck Arm Co. v. Hood (1864)* Third Day, Feb. 15, 1864, *The British Colonist,* Feb. 17, 1864, p. 3.

123. "Letter from Vancouver's Island," *Daily Alta California,* April 4, 1861, p. 1.

Francisco. Arriving alongside the steamship committee, these carriers would become the only outside source of smallpox during the epidemics that would then sweep the indigenous population of the entire British pacific. Given the pattern of the disease's subsequent distribution, and not the least from how its course can be documented in Tsilhqot'in and Nuxalk territory, each new consistency of detail adds proof that the steamship committee deliberately "imported the disease" here within a larger Regime-wide colonial policy.[124]

II
A road from the north coast to the interior.

As Cary was organizing the steamship committee in March 1861, Edward Green began laying the groundwork of a road. Without a road, the land and the subsidy would be of little lasting value.

What value did the investors expect from a road? Green testified that they paid the Colony $2000 after staking three locations and that they then decided to focus first on their North Bentinck Arm claim at Bella Coola. If one includes the initial outlay for the road, the final cost of acquisition may have been $4.00 an acre. In *Bentinck Arm v. Hood*, Green testified that, if Hood had completed his contract, he expected the land to have been *worth $50 to $60 an acre, perhaps $100.*[125] Cary testified that, before the road contract, *St. Ours* [a businessman] *offered me $1,600 for 40 acres* [or $40 an acre.]... *I would not have taken double that.*[126] So, with a road, the speculators expected profits of perhaps 1600 percent. This was not unreasonable. Similar pioneers at Victoria, *having bought property three and a half years ago...made 500 to 1000 percent on their purchase.*[127] Gaining control of resources for little and selling them for windfall profits, speculating in land that is, was always the true B.C. gold rush.

Such prospects provide a powerful motive to create the necessary pre-conditions. Realizing these profits assumed British jurisdiction,

---

124. The verb applied by Regime insider John Sheepshanks, *Bishop in the Rough* (New York: E.P. Dutton, 1909) p. 70.

125. Testimony of Edward Green," *Bentinck Arm v. Hood,* Day One, Feb. 11, 1864, *The British Colonist*, Feb. 12, 1864, p. 3.

126. Testimony of George Cary, *Bentinck Arm v. Hood,* Day Three, Feb. 15, 1864, *The British Colonist,* Feb. 17, 1864, p. 3.

127. *Victoria Daily Press*, March 28, 1862, p. 3.

vacant possession and fee simple titles. That is, to depose the *de jure* authorities, to dispossess the indigenous occupiers and to institute a new political regime with a new land system. All in a timely way.

In April 1861, investing $1000 on New Aberdeen's account, Edward Green sent James Kenny and Colin McKenzie from Ft. Alexandria across Tsilhqot'in territory to Bella Coola as his agents.[128] McKenzie had crossed Tsilhqot'in territory six months before with the H.B.C.'s Ft. Alexandria manager.[129] Since McKenzie already knew the way, seeking permission for this expanded usage and for the related services was the only reason for them to have spent several days visiting Tsilhqot'in leaders on this occasion.

Kenny and McKenzie reported a cool reception in the East Tsilhqot'in.[130] Nits'il?in Alexis inconvenienced them by moving just before they arrived. His community then pled scarcity for an inability to supply them. Most telling, after several days, Alexis still declined to provide guides. Since McKenzie already knew the way, guides were only a formality, an endorsement.

Their West Tsilhqot'in reception went better. After several days, at Nagwentlun, Nits'il?in Anaham provided a party of nine guides to Bella Coola.[131] The size of this party argues that the Tsilhqot'in also had assumed some control of the mission. At Bella Coola, Staltmc Pootlass gave a large feast. All this is most consistent with these agents having gained permission for a road from the indigenous authorities.

Anaham's nine guides seemingly included "War Chief" Solyman from an Upper Valley community. Solyman continued to Victoria.[132] Kenny surely introduced him to his employers. Solyman remained for several months. He became fluent in English. In spring 1862, he returned to supervise indigenous packers serving miners crossing to the Cariboo mines. During winter 1862/63, Solyman would execute a non-

128. Testimony of Edward Green, *Bentinck Arm Company v. Hood,* Day One, Feb. 11, 1864, *The British Colonist,* Feb. 12, 1864, p. 3. Say, $40,000 today.

129. The *Fort Alexandria Journal* indicates that the Post Manager, John Saunders, and McKenzie left Oct. 22 and returned for Nov. 16. See also "Encouraging Mining News," *The British Colonist, December* 22, 1860, p. 3., which reports their return and the first hint of the rich Cariboo gold discovery in the same article.

130. "Arrival of an Exploring Party from Fort Alexandria to the Coast," *The British Colonist,* June 12, 1861, p. 3.

131. "...they descended the River to Noo-tie-och with nine Chilcotin Indians. Then they took canoes about midday and arrived at Bella Coola the same day," See "Arrival of an Exploring Party..." The British Colonist, June 12, 1861, p. 3.

132. "The Murder of Bob McLeod," *Evening Express,* April 26, 1863, p. 2.

indigenous packer for violating the law of the land.[133] The Colony did not react, underlining the fact that it had not yet extended any jurisdiction to these territories. Solyman's apparent role in all this reflected the fact of pre-existing licensing and regulatory oversight along these trails. All this space was occupied in a political sense.

A new set of prospective developers, Ranald McDonald, George Barnston, J.B. Pearson and Gilbert Tompkins soon followed.[134] These also reported an initial lack of Tsilhqot'in enthusiasm. However, after two days, Anaham provided them with a guide. There may have been some confusion about the relationship between this new request and the permission already given to the previous visitors.

At Bella Coola, Barnston said the Ancestors received them, *(W)ith the greatest hospitality and [we] were feasted at the different villages on salmon and eulachon oil in every imaginable style.*[135] He also noted that Bella Coola natives were *(P)erfectly well acquainted with all the trails into the interior as they make annual excursions to trade for furs with the inland tribes, making a handsome profit by reselling them to the [H.B.C.'s] Labouchere and traders on the coast.* This native-to-native trade had flourished for years. H.B.C. records show that fully 40 percent of the trade at Ft. McLoughlin in Heiltsuk territory in the 1830s was with Bella Coola traders reselling furs that they had purchased in Tsilhqot'in or Dakelh territory.[136]

In other words, these trails already supported an established commercial industry. This implies customary practices. Participants in any customary trade usually adapt these customs to changing methods, means or goods as the root of commercial law. That is, the non-indigenous community's commercial needs could have been met by the established framework and without outside interference. Settlers, however, also had sweeping political objectives.

133. See discussion in Chapter 10.

134. "A Trip from Alexandria to the Coast," *The British Colonist*, August 16, 1861, p. 2. Barnston met with the Governor just before leaving for this trip. He wrote this letter July 24, on his return to the Bonaparte River. However he did not send it for publication until after he had applied to the Governor for a toll road license. In what will soon seem a pattern of deceit, his letter says they arrived at the Fort July 10 but the Fort *Journal* recorded their arrival there July 12: that is, Barnston made it appear that it took less time than it did.

135. "A Trip from Alexandria to the Coast," as above.

136. HBCA. B.223/b/20, p. 71, James Douglas to Gov. Simpson, March 18, 1838.

McDonald and Barnston returned to Ft. Alexandria July 12.[137] The oldest son of a P.S.A.C. founder and his lawyer, these men had intimate connections within the Douglas Regime. In fact, Barnston met with Douglas just before leaving for Bella Coola.[138] On the 13th, they went to Williams Lake where the Colonial official with regional responsibility for indigenous relations resided. Since the Colony had not approached the Tsilhqot'in yet for any reason and since official contact might smooth their way, they had every incentive to visit him.

Alexis and Lhats'as?in accompanied McDonald and Barnston to Ft. Alexandria and remained there.[139] Representatives from Klus Kus and other Southern Dakelh communities soon joined them. This seems an inter-tribal conference to discuss the coming prospect of an increased non-indigenous presence.[140] The timing, hard on the heels of McDonald and Barnston's return, suggests they expected a Colonial representative to join them. Those attending this conference represented the true sovereign authorities here. The "Honor of the Crown" and the non-indigenous community's safety each required that the Colonial government send an agent to learn their terms. Yet the Douglas Regime had delegated little of the appropriate authority. This inaction may have been from gross incompetence, a lack of care for the dignity of its hosts and the safety of settlers, or the pursuit of an undeclared policy. For their part, whatever considerations were canvassed at this conference, in the result, all these communities and the Ancestors then received travelling miners in peace.

Kenny and McKenzie crossed again in September, now with Denis Cain and Cavendish Venables. Dr. J.B. Wilkinson also seems to have accompanied this party. In the light of what would take place just a few months later, the presence of a doctor in this prior period stands out as calling for notice. Cain paused to stake the first settler's claim

---

137. *Fort Alexandria Journal,* July 12, 1861.

138. Douglas to Secretary of State for the Colonies, Oct. 24, 1861, p. 18, Dispatch No. 20 in *Papers Relating to British Columbia,* 1862, p. 52.

139. On the arrival of Alexis with a large party of Tsilhqot'in at the same time as McDonald and Barnston returning from Nagwentlun and the coast see, *Fort Alexandria Journal,* July 12, 1861. When Rev. Lundin Brown subsequently met Lhats'as?in at Ft. Alexandria on Aug. 18, 1861, he said that Lhats'as?in had come there from Nagwentlun. See: *Fort Alexandria Journal* Aug. 18, 1861 and Brown, *Klatsassan,* s. 1, reference to his party as from "Nicootlem." As "War Chief" from a community near Tatla Lake, Lhats'as?in ordinarily would not have been said to come from Nagwentlun.

140. "A good number of Indians, Chilcotin, Klooskas, and Porter [Carrier or Dakelh]" *Fort Alexandria Journal,* July 18, 1861.

in Tsilhqot'in territory, at Chilcotin Lake.[141] Venables made a point of having secured guides from Anaham.[142]

This party followed Anaham's recommendation of Mackenzie's route to Nautlieff/Nutl'lhiixw.[143] On Sept. 30, 1861, Venables staked 1000 acres upriver of New Aberdeen's 960 acres.[144] He covered his bets with a claim on the Dean Channel. As Venables staked the portion of Q'umk'uts given up by New Aberdeen, Denis Cain staked the ground under Soonochlim.[145] Dr. Wilkinson staked a 160-acre claim in the Tallyu precinct at South Bentinck Arm.[146] Each new claim was to land unmistakably within the immediate precinct of long-established, permanent, indigenous communities.

So far every visitor seeking an interest in these foreign territories had sought permission from the true *de jure* authorities. Everything seemed suggestive of good faith. All these visitors did was to mark some trees and leave. There was little in this activity to raise alarm bells. Nothing suggested the reality that these settler vanguards were harbingers of a colonial movement seeking to displace the authorities.

Venables remained in the Ancestors' territory for four months. He scouted locations and made plans. Returning to Victoria, he said,

> *The Bella Coola Indians are very friendly and so are the other tribes round about. They are only too anxious for white men to come among them. They are mostly fine strong men, ready and eager to be employed packing to the mines.... They would gladly pack I imagine to the mouth of Quesnel River or Alexandria for 10 or 12 cents and be then well paid...at the outside ten days.... I assure [any miner] he will have no difficulty in packing [with] Indians.... The Anaham and Chilcotin [Chilcotin Lake and Puntzi] Indians have a good many horses, which might be turned to good use for packing.*

141. BCARS. GR-1182. British Columbia Dept. of Lands and Works, Cariboo, Lytton and Lillooet pre-emption records, Folder 1, Claim of Denis Cain, records taken by P. Nind and T. Elwyn, Alexandria District, 1860-1863.

142. "Bentinck Arm Route," *The British Colonist*, Jan. 29, 1862, p. 3.

143. "Route from Alexandria to North Bentinck Arm," *The British Colonist*, Oct. 28, 1861, p. 3.

144. BCARS. British Columbia. Colonial Correspondence. B01372. F1798. Cavendish Venables to the Department of Lands and Works, Bella Coola, Sept. 30, 1861. BCARS. Map of Cavendish Venables, Sept. 30, 1861, CM-B91.

145. Venables' map, BCARS CM/B91.

146. BCARS. GR-1182. British Columbia Dept. of Lands and Works, Cariboo, Lytton and Lillooet pre-emption records, Folder 1, Claim of J.B. Wilkinson, records taken by P. Nind and T. Elwyn, Alexandria District, 1860-1863. No sketch included.

I must say a few words of the Bella Coola Indians. Since I have been there, they have in every way been kind and friendly. Although we often have nothing to exchange, they always supplied us with fish and game. The old Chief, Pootlass, went out purposely to shoot for us and brought 20 deer. When we left...he made us promise to return and so, to the last, they were ready in every way to oblige us. They have seen less of the white man than other tribes and it is a great pity that they should, like the others, be spoiled by that poison, which is continually sold on that coast. About every fortnight small schooners pass and leave their mark behind. In almost every instance from 300 to 400 gallons of liquor is part of the cargo.[147]

III
An honorable duty of intervention.

Protecting the Crown's honor and, thereby, the non-indigenous community's interests now required that officials: 1) approach the Ancestors for a political treaty outlining non-indigenous intentions while protecting indigenous rights of self determination; 2) take steps to forestall conflict when the indigenous authorities might be moved to protect their own interests, as in Tsilhqot'in territory; 3) control speculators as they began pursuing strategic locations in any territory and attempting to drive up the value; and 4) control outlaws preying on indigenous communities and then escaping beyond their reach. One might have expected the Governor's formal legal adviser to raise these issues. But this was Attorney General George Cary.

In fact, the Douglas Regime did not operate in contemplation of the Crown's honor anywhere, only in the opportunistic growth of its reach. In lieu of approaches to indigenous communities in good faith, Douglas steered the Pacific Colonies along a course dominated by a propertied class diametrically opposed to indigenous interests. One leading representative, while supposing that all human beings are no more than dishonorable beasts, candidly noted that, in relations with the indigenous Peoples, the Colony had practiced only, "The survival of the fittest."[148] This official disavowal of the Crown's honor was the true spirit of regime change at the founding of British Columbia.

---

147. "Bentinck Arm Route," *The British Colonist,* Jan. 29, 1862, p. 3.
148. John Sebastian Helmcken, *Reminiscences.* (Vancouver: U.B.C. Press, 1975) p. 331.

In the Island Assembly during summer 1861, Attorney General Cary introduced a racist Bill to diminish native rights. He sought to remove the "expensive and insufficient" procedures protecting people under British jurisdiction and to substitute in their place an apartheid-style "Indian commissioner" to try "Indian criminals."[149] This racist inclination to disrespect indigenous residents as a sub-class reflects on those with the most urgent stake in relations with the Ancestors. Such men seem more likely than others to contemplate extermination to rid themselves of a sub-class considered a source of nuisance.

Cary also proposed lifting restrictions on trading liquor into indigenous communities.[150] Coincident with this legislative proposal, a notorious liquor-for-furs trader,[151] Capt. Jim Taylor of the *Petrel*, a "floating whiskey tap"[152] relocated to Bella Coola as an agent for Cary's enterprises.[153] Taylor would assist Venables and Cain as they staked land under the Bella Coola villages in Sept.[154] With Angus McLeod as a colleague, Taylor's purpose was to protect the absentee claimants from later claim jumpers.[155] And indeed, in 1862, the first settlers reported two men here who threatened them with violence, if they interfered with the rights of prior claimants.[156]

Notice that these developers were taking steps already in summer 1861 to counter foreseeable settler claim jumping. They seem equally as likely, therefore, also to have begun planning at the same time to counter indigenous occupation and the even more readily foreseeable probability of violent resistance. Remember that two smallpox carriers would arrive

---

149. "House of Assembly," *The British Colonist*, August 2, 1861, p. 3.

150. See above, "House of Assembly," Aug. 2, 1861.

151. The *Fort Simpson Journal* describes Taylor and the *Petrel* in action Dec. 10-13, 1862. BCARS./A/C/20/ si William Henry McNeil, *Fort Simpson Journal*, 1859 – 1862. Taylor and the *Petrel* were a regular source of furs for the H.B.C. see: "From Fort Simpson," *Victoria Daily Chronicle*, Jan. 18, 1863, on the furs collected by this means.

152. *H.M.S. Devastation* caught the *Petrel* in a sweep during April 1863 for avoiding customs duties on imported liquor. Taylor fled without paying the fine in New Westminster. Ultimately, Dr. Tolmie, General Manager of the P.S.A.C. went to claim her. Coverage in the colonial newspapers begins May 1, 1863 and continues over several days.

153. "Coast Route Explorer," *The British Colonist*, July 22, 1861, p. 3. And see "Threatening Settlers," *The British Colonist*, March 31, 1862.

154. "The North Bentinck Arm," *The Daily Press*, Dec. 5, 1861, p. 3.

155. See the Testimony of Edward Green, *Bentinck Arm Co. v. Hood*, Day 1, Afternoon Session, "The Coast Muddle," *Daily Chronicle*, Feb. 12, 1864, p. 3 and "A Trip to the Head of Bentinck Arm…" *The British Colonist*, Aug. 19, 1862, p. 3.

156. "Threatening Settlers," *The British Colonist*, Mar. 31, 1862, p. 3.

on the steamship committee's sailing of March 12, 1862, eight months later at the start of the 1862 season. This is perfectly consistent with the creation and adoption of a plan in summer 1861. Indeed, it is just what premeditation would look like.

Given the timing, Cary's liquor bill seems perhaps some *quid pro quo* with Taylor, a potential great beneficiary. Nor should one discount the political significance of Taylor relocating here under these circumstances with Cary's sponsorship. Settlers frequently undermined the cohesion of indigenous communities by creating widespread addictions through distributing cheap liquor. Francis Poole documented natives *mad-drunk, the [H.B.C.'s] Labouchere having...supplied them with an immense quantity of whiskey in barter for furs.... The surprise of the Indians at our own refusal told its own tale. During the night, numbers came alongside in a shocking state of intoxication openly proclaiming that the H.B.C. regularly sent liquor around.... Fearing treachery from these besotted Indians, we stole away at daybreak.*[157] If this practice produced higher profits in fur trading, then why not use it in the acquisition of land?

The profit-at-any-cost attitude minimally behind this trade is especially pertinent here for the bulk of New Aberdeen adventurers came from within H.B.C. circles, including Capt. John Swanson of the *Labouchere*. Capt. Swanson, Taylor and McKay each would build houses on claims near the road by spring 1862.[158] These were the kind of strategic front running investments that could generate quick profits once titles could be registered and the road had traffic. The prospect of quick profits provides an immediate motive for bringing about the necessary conditions: vacant land, in this case.

In any case, participating in this illegal trade shows the character of these men as capable of rationalizing criminal behavior when convenient for their purposes. It also reveals their willingness to take advantage, given tolerance in their own social entity, for abusing those in another. These are just the kind of considerations that one would expect to find in circumstances conducive to genocide.

To begin 1862, then, the Victoria adventurers had the requisite local permissions for a road and its ancillary services. To realize their expected profits, they had only to generate traffic, secure registration of their land

---

157. Francis Poole, *Queen Charlotte Islands*, pp. 184-187.

158. BCARS. Map of Cavendish Venables, Sept. 30, 1861, CM-B91. And Viator, "A Trip to the Head of Bentinck Arm on the Steamer Labouchere," serialized in *The British Colonist*, August 18, 19 and 20, 1862.

claims, subdivide and sell lots. By, say, early June, they could be rolling in profits with Victoria's economic future secured.

The greatest uncertainty in this plan remained the disposition of indigenous residents as their territorial control became compromised and as they became dispossessed from the ground to which they had inalienable ancestral rights under the law of the land. So long as indigenous residents vastly outnumbered incoming settlers, the *de jure* authorities could remain confident of asserting their *de facto* control as and when they might choose. But the settler community nowhere contemplated the continuation of any such status quo.

9

The Bentinck Arm Company's Road

On application by George Barnston for his client Ranald McDonald after their July 1861 trip through the Ancestors' and Tsilhqot'in territory, Governor Douglas granted a Charter authorizing McDonald to collect tolls on goods and cattle transported via a mule trail connecting Bentinck Arm to the Fraser River.[159] The Charter contemplated higher tolls after the trail's conversion to a wagon road.

The privileged son of a prominent H.B.C. manager, McDonald had no experience with roads or trails. With a dilettante's confidence, he told *Bentinck Arm v. Hood, I never constructed a road but [had] seen a good deal of it.*[160] He bragged, *I could have made a good trail in three months... [or] laid down a passable line for a wagon road in 36 days.*[161] On seeing the terrain and with experience in B.C., Lt. Palmer of the Royal Engineers said that simply blazing a suitable line by itself would be, *(T)he work...of months.*[162] Of McDonald, William Hood testified, *I did not wish to have anything [more] to do with Ranald McDonald [who] I had seen bruised from fighting, and had been told that he was in the custom of fighting when he got into liquor...not of infrequent occurrence.*[163]

Leaving the road in McDonald's hands, then, would have been a risky proposition for New Aberdeen. George Cary and Edward Green immediately purchased the Charter from McDonald. While this took pressure off McDonald, it delayed work while they created a limited

---

159. See page 4, *Prospectus of the Bentinck Arm and Fraser River Road Company Ltd.*, Victoria, Printed at the British Colonist, 1862, microfilm identifier cihm 17091.

160. Testimony of Ranald McDonald, *Bentinck Arm Co. v. Hood*, Fourth Day, Feb. 16, 1864, *The British Colonist*, Feb. 17, 1864, p. 3.

161. Testimony of Ranald McDonald, *Bentinck Arm Co. v Hood*, Fourth Day, Feb. 16, 1864, *Daily Chronicle*, Feb. 17, 1864, p. 3.

162. BCARS. GR-1372. British Columbia. Colonial Correspondence. B01353. F. 1302a. Lt. Henry Palmer to Colonel Moody, August 17, 1862.

163. Testimony of William Hood, *Bentinck Arm Co. v. Hood*, Seventh Day, Feb. 19, 1864, *The British Colonist*, Feb. 20, 1864, p. 3.

liability company and found a suitable contractor. As an incentive for the sale, Cary agreed to leave McDonald with a substantial minority interest, to make him a company director and to add him to the land syndicate. Green also paid McDonald's expenses while he assisted in promoting the route. In this connection, McDonald accompanied Cary's steamship committee to San Francisco and returned on the boat bringing smallpox.[164] Had the Bentinck Arm Road opened on schedule, McDonald would have been its greatest beneficiary after Cary and Green. He had considerable personal motive for backing an extermination policy as he helped mark out the Company's route for Poole's party taking smallpox to Chilcotin Lake and elsewhere.

I

A provocation of war within The Settlers' Insurrection.

In the beginning, every prospective operator acknowledged the true political realities with visits to the indigenous authorities. Yet the Charter given by Douglas now licensed its owner to collect tolls on traffic using established trails in several foreign territories where the Colony had not yet made approaches or acquired rights of any kind.

Without approaching the territorial authorities, Douglas had no lawful jurisdiction for authorizing any settler activity, let alone the legal authority for unilaterally setting tolls on indigenous trails. The "Indian trail" in question here may have been in use as a public utility for hundreds of years. Suppose the United States began collecting tolls on Canadian highways simply because American companies wanted to use them. Then imagine that those companies refused to pay Canadian tolls or to appear in Canadian courts, all the while American aircraft carriers cruised Georgia Strait. Similarly, this Charter was a provocation of war within The Settlers' Insurrection.

In addition to slighting the indigenous authorities, Douglas favored McDonald without considering other proposals. This reeked of corruption. Douglas also did not seek input from Colonel Richard Moody, B.C.'s Chief Commissioner for Land and Works. As the highest-ranking official actually resident in the Colony, Moody represented the citizens of New Westminster who understood a Fraser Canyon Road as

---

164. He was listed among the passengers, along with the committee, when it arrived back in Victoria March 12, 1862. See, "Passengers" per *Brother Jonathan*, *The British Colonist*, March 13, 1862, p. 3.

more in their interest. Following the sting of Douglas' corrupt licensing, Moody knew Cary's subsequent involvement for what it was: an attempt by Victoria interests to interfere on the mainland at New Westminster's expense. Moody wrote a blistering confidential letter to Douglas describing all this as "perfectly notorious."[165] New Westminster officials then began bureaucratically delaying Bentinck Arm at every chance.

II
The Bentinck Arm Company.

With the Charter in hand, Cary created the Bentinck Arm and Fraser River Road Company. His *Prospectus* had three parts: a business plan, an "Appendix" describing the new coastal route's sea leg, Victoria to North Bentinck Arm, and a "Report" by McDonald and Barnston on the land leg to the Fraser River.[166] The initial public offering began in April 1862 with shares priced at $250 each.[167]

A prospectus is a formal requirement before a company can offer shares to the public. Prudent investors read them for their failures. In the excerpts below, notice how preserving Victoria's economic place was a central theme of this private endeavor. Since public objectives were unmistakably at play in its purpose, so also there would be public motives in any extermination policy; supposing, that is, the company or its agents might be found to have participated in one. Official policy is the difference between mass murder and genocide.

Except once, the document is silent about indigenous interests. Yet these were a material fact for a Company planning to operate in several foreign territories. It mentions toll revenue that the Company expects under its Colonial charter. However it does not estimate the cost of satisfying indigenous interests. In addition, no prudent person could ignore the business risk of operating in territories where there had been no diplomatic approaches by the Colony. Only if the author

---

165. BCARS. British Columbia. Colonial Correspondence. B01372. F1798. Colonel Richard Moody to the Colonial Secretary (confidential), March 17, 1862.

166. *Prospectus of the Bentinck Arm and Fraser River Road Company Ltd.*, Victoria, Printed at the British Colonist, 1862, microfilm identifier cihm 17091.

167. Victoria had public companies with shares available for trading by the end of 1861, an agent for the London Stock Exchange by 1862, and a Stock Exchange Board with a list of transactions and shares on offer by the end of 1863. However, a cursory search does not turn up any transactions of Bentinck Arm Company shares. It is difficult to determine just when the shares began falling in value, or when there was no market for them.

had faith that there was some plan to render the indigenous regimes ineffective does the document make sense. Although he prepared it as a private solicitor, the Attorney General was perfectly positioned to know the Douglas Regime's actual plan to counter the certainty of violent indigenous opposition to their rude dispossession.

In that regard, it should be noted then that, when Cary published this document April 5, 1862, smallpox already had arrived in the Colonies on his steamship committee's sailing of March 12. Douglas already had acknowledged its presence at Victoria. His administration was just three weeks away from implementing a set of policies that were certain to accelerate its distribution. If the steamship committee had imported the disease as part of a larger official plan, then the administration already expected to facilitate its spread as Cary wrote this prospectus. In that light, the document's cavalier lack of concern for the cost of satisfying indigenous interests, or for overcoming their opposition, is less surprising. The Colony already was taking care of it. Cary had only to do his part.

The *Prospectus* outlined the business plan as follows,

> *The object for this Company is the construction of a road* [either for mules or wagons] *from the North Bentinck Arm...to a point on the Fraser River at or near the mouth of Quesnelle or Swift Rivers....*

> *North Bentinck Arm possesses an excellent harbor sufficient to accommodate the largest of fleets at all seasons.... The town site of Bella Coola is admirably adapted for the formation of a Commercial Depot for the northern portions of British Columbia, being accessible by steamer from Victoria in forty hours in all seasons....*

When Cary wrote this, there was no "town site of Bella Coola." There was only Q'umk'uts and Cary's plan for New Aberdeen. When the progress of his plans for New Aberdeen are analyzed in a later chapter, it will be clear that, as Cary wrote this in April 1862, the syndicate already expected to sell lots in June for this "town site." It is this to which he was referring. His notice in the road company's *Prospectus* proves again the integration of his various plans. Again, proof of planning is also proof of premeditation.

> *The average freight from the head of Fraser to the Cariboo mines has not been less than 40 to 50 cents [a pound.] It is anticipated that over*

the proposed road an immediate reduction of at least 15 cents a pound will take place, to be reduced in time....

If we estimate the probable immigration during the season as eight thousand, they will require a monthly supply of nine hundred tons of goods. [If half of the traffic passes over the proposed road] the toll will amount to eighty-one thousand dollars [$81,000].... The expense of constructing a mule trail is estimated [at less than] 35,000 dollars.

Since the Company had authorized 240 shares at $250 each to raise $60,000, it was made to appear that this would supply sufficient working capital until the toll revenues began flowing. On the figures given, even the first year's return would be astronomical. Prudent investors perhaps filed this under, "Too Good to be True." Yet, was it possible that one of the Douglas Regime's highest officers and some prominent H.B.C. figures might be no more honorable than penny stock con artists? How reliable were these projections?

Green eventually approached John Morris, a civil engineer with road experience, to visit the route and reflect on the cost. In *Bentinck Arm v. Hood*, Morris testified that he could not make the road for $60,000, let alone $35,000.[168] In 1862, Lt. Palmer estimated a cost of $9,000 to $10,000 just to accommodate packhorses.[169] Meanwhile, upgrading to a wagon road "would cost a great deal."[170] Reflecting on Hood's contract as a means of fulfilling McDonald's Charter, Palmer said there was, *No chance of anybody's fulfilling the present charter. A toll of 4 cents a lb. wouldn't pay. Everything has been awfully misrepresented and I am beginning to believe in <u>nobody</u>.*[171] Palmer was expressing here the same sense of surprise as William Hood at George Cary's apparent lack of care as an officer of the Crown. Palmer himself had been misled into shipping horses he could not use. He was feeling the sting of being a "sheep ready for shearing."

So also would the Company's shareholders. Following Morris' analysis, even with all the shares sold, the company would have been

---

168.   Testimony of John Morris, *Bentinck Arm V. Hood*, Third Day, Monday Feb. 15, *The British Colonist*, Feb. 17, 1864, p. 3.

169.   BCARS. GR-1372. British Columbia. Colonial Correspondence. B01353. F. 1302a. Lt. Henry Palmer to Colonel Moody, August 16, 1862.

170.   Palmer to Colonel Moody, letter of August 16, 1862.

171.   BCARS. GR-1372. British Columbia. Colonial Correspondence. B01353. F. 1302a. Lt. Henry Palmer to Colonel Moody, August 13, 1862. Emphasis is in the original.

under-capitalized. That road leads only to bankruptcy. Equally as deadly to shareholder interests, more apparent bad faith took place during Cary's negotiations with Hood. Without sufficient working capital, the Company could not pay Hood to build the road. So Cary negotiated that, in return for financing construction on his own account, Hood would have two-thirds of the toll revenue. In the same agreement, Green and Cary would share the remaining one-third themselves.[172] This left no future income stream for shareholders. Shareholders had another surprise in store. When the jury interpreted this agreement as giving Hood two-thirds ownership of the Company, he liquidated it to cut his own losses. Shareholders received nothing.

The *Prospectus* "Appendix" was made to seem objective through figures supplied by Captain Swanson of the H.B.C.'s *Labouchere*. Yet, as a New Aberdeen shareholder, Swanson had an undisclosed personal interest and, therefore, a clear motive for deception.

> *Coast route to the northern mines from Victoria to Bentinck Arm, thence to Cariboo. The following is the time of the Labouchere, Victoria to Nanaimo, 7 ½ hours; Nanaimo to Fort Rupert, 20 hours; Fort Rupert to Bentinck Arm, 18 hours.... A suitable boat ought to make three trips a month....*

Notice the time represented for a one-way trip from Victoria to Bella Coola: less than 48 hours. The time required for this passage is an issue here and later will become important in another respect. As documented in a later chapter, an actual one-way outbound voyage of the *Labouchere* required eight days, without even time for loading or resting the crew. Three return trips a month seems highly improbable.

> *The distance by each route [inland is] about equal but [there is] a saving to passengers [on the coastal route] of 12 days, of cost $40 to $60; in transportation of goods, 15 days, saving of $300 per ton....*

The Appendix also made the only representation concerning the Ancestors' disposition toward the road and its ancillary aspects.

---

172. Testimony of George Cary, *Bentinck Arm v. Hood*, Third Day, Monday Feb. 15, *The British Colonist*, *Feb.* 17, 1864, p. 3.

The Bella Coola Indians are of the most-friendly kind, ready to give every assistance in packing over the road, and very anxious for the settlement of white men at Bentinck Arm....

As it would turn out, all these representations were unreliable, leaving little reason to trust this last one simply as stated. The best evidence seems that the Ancestors were friendly and ready to pack: but for the right price. Indeed, they had approved a depot and a road. This document provides nothing about their terms and conditions. Nor is there any reason to doubt that they were open to receiving immigrants who respected the laws and the People. The same thing was said of the Tsilhqot'in, until the Chilcotin War. Guests ideologically motivated by European colonialism were a completely new phenomenon to these prospective host communities.

Finally, the "Report" underlined the prospect that this road would become part of some future transcontinental crossing linking the British North American colonies. This was the "National Dream" of Canadian imperialism. It supplied another layer of public motive for an extermination policy; again should the evidence show in due course that agents of the Company participated in one.

The opening of the proposed road would have the following effect: Bella Coola would become the depot for the supply of the northern mines... on the [competing] river routes there are no depots at all...not New Westminster...Victoria is, as it always has been, the only depot for British Columbia...Bella Coola would become a branch town of Victoria, and Victoria [would remain] the depot for the river trade and [become] the main depot for the coast trade....

(A)t some point in the not far distant [future] a road will be made across the continent, connecting the British provinces of the Atlantic with the colonies of the Pacific. Such road there is every reason to believe will pass through...the Rocky Mountains via Tete Jaune Cache to Fort George, thence, provided it is open, there is no doubt that it would go to North Bentinck Arm. So that it appears probable enough that [a] future town [at] Bella Coola will yet be the terminus of the much-talked Pacific Road through British territory.

Notice the reference now to some "future town" at Bella Coola. This recognizes that when this document was published in April 1862 the Bella Coola town site contemplated did not yet exist. Notice, too, its correlative silence about the large existing indigenous occupation. This document makes it seem the space in question was only awaiting development as vacant land with "no Indian settlement."[173]

Despite this document's presumption, out on the ground as of April 1862, this space can only ever have been the Nuxalk Ancestors' territory and in nothing but an imaginary sense part of "British territory." No British official had even visited yet! A long-established regime with its own constitution still governed all legal or duty-creating relationships here, not English law, not Parliament and not the Crown. How could this be British territory before there was ever any actual official British presence? There had been, as yet, no real assertion of control over either land or citizens by the thousands.

In any case, the underlying business plan called for the road to be profitable on its own terms while increasing New Aberdeen's value. The operators also undertook two public objectives for the Colony of Vancouver Island: 1) to retain the benefits Victoria had come to enjoy via the H.B.C. from exploiting the B.C. hinterland; and 2) to position it for the benefits of hosting the terminus of a transcontinental road.

As events turned out, did the indigenous authorities apply their *de facto* regulatory control to the surprise and cost of non-indigenous operators before these smallpox epidemics? If so, then the predictable costs associated with assertions of indigenous sovereignty underline the public motive for their anticipation and subversion.

---

173. So Cary would describe it. See Chapter 11, s. iv.

10

Freighting to the Gold Rush Before Smallpox and The Settlers' Insurrection

The 1862 season began with Venables' return from Bella Coola. On Jan. 27, a Victoria newspaper editorialized,

> *Whether or not the Bentinck Arm Company [opens a trail] we are assured by Captain Venables...that the Bentinck Arm Indians intend engaging in the packing business.... Ten cents a pound is the price they expect for freight carried from Bella Coola to the mouth of the Swift or Quesnel rivers...in 12 days. We have very grave doubts whether our miners will find it much to their advantage...depending on Indians for transportation. If a chartered company were to open the route and make it travelable, it would be a different matter.*[174]

On Feb. 19, Capt. McKay left for Bella Coola with the first non-indigenous party expecting to transport goods inland using native packers contracted through Pootlass. His passengers included Bob McLeod. Edward Green had paid McLeod to improve the landing, a first step for the road.[175] Using native packers to haul goods, McLeod was then expected to lead the first party using the Company's route.

On his return, McKay reported that McLeod had secured packers and started for the Cariboo mines. He also advertised that, *(I)f necessary 2000 able-bodied Indians who will pack 100 pounds apiece can be obtained to pack at eight cents a pound to Ft. Alexandria.*[176] Through his previous visits in the fur trade, McKay was the most knowledgeable outside source concerning the pre-smallpox adult male population within easy

---

174. "Bentinck Arm Route," *The British Colonist*, Jan. 27, 1862, p. 2. For a 100-pound pack, ten cents a pound represented about three blankets; and for a 75-pound pack a little more than two blankets.

175. Testimony of Edward Green, *Bentinck Arm v. Hood*, First Day, Feb. 11, 1864, *The British Colonist*, Feb. 12, 1864, p. 3

176. "From Bentinck Arm and the Coast Route," *The British Colonist*, March 31, 1862.

reach of Bella Coola. His estimate of able-bodied adult males might project to a total population of men, women, children and elders near 10,000. This casts a wider net and seems consistent with the estimate of 4000 for the lower valley alone that Francis Poole would make just five months later.[177] Neither figure would have included the whole Nuxalk Ancestral population.

McKay's estimate of 2000 able-bodied Ancestors within easy reach of Bella Coola, men capable of carrying 100 pounds for long distances, was also effectively an estimate of the pre-smallpox force of warriors available to the Ancestors here alone. That is, this was the source of *de facto* sovereign power for administering the law and defending territory. Before smallpox, there was never any time at which this force could not have imposed the sovereign will of the host citizenry on a small and dispersed settler population.

At a bare minimum, to impose non-consensual rule by a colonial government, The Settlers' Insurrection would have to overcome these 2000 warriors while dispossessing and subjugating the residents to a new administration. Before the Governor would demonstrate the military power of the British Empire here on June 18, 1864, the Ancestors never saw more than perhaps 50 settlers at any one time, a number they are always sure to have been able to control if needed.[178]

McKay also reported interior natives said to be "from the large lakes." That is, Tsilhqot'in. McKay reported these as saying that they, too, *were ready and anxious to pack for the whites whom they say they wish to settle there.*[179] This seems a clear reference to Alex McDonald's group at Puntzi Lake. McDonald either came with his supplies shipped here via McKay's boat or he arrived here now in the company of these Tsilhqot'in to pack them inland. With McKay was Major William Robertson who planned opening a store at Q'umk'uts. He separately noted this Tsilhqot'in party's arrival.[180]

The Bentinck Arm route, then, was made to seem open with both key indigenous communities unconditionally on board. Was this true? Or were McKay and Venables dishonorably misrepresenting the true

177. Poole, *Queen Charlotte Islands*, p. 181.

178. On the first appearance here by a Colonial governor, see Chapter 17.

179. "From Bentinck Arm and the Coast Route," *The British Colonist*, March 31, 1862, p. 3. Alex McDonald also was at Bella Coola near this time.

180. "From Bentinck Arm and the Coast Route," *The British Colonist*, Mar 31, 1862.

conditions to attract traffic and, thereby, to increase the prospective value of their own interests?

McKay implied that entrepreneurs could plan for paying $8.00 to ship 100 pounds of freight from Bella Coola to Ft. Alexandria. With the market rate at $3.00 to $3.30 each, this represented two to three blankets per packer for this trip.[181] Was this the market rate for labor?

In May, a frustrated miner brought back the first report. Actually, McLeod had not gone through at all.[182] Apparently, McKay had lied. Why? One explanation begun by Alex McDonald was that snow had closed the trail.[183] But the man bringing this report said he knew first-hand that the trail was open. He said Tsilhqot'in packers were going through almost every day. But they were asking 22 blankets each. This was almost ten times the rate quoted by McKay. McDonald and McKay each had deceived their own public about the true situation.

A second explanation had it that, either the Tsilhqot'in had refused to allow Bella Coola packers to cross their territory, or that Bella Coola packers had refused to enter Tsilhqot'in territory without freighters paying an additional fee, a public tax.[184] In other words, while both indigenous communities were ready to accommodate non-indigenous needs, they also expected people doing business in their territories to pay the usual taxes and follow the established laws. Why anyone should find this surprising is a mystery of colonialism.

These colonial-minded settlers were denying the necessity of recognizing the indigenous regimes while those regimes still had the *de facto* power that comes from the ability to project a real political presence. It was this mindset among the settler community that underpinned the choice of an insurrection rather than treaties.

This highlights two common misunderstandings while all this activity remained under supervision by indigenous authorities. The first was about the price of indigenous packers. The second was about indigenous taxes for benefitting from territorial access.

181. Blankets were a form of currency. The 3000 blankets distributed at a single potlatch were estimated to have a value of $10,000. "Kultis Potlatch," *The British Columbian*, Oct. 3, 1862, p. 3. In today's values, using the price of gold as a common standard, this might be $400,000. This is an indicator of the comparative wealth enjoyed by the indigenous Peoples before colonization.

182. "From North Bentinck Arm," *The British Colonist*, May 13, 1862, p. 3.

183. "Letter from Bentinck Arm," *Daily Press*, June 5, 1862, p. 3.

184. "From Bentinck Arm," *The British Colonist*, June 14, 1862, p. 3.

On the first issue, unlike the case with slaves or demoralized labor, while the indigenous regimes remained in control, prices were negotiated between equals where conditions favored labor. Some miners who had believed McKay's representations, gave this report,

> *Some 60 miners arrived at Cariboo about the 1ˢᵗ of June via Bentinck Arm. They were six weeks making the journey from the Arm and were obliged to abandon the greater part of their stuff on the way, as Indians could not be induced to go with them as packers or guides. As many of these people were induced by the representatives of parties at Victoria to ship considerable quantities of provisions with the expectation of getting Indians to pack, they have been obliged to abandon a considerable amount of stuff where they disembarked, what will doubtless fall into the hands of Indians.*[185]

At the Bella Coola end, a newspaper correspondent gave this report from observations made in early July,

> *Under the circumstances it was exceedingly cruel and very reprehensible without better foundation to assure miners that the trail offered no difficulties, and that they could get their several hundred pounds of provisions packed through to Fort Alexandria at 10 cents a pound by the Bella Coola's, of whom not one has packed any provisions through* [i.e., they packed only to Tsilhqot'in territory.] *Some have left the bulk of their provisions with Pootlass, the Bella Coola chief...others with Barney Johnson...some at the head of navigation with Mr. Spring...a few at the slide with Venables....*[186]

In point of fact, natives could be induced as packers and guides. The witness reported above noted that Tsilhqot'in packers were going almost every day. Yet they were not laborers seeking wages. They were entrepreneurs offering a service at their own price.

The problem was that some operators arrived unprepared for the market rate and for the usual conditions applied under the local regulatory regimes. They had been misled by greed or by the colonial "world view" denying the accord of human dignity to the indigenous people. These expected, as a matter of course, to exploit native labor at slave rates. Yet, before the Insurrection, natives could be confident

---

185. "News from Cariboo," *The British Columbian*, July 2, 1862, p.3.
186. "A trip to the Head of Bentinck Arm..." *The British Colonist*, August 20, 1862.

of a traditional livelihood. This provided them with "take it or leave it" bargaining power. After the Insurrection, this power slipped away. Confidence gave way to powerlessness and poverty.

Confirming the pre-smallpox conditions on the ground, one of Pearson's party arriving at Bella Coola May 27, gave this report,

> *Being informed here* [in Victoria] *previous to leaving that the Indians at Bella Coola were not only willing but anxious to pack, receiving payment in blankets, shirts, tobacco, etc., our party supplied themselves with these things in large quantities. On arrival we found this was not the case,* "but that it has never been known of a Coast Indian going through to Fraser River alone, and no packing would be done." *However, the party engaged ten who were willing to pack 75 pounds... arranging with the Chief and paying before the work was done, we got canoes to carry provisions to the head of navigation (about 35 miles) for which was paid 25 blankets for each canoe and four men, taking about 1000 pounds.*[187]

These men found packers. They paid 25 blankets for four Bella Coola men to freight goods 55 km by canoe: about $20 per packer to cover less than one quarter the distance. This took them, roughly speaking, to the point where goods were transferred for shipment by land. For the remaining 250 km, they negotiated with 10 Tsilhqot'in willing to pack 75 pounds rather than the 100 pounds advertised by McKay. The writer did not give the price for this leg, but reducing the load already increased the cost by one quarter.

On the whole, then, market prices may have been ten times what McKay had advertised. In effect, some of the out-sized profits made possible by the gold rush were accruing to the Ancestors. This was only justice. Yet this also provided settlers with a public motive for ending the existing regimen where indigenous considerations and values might influence prices and business conditions.

On the second commonly misunderstood issue, this last party negotiated its way around the relevant fees. It hired Bella Coola packers in their territory and Tsilhqot'in packers for theirs. There is nothing remarkable about such taxes. Their existence only proves the reality of

---

187. "Coast Route to Cariboo," *The British Colonist*, July 23, 1862, p.3.

what everyone otherwise takes for granted. If one wishes to operate in France, then one must expect to pay French taxes.

Settlers who experienced this situation as problematic seemingly had no expectation of satisfying other political regimes. Encouraged by the Douglas Regime's insurrectionist bad faith, some perhaps mistakenly believed that they were still within the Colony of British Columbia. They were not. They were visiting two foreign territories where no Colonial official had ever yet even stepped foot.

One traveler explained McLeod's reaction to the tax this way,

> *The Interior Indians, it appears, have always paid the coast Indians for the privilege of passing through the latter's territory and trading within its borders; and now that the coast Indians wish to visit the interior they are refused permission unless they pay a considerable sum of money. Packing was therefore at a deadlock. But McLeod was daily expected to return from the Fraser with animals to take the goods through.*[188]

Packing was deadlocked only for those with an insurrectionist mindset. Others were going through almost daily. McLeod failed because he had refused in principle to pay the Tsilhqot'in tax. Most likely, it had been one of the specific conditions required by the Tsilhqot'in before they had approved the road at Nagwentlun during summer 1861. Why else would they allow something of benefit only to outsiders? McLeod would not pay any indigenous tax even at the cost of losing business. Instead, he changed his business plan.

Setting an appropriate precedent with the first non-indigenous freighters, it was Solyman who demanded the tax from McLeod. Since he could speak "fluent English," communication was not an issue. According to reports in Victoria, McLeod then became violent with Solyman and "beat him in a temper."[189] But the Bella Coola packers then stranded McLeod. Showing the settler mindset, Alex McDonald, who was with McLeod, said, *The Bella Coolas behaved very mean to us....*[190] Yet every authority treats tax cheats the same.

188. "From Bentinck Arm," *The British Colonist*, June 14, 1862, p. 3.
189. *Victoria Evening Express*, April 26, 1863, p. 3.
190. "Letter from Bentinck Arm," *Daily Press*, June 5, 1862, p. 3.

At the end of the season, as described in a later chapter, Solyman executed McLeod. Natives celebrated him. In their turn, since settlers expected the Douglas Regime to backstop their lawless behavior, those at New Aberdeen imagined that Douglas' failure to respond in this case was a betrayal and a factor encouraging the Chilcotin War.

John Morris hired packers near the end of June as smallpox had begun taking its toll. Morris testified in *Bentinck Arm v. Hood* that, *The Indians were very troublesome to us. They levied blackmail on us.*[191] And again, *We had to pay twelve blankets for the use of four Indians and they levied blackmail of four more.... It cost about 60 cents a pound [to freight goods all-told to the mines]; the Indians [ate] up a great deal [of the profits.]*[192]

The four extra blankets that Morris resented paying probably were the Tsilhqot'in tax. Notice that, with the advent of smallpox, the price of indigenous labor collapsed. Morris paid only three blankets per packer, about the rate McKay had advertised. The Nuxalk could not have seemed troublesome because they held out for higher prices. They did not. This "troublesomeness" seems from anger, insecurity, resentment or fear as the old regime suddenly collapsed around them.

Smallpox decimated the availability of native packers. Yet this labor shortage did not create economic problems. In August, Hood left Nuxalk territory with 27 packhorses, McLeod with 6, Alex McDonald with 11, and Pollard & McGee with 11.[193] Horses carried 200 pounds each. They ate grass for which their operators paid little. Every non-indigenous participant knew from before even the first day that native packers would be unnecessary with any upgraded trail. With its labor then only of marginal value, the indigenous presence would go from being economically important to a potential nuisance. For their part, once freighters turned to horses, indigenous residents no longer had access to the excess profits enabled by their location.

In sum, Attorney General George Cary's business associates misrepresented the cost of doing business along the coastal route. They did this in large measure through denying indigenous economic and political interests. While the existence of these interests was certain, and

191. Testimony of John Morris, *Bentinck Arm v. Hood*, Third Day, Monday Feb. 15, *The British Colonist*, Feb. 17, 1864, p.3.

192. Testimony of John Morris, *Bentinck Arm v. Hood*, Fifth Day, Wednesday Feb. 17, *The British Colonist*, Feb. 18, 1864, p.3.

193. "Four days later from Bentinck Arm," *The British Colonist*, Aug. 27, 1862, p.3.

the greater probability is that acknowledging them had been a condition of indigenous approval, Cary and his cohorts treated these interests as if they did not exist. In this, they were merely following the Douglas Regime's general pattern.

This disrespect for the indigenous regimes seems evidence of dehumanization, a common feature in circumstances of genocide. In addition, it would seem that such an unscrupulous class of individuals as these settlers were, men willing to abuse even their own community in order to advance their cause and their profits, could be expected to treat with even less care an indigenous population to whom they felt superior and towards whom they revealed no sense of civic or human obligation.

Ignoring the established regimes while they still had real *de facto* power had some painful consequences. It cost McLeod his life. It cost others the loss of goods or opportunities in the gold fields. All this provided an incentive for diminishing indigenous *de facto* power until it could have no effect on price or access to resources. In the end, it was smallpox, and not negotiation, that brought the economic regime change desired by the settler community.

From taking control of travel corridors without accommodating indigenous political or economic interests, we turn to appropriating land without paying or concern for indigenous livelihoods.

11

Land Rush to the Ancestors' Territory

Those seeking constitutional change in B.C. desperately needed to leverage their gold rush for a land rush. Gold rushes typically leave little civic legacy, except ghost towns. Time became of the essence. To great applause, a prominent settler had advised Cary's steamship committee to go all-in, *Don't let these golden moments slip.*[194]

Yet the Crown's honor and every civil consideration required that the Douglas Regime approach the Ancestors for a treaty before creating any circumstances that might necessitate some use of the Crown's *de facto* power in their territory. These same considerations required that the Crown purchase some color of legal right to share in the resources used by others under the existing system before inviting settlers to invest time, labor or capital under a new system.

The Douglas Regime did neither. From the Colony's creation, its implicit main policy was to draw sufficient settlers until the *de facto* power of the existing authorities could be displaced without notice. This was the main strategy of The Settlers' Insurrection. This original pattern has remained the underlying strategy of all levels of Canadian government in British Columbia ever since.

To create the illegal land rush that was an integral part of the Insurrection, the Colony would offer for sale to settlers: 1) land that was located in foreign territories where no formal approaches had been made to the local authorities; 2) land that was communally "owned" by indigenous entities even under English law, let alone its status under the law of the land; 3) land that was wholly occupied by indigenous residents, often by whole villages; and 4) land that was required for indigenous livelihoods. It would do all this without compensating in

194. "The Steamship Meeting," *The British Colonist*, Mar. 18, 1861, p. 3.

any way those with rights of occupation under the pre-existing schemes of resource distribution.

Through successive unilateral Proclamations concerning land, the Douglas Regime would fraudulently misrepresent indigenous land as if the Crown had acquired some color of right to it. This defrauded subsequent purchasers and created widespread indigenous rights of restitution. Whether there might be some Statute of Limitations on these rights is not a question for English law, but for the law of the land. In 2014, while expressing "profound sorrow" for the wrongs of previous governments, B.C.'s Premier specifically noted the Douglas Regime's dishonorable land policies as first among them.[195]

In Feb. 1859, pretending that his signature on an executive order could change the nature of resource ownership lawfully in the Ancestors' and other territories where the Crown was a foreign power without any presence, Douglas declared by a dictatorial fiat that the Crown had come into a tenure known to settlers as a "fee simple" ownership of all land, mines and minerals.[196]

If, today, the ambassador for a foreign government would issue a similar executive order purporting to give his government a constitutional right to all the land and minerals in Canada, one would little expect this to have any legal effect. Not without violence or its imminent threat. It was only the eventual overthrow of the existing indigenous constitutions, as described here, that allows this order to serve as the basis of land ownership in British Columbia today.

Douglas' executive order included all the land for which all the Ancestral families held an undisputed title extending for countless generations under the existing system. His Regime made this claim without notice and without any delegation of the necessary legal or moral authority from the citizenry as is required for legitimacy. In the result, the Crown purchased no color of title to resources anywhere on the mainland and would rely instead on the application of violence or the threat of it. This executive order was another provocation of war by the Douglas Regime within The Settlers' Insurrection.

195. Hansard, Thursday Oct. 23, Vol. 16, Number 2, p. 4860. The statement can also be found at www.shawnswanky.com/articles/canadas-war/exoneration -of-the-chilcotin-chiefs/

196. Douglas refers to "the constitutional rights of the Crown to all the lands in British Columbia" in his dispatch to London, Douglas to Lytton, Feb. 19, 1859, National Archives of the UK, 3826 CO 60/4 *The Colonial Despatches of Vancouver Island and British Columbia 1846-1871*, James Hendrickson and the Colonial Despatches project, University of Victoria. http://begenesis.uvic.ca/getDoc.htm?id=B59104.scx

I
Targeting Q'umk'uts and its precinct.

Q'umk'uts in the Ancestors' territory became among the very first targets of the Douglas Regime's dishonorable land grab. While Douglas' various Proclamations nominally contemplated supposedly vacant ground suited to European-style agriculture, it is difficult to imagine any space less so suited than Q'umk'uts and its precinct. Perhaps 2000 Ancestors called this home. Further, the first settlers noted that these already had considerable land under cultivation.[197] Settlers staked it anyway and destroyed the Ancestors' crops. During the Chilcotin War, an eyewitness to what had happened in the first rush of settler activity at Bella Coola noted that one of the indigenous population's legitimate grievances was the way in which settlers had rudely turned the Ancestors off their cultivated land.[198]

It should go without saying that no one begins targeting the rightful occupiers of any land for dispossession without first having anticipated the certainty of a violent response. It comes as no surprise then that the Douglas Regime also well understood that risk. In a Jan. 1861 session of the Vancouver Island Assembly, M.L.A. Dr. William Tolmie, head of the P.S.A.C., *moved that the House petition the Secretary of State for the Colonies [in London] relative to the extinguishing of Indian Titles – and referred in a few words to the fact that the Indian wars of Australia and other colonies had arisen from the land being purchased and the owners not being able to occupy them on account of Indian aggression.*[199] Precisely. Except that, rather than "Indian aggression," he ought to have referenced any legitimate occupant's natural sense of justice. Would you go quietly if developers moved into your home after a third party in another country sold it to them?

Although senior officials already knew that London considered the purchase of "Indian title" a local expense, the Assembly would buy time arguing that, as one member would put it, *the question should be settled [between] the Imperial Government [and the Indians as sovereign nations] and the land given to the Colonial Government [so it, in turn, could grant]*

---

197. BCARS. Cavendish Venables. Bentinck Arm. Map reference CM/B91.

198. "Emergency Meeting," *The British Colonist*, June 2, 1864, p. 3. C.B. Young visited Bella Coola at the same time as Lt. Palmer's party. His stay there began July 2, 1862.

199. "House of Assembly," *The British Colonist*, Jan. 23, 1861. p. 3.

perfect titles [to settlers.]... (I)f we [the Colonists] *had to quit* [were held responsible for the cost of purchasing Indian title] *we ought to refuse....*[200]

Notice that all this discussion about purchasing title took place after Douglas already had seized a supposed fee simple ownership of indigenous lands for the Crown on paper. The settler community knew that both justice and securing quiet occupation required more.

If the Colonies were to refuse the cost of purchasing title, as they did, then how did they then plan to avoid the readily predictable violence when indigenous residents refused to vacate land that the colonial governments had sold to incoming settlers? What was the Douglas Regime's Plan B? On this issue, the three Pacific colonies all shared the same position. So the Imperial response to Vancouver Island also necessarily influenced events in Nuxalk territory.

Although George Cary listened to this "land title" discussion in the Assembly, the Attorney General remained silent. Yet, is this not the kind of issue where one expects the government's highest legal officer to lead? Cary's silence suggests that, while his actions show he disagreed with the very premise of "Indian title," he saw some value in letting this course play out while waiting for Plan B.

M.L.A. Dr. John Helmcken, also an H.B.C. executive and the Governor's son-in-law, concluded the discussion with this statement, *without these claims quieted in some way we may always expect annoyance from the Indians.*[201] Precisely: we may **"always expect."** Prudent administrators invariably begin making plans in such cases.

Dr. Helmcken's equivocal **"quieted in some way"** opens the door to other means besides purchase. Given the dishonorable nature of most other means, one should not expect to find them freely disclosed. Still, Helmcken observed in his memoir, *All men must die. Indians obeyed the mandate perhaps a little earlier than they otherwise might. Socially, probably, their death is of little consequence; politically, it may be of more importance.*[202] This is an understated admission that they died otherwise than in the natural course. He also underlines the political significance of this fact: these unnatural deaths were key to the unconstitutional transition of power in the British Pacific Northwest. Remember that it was Helmcken

---

200. "House of Assembly." *The British Colonist*, Jan. 29, 1861, p. 3.

201. "House of Assembly," *The British Colonist*, Jan. 29, 1861, p. 3.

202. *The Reminiscences of Doctor John Sebastian Helmcken,* ed Dorothy Blakey Smith. (Vancouver: UBC press, 1975) pp. 329-331.

who said that the Colony had relied on "survival of the fittest" in its displacement of the indigenous regimes.

In March 1862, Douglas released the news of London's refusal to purchase "Indian title" exactly coincident with it becoming known that: 1) London was sending 500 rifles with ammunition to arm colonial militias, apparently in anticipation of "Indian wars" given a decision not to pay for land; and 2) the smallpox carriers from the steamship committee's sailing had spread the disease to a native community.[203] As a supposed coincidental outbreak of disease, this was extraordinary. If smallpox did its usual work, settlers would need to budget neither for "Indian title" nor for "Indian wars." This seems "too good to be true" for "just lucky" as a good explanation. Plan B was to rely on fraud, force and fear. Given this choice, and given that the native citizenry greatly outnumbered settlers in every territory, distributing smallpox would seem a most efficient policy choice.

II
The private dispossession of Q'umk'uts on settler paper.

How, then, did the dispossession of Q'umk'uts proceed? Under a little used section of a subsequent land Proclamation dated Jan. 4, 1860, Attorney General Cary had the Colony sell the land under Q'umk'uts and its precinct to the New Aberdeen syndicate.[204] The resulting deed has not survived, but it is noted elsewhere and during *Bentinck Arm Co. v. Hood.*[205] Cary eventually produced a plan of this property that was dated Nov. 1860.[206] (See map p. 185.) He may have created the deed for it as early as April 4, 1860 but no later than November.

This clause in the Proclamation provided that,

---

203. "House of Assembly," *The British Colonist,* Mar. 20, 1862, p. 3, and Mar. 21, p. 2.

204. See Clause 7, "British Columbia. Proclamation," *The British Colonist,* Jan. 12, 1860, p. 3. Proclamation dated Jan. 4, 1860.

205. BCARS. GR-1372. British Columbia. Colonial Correspondence. B01313. F275. No. 68 Attorney General Henry Crease to Colonel Richard Moody, Chief Commissioner for Lands and Works, June 19, 1862. Para. 6-14. The court may have supplied the date of the original deed, April 4, 1860, in "Supreme Court," *The British Colonist,* Feb. 24, 1864, p.3.

206. BCARS. GR-1372. British Columbia. Colonial Correspondence. B01313. F275. George Hunter Cary to the A.G. for British Columbia, Henry Crease, June 4, 1862.

7. Any person...may purchase in addition [to pre-empting land for agriculture] any number of acres not otherwise appropriated...for five shillings down and the rest at the time of survey.[207]

Without the limitations of "pre-emption" claims, Cary, *felt assured that a title of this character is, except so far as the [formal] legal estate is concerned, equally as good as a Crown grant in fee simple.*[208] Whereas a *title under a pre-emption is not nearly so perfect as one under an absolute purchase from the Crown.*[209]

The Nov. 1860 plan outlined the original New Aberdeen claim as more than a mile wide and extending two miles (three km) upriver.[210] It covered 1600 acres. When Lt. Palmer arrived here in 1862, he said, at the harbor straddling the River, *are situated two Indian villages, forming a settlement named Ko-omko-otz...two miles further up the south bank is another large village named Soonochlim...the whole population numbered when I was there, 1200 souls.*[211] So Cary's original claim included all the land under Q'umk'uts and extended to Soonochlim. (See map p. 184.) All this land was visibly and unmistakably occupied. And Cary had had the opportunity to begin planning for the means to counter this occupation from Sept. 1860.

Now, when Palmer "was there," smallpox already was shrinking the population. Colonel Foster estimated the pre-smallpox population at 2000.[212] Francis Poole, who had the best opportunity from direct observation before the epidemics began, estimated 4000 residents in these two villages, more or less.[213] Poole's estimate was consistent with that of 2000 day-laboring-suitable adult males nearby as made by Capt. McKay in 1861. Whatever the best number, the New Aberdeen claim directly affected Nuxalk Ancestors by the thousands.

207. "British Columbia, Proclamation," *The British Colonist,* Jan. 12, 1860, p. 3. Proclamation dated Jan. 4, 1860.

208. BCARS. GR-1372. British Columbia. Colonial Correspondence. B01313. F275. George Hunter Cary to the Attorney General for British Columbia, Henry Crease, June 4, delivered in person June 11.

209. Cary to Crease, June 4, as cited above.

210. Cary attached the map, dated November 1860, to his letter of June 4, cited above.

211. Henry Spencer Palmer, *Report of a Journey of Survey, from Victoria to Fort Alexander via North Bentinck Arm.* (New Westminster: Royal Engineers Press, 1863) p. 6.

212. See Anglican Archives of B.C. B8/S1 Bishop George Hills, *Diary,* July 22 to Dec. 31, 1862, p. 135, on meeting Col. Foster as he arrived at Alexandria from Bella Coola.

213. Francis Poole, *Queen Charlotte Islands,* p. 181.

On this plan, this space looks like vacant land. In fact, under the Douglas Regime's land redistribution scheme, it was vacant land: it was "Crown land" unencumbered by any private property right. In the Douglas Regime's land theory, indigenous residents occupied space only at the will of the Crown. Once settlers claimed some land to be surveyed for conversion to a "fee simple" title, the indigenous occupiers became trespassers subject to eviction.[214]

Settlers soon contested with each other for land. *Considerable ill blood has been engendered between settlers at the head of Bentinck Arm, in consequence of conflicting interests in pre-empted land.*[215] If settlers felt strongly about "claim jumping" from other settlers, a child could anticipate that indigenous residents eventually would protect their livelihoods with violence. Except that the true *de jure* authorities would have authorized this indigenous violence and it would be backed by the certainty of having the high moral ground.

In April 1861, apparently insecure about this transaction, the syndicate filed new claims under the pre-emption provisions. (See map p. 186-187.) Six men claimed 160 acres each, or 960 acres, "at the delta formed by the Bella Coola River" and "at the delta formed by the Dean River."[216] Anticipating the B.C. government's unhelpful inclinations, they filed identical applications at New Westminster and Williams Lake. The syndicate now had three claims to most of the same land. This shows a consistent determination to prevail. It goes to motive and intent.

These individual pre-emption claimants included Samuel Price and Fred Green. When the sale of lots did not proceed and when the Bentinck Arm Co. failed, these two claimants defaulted on mortgages given elsewhere to finance their adventures. Highly leveraged individuals may countenance desperate measures to avoid the humiliation of default. This goes to motive. It also gave their investment banker a financial interest in their success at Bella Coola. On their failure to pay, this banker had the properties seized and sold.[217] The investment banker with an interest in New Aberdeen's success was Donald Fraser, a friend

214. Clause 13. "British Columbia. Proclamation." *The British Colonist*, Jan. 12, 1860.

215. "From North Bentinck Arm," *The British Colonist*, May 13, 1862, p. 3.

216. BCARS. GR-1182. British Columbia Dept. of Lands and Works, Cariboo, Lytton and Lillooet pre-emption records, Folder 1, Records taken by P. Nind and T. Elwyn, Alexandria District, 1860-1863. Unlisted among pre-emption claims accepted, the document remains in the back of the folder.

217. The court order was dated July 23, 1863. The properties were advertised for sale throughout the fall. For example, "To be Sold," *The British Colonist*, Oct. 19, 1863, p. 4.

of Governor Douglas, a member of his Executive Council and a key propagandist for the Colonies through the *London Times*. These facts extend the blanket of private motive to others in the Governor's circle and add another layer to the issue of public motive.

In making these pre-emption claims, the syndicate scaled back its claim from 1600 to 960 acres. This seems in contemplation of Cavendish Venables' trip to Bella Coola with James Kenny in Sept. 1861. Venables claimed all the land released by New Aberdeen and 360 acres more, for 1000 acres. He prepared a map outlining his claim and all others staked in the Lower Valley.[218] He also showed the four indigenous settlements controlling the space, along with their gardens and fishing weirs. Every acre had been staked for five miles from the proposed landing, including all land under the villages.

Venables' claim dovetails perfectly with these other claims and that of New Aberdeen. So, either all these claims were staked then, or Venables was a stalking horse for an undisclosed interest associated with Cary's prior claimants. He would have flipped the claim once it was registered and available for resale to third parties. In March 1862, a newly arrived settler made just this charge. *A great many monopolizing companies in Victoria and elsewhere have registered thousands of acres of the best land here and sent one man to represent it.*[219] This was an unmistakable reference to Venables as a stalking horse for the H.B.C. or P.S.A.C. It underlines that these first claimants were speculators with little incentive for long-term regard.

Except for the syndicate, none of the other claimants seem to have applied for registration of the claims outlined on Venables' map. Indeed, until some precedent was set, their validity was uncertain. Venables also did not file an ordinary pre-emption claim. He asserted that, as a "retired officer in the 74th Highlanders," he was entitled to land on being decommissioned.[220] He also encountered bureaucratic delays and never proved his commission or his discharge.[221] Venables abandoned

218.   BCARS. Cavendish Venables. Bentinck Arm. Map reference CM/B91. This map forms part of the basis for *Claims Staked at Bella Coola Before Smallpox* in the Maps and Illustrations section (p. 186-187).

219.   "From Bentinck Arm and the Coast Route," *The British Colonist*, Mar 31, 1862.

220.   BCARS. British Columbia. Colonial Correspondence. B01372. F1798. Cavendish Venables to the Department of Lands and Works, Bella Coola, Sept. 30, 1861.

221.   Venables did serve with the British Army's 4th Division in the Crimea but the 74th Highlanders, a famed regiment, had been disbanded several years before then.

this claim when the road failed. On Nov. 3, 1863, the Nuxalk "pulled down" the house built as a token of his occupancy.[222]

All this shows that the motive for supporting or participating in an extermination policy extended beyond George Cary and Co.[223] It also reconfirms that the Attorney General was perfectly acquainted with the extent of indigenous occupation. And, therefore, of his need to anticipate resistance, or "an Indian war," as the land was sold from under the indigenous residents.

III

Q'umk'uts publicly seized on paper by the Colony of B.C.

The struggle between Victoria and New Westminster took a new turn on March 27, 1862. Under a Proclamation provision permitting the government to reserve land for public purposes, Colonel Moody seized the Bella Coola and Dean River deltas, and all Fraser River junctions noted as possible Bentinck Arm Road destinations.[224]

This order included New Aberdeen's whole claim at Q'umk'uts. (See map p. 190.) This was not done to prevent indigenous dispossession. Rather, it was part of an internecine squabble over the distribution of spoils: in what proportion should the profits from selling unceded indigenous land be divided between developers and the government?

With respect to the indigenous regimes, Moody's administrative action was another provocation of war in The Settlers' Insurrection. This was one political entity assuming a unilateral right to control land in the jurisdiction of three others. Suppose Germany suddenly revealed plans to dispose of land in Poland, Belgium and France: everyone soon would see that as a provocation of war.

Understanding the true intent behind the Proclamation's "public purposes" clause, Cary immediately countered in a letter of April 14,

> *My clients are prepared to surrender to you the land in question. You as Chief Commissioner to cause the same to be laid out as a town site and*

---

222. "News From Bentinck Arm," *The British Colonist*, Nov. 20, 1863.

223. As a matter of interest, Venables' map came to the B.C. Archives not through the land department but through the files of the Puget Sound Agricultural Company.

224. This included the mouth of the Homathko River as well to freeze all the Victoria sponsored projects. See the two "Public Notices," *The British Colonist*, April 18, 1862, p. 4. At Quesnel, after the government sold lots in their stead and without making any Indian Reserve on account of all the natives being dead, the displaced pre-emptors were offered a land swap as justice but the new land had little present value.

sold as such in Victoria, as soon as may be advisable. The government [would be] entitled to such reasonable reservations for the site of public buildings as you may select without compensation. The government to retain one-third of the gross price of the sales and pay over the other two thirds to my clients.[225]

Notice Cary's assertion of a prior legal property right in the land. Yet the resident occupants had not sold any rights to anyone. Moody referred this letter to Cary's replacement as attorney general on the mainland, Henry Crease. Crease's first position was that: if the supposed title were good, then it should be considered, with expenses borne by the proprietors, and that B.C. towns must be sold in B.C.[226]

Crease added, *Indian reserves must be carefully provided.* This was the first notice of the Ancestors' interests. It also distorted the legal reality in the most typical way for the Douglas Regime. In fact, Pootlass as their Staltmc and the Ancestors still represented the only legitimate sovereign authority at the time and in the place concerned. The Colony had made no approaches to them for some constitutional share of jurisdiction. Therefore, neither Douglas, nor Moody, nor Crease, nor Cary, nor the Colony of British Columbia had any legal or moral right to dispose of land here, let alone any legal authority to limit the indigenous residents' freedom of access, to confine them on refugee camps or "reserves," or to dispossess them by any means. Crease's position contained the same mistaken legal assumption that would see the wrongful hanging of the "Chilcotin Chiefs."

In addition, what ordinarily prudent political actor ever would expect, all things being equal while they still might be so numerous as to have real *de facto* power, that indigenous citizens would freely abandon their homes and migrate happily to small reserves? Would Canadians happily abandon their homes at the first instance of a foreign power seeking to reallocate our economic space? It would be laughably absurd to expect so. So Crease's "reserve" conception, too, required the unstated premise of a rapidly shrinking indigenous population with reduced *de facto* capabilities. In this regard, Crease and Cary were on the same page of the Douglas Regime's playbook.

225. BCARS. GR-1372. British Columbia. Colonial Correspondence. B01313. F275/5. George Hunter Cary to Colonel Richard Moody, Chief Commissioner for Lands and Works, April 14, 1862.

226. BCARS. GR-1372. British Columbia. Colonial Correspondence. B01313. F275. Attorney General Henry Crease to Colonel Richard Moody, Chief Commissioner for Lands and Works, April 16, 1862.

Cary then immediately brought to Moody and Crease's attention that his clients intended to sell subdivided town lots "in early June." This expectation was common knowledge in Victoria. Even a San Francisco newspaper had reported in March that, *within a month or two...Bentinck lots will, doubtless, be all the rage.*[227] The New Aberdeen speculators were poised to realize their 1600 percent profits. The stakes had been raised. If Cary had a plan to deal with indigenous occupation, it now had a deadline: early June 1862.

Cary wrote to Moody,

> *My clients are anxious for your reply...although they are desirous of affording every facility to the government in laying out a town site... yet they feel that their interests will suffer by any delay. It is their intention, should the government decline their proposal, to lay out the land themselves and sell it in Victoria in the early part of June at latest.... In the event of my clients selling on their own, I must request you insert a notification in the government gazette exempting the 960 acres from the [government] reservation...without [this] modification [it] would seriously prejudice the sale.*[228]

Since this timing now assumes a greater significance, it should be underlined: before March 1862, that is, before two smallpox carriers arrived on the same ship as Cary's steamship committee, Cary already had fully formed plans to sell lots at New Aberdeen, a plan that required vacant possession in early June. This is what premeditation looks like. It greatly reduces the odds of coincidence at any stage in the disease's subsequent distribution.

Cary's reply ignored Crease's note on indigenous occupation. Now, when property developers do not respond to explicit concerns raised by government officials whose approval they need, the best explanation is that they believe the concern is being addressed. Yet, as of Cary's April 20 letter, this land was still under the control of a foreign system of governance and home to perhaps 2000 indigenous residents. Nevertheless, the developers' plans called for the delivery of English-style fee simple titles in early June. How?

227. "Letter from Victoria," *Daily Alta*, Vol. XIV, No 4415, March 23, 1862, p. 1. This information was brought down on the same ship as had delivered the smallpox carriers.
228. BCARS. GR-1372. British Columbia. Colonial Correspondence. B01313. F275. George Hunter Cary to Colonel Richard Moody, Chief Commissioner for Lands and Works, April 20, 1862.

To better see the challenge facing Cary, one should understand that fee simple vendors must deliver vacant possession. Purchasers have a legal right to take possession of fee simple properties free from any form of prior occupation. By early June, then, these vendors needed to create the conditions under which purchasers could register fee simple titles and take up occupancy of their vacant property.

Purchasers who might have arrived after an early June sale to find 2000 indigenous residents still occupying their land would have had a right to demand their money back or to have the government evict them with police violence. How could the speculators be expecting to realize their profits "in the early part of June," if they did not have a plan to deliver vacant possession then? It is impossible that there was no plan. Nor was this just a local challenge. As Dr. Tolmie had told the Island Assembly in 1861, with Cary listening, *the Indian wars of Australia and other colonies had arisen from land being purchased and the owners not being able to occupy them on account of Indian aggression.*[229] Why was there no war here?

By May 15, Cary had contacted a surveyor and was pressing Crease on the issue of title.[230] If the purchasers could not receive fee simple titles capable of registration at the Colonial land office, they would be unable to arrange financing. The land would be worth less. Once again, Cary did not address the issue of indigenous occupation. His lack of concern underscores his apparent comfort on this issue. Having no response by May 25, and with time now increasingly of the essence, Cary wrote to Crease,

> *I received your letter of May 16 in which an answer is promised by nearest day. Fearing that pressure of business has prevented your promised letter I venture to call your attention to the subject. I would add that previous delays have almost frustrated the formation of the Bentinck Arm route and that if my clients fail to receive an...answer without delay it will be impossible to complete the arrangements necessary to carry out their desirable object.*[231]

---

229. "House of Assembly," *The British Colonist*, Jan. 23, 1861, p. 2.

230. BCARS. GR-1372. British Columbia. Colonial Correspondence. B01313. F275. George Hunter Cary to B.C. Attorney General Henry Crease, May 15, 1862.

231. BCARS. GR-1372. British Columbia. Colonial Correspondence. B01313. F275. George Hunter Cary to B.C. Attorney General Henry Crease, May 25, 1862.

One can feel the sense of urgency in Cary's tone as "early June" approached. Indigenous occupation received no mention once again. Stonewalling, Crease saw a need for yet more information, and again later yet still more.[232] Of course, every new delay that "frustrated a Bentinck Arm route," allowed the even more desirable objective, for New Westminster, that Fraser Canyon should open first and prevail.

May 27, Crease finally sent notes to Moody and Cary, making the same points to each. Most importantly:

> *2. The extracts from the Pre-emption Books and the returns from your [Moody's] office do not afford the information necessary to establish the desirability or otherwise of [Cary's] proposal.... 4. The position of the Title would also have first to be ascertained, by whom the land is occupied and if there be competing claimants. 5. The extent of the public and Indian Reserves in the vicinity.*[233]

With early June upon them the situation was at a crisis level. Cary began clearing his legislative calendar as Premier so that he could visit New Westminster and force a resolution face to face. On June 9, Cary visited the neighboring Colony. The public there so disliked Cary that an unruly mob formed spontaneously at news of his arrival. John Sheepshanks and others rescued him while the crowd "drowned him in effigy," expressing this public's outrage over the steamship subsidy.[234] It was this widespread anti-Victoria sentiment that gave Crease and Moody cover for their official foot-dragging.

At New Westminster, Crease and Moody continued to refuse Cary accommodation for New Aberdeen's preferred timetable to sell lots. Yet they did agree to assess Bentinck Arm's potential for a road. A few days later, Moody dispatched Lt. Henry Palmer on this first official mission by an agent of the Crown to the Ancestors' territory.

232. BCARS. GR-1372. British Columbia. Colonial Correspondence. B01313. F275. No. 68. Attorney General Henry Crease to Colonel Richard Moody, Chief Commissioner for Lands and Works, June 19, 1862.

233. BCARS. GR-1372. British Columbia. Colonial Correspondence. B01313. F275. No. 58. Attorney General Henry Crease to Colonel Richard Moody, Chief Commissioner for Lands and Works, May 27, 1862.

234. "Don't Seem to Like Him," *The British Colonist*, June 13, 1862, p. 3.

Cary returned to Victoria June 14.[235] Said to be absent from the legislature "prostrate from the effects of physical suffering" with an eye infection, Cary now focused on Bentinck Arm Co. business from home.[236] William Hood had approached Edward Green about becoming their road contractor. In the face of an insufficient return from the sale of shares and under urgent pressure from the Charter's time limit, Green and Cary needed to entice Hood to fund the road himself. Between June 20 and 25, they negotiated with him at length. Cary produced a contract only at the last minute. Hood signed and raced to the harbor where his supplies and 11 men, including M.D. Barron, already were loaded.[237] On the same sailing were Lt. Palmer's Royal Engineers party, including Island M.L.A. and commander of its Colonial militia, Colonel George Foster, a hostile correspondent from the Douglas Route and entrepreneur C.B. Young.

At this juncture, it can only have seemed to Cary that the road would open sufficiently to meet the Charter's requirement and that New Aberdeen would sell vacant lots for a settler town site at Bella Coola. His advantage would not begin slipping away until the end of July when the Charter and the steamship subsidy each would expire.

IV
"There is no Indian settlement."

In his letter of June 4 that Cary delivered in person at New Westminster on June 11, he finally addressed the issue of indigenous occupancy. Cary ignored the Ancestors' prior sovereignty and the urgent need to approach them for a treaty before negotiating compensation for some color of right to land. Instead, in a declining order, he advanced three gambits typical of the Douglas Regime's public policy toward its indigenous hosts. He began,

There is no Indian settlement on the land in question....[238]

235. "A False Report," *The British Colonist,* June 15, 1862, p. 3. (Actually, June 16 – the paper dated its edition incorrectly.)

236. See "A False Report," above.

237. Note reference to the subsequent pre-emption claim that Barron would make and the second wave of smallpox of Oct./Nov. 1862 in Chapter 15.

238. BCARS. GR-1372. British Columbia. Colonial Correspondence. B01313. F275. George Hunter Cary to B.C. Attorney General Henry Crease, June 4, 1862, delivered at New Westminster June 11.

This statement violated every connection with reality. (See illustration p. 185.) One of the Douglas Regime's highest officials here expressed the essence of B.C. colonialism in a single phrase. If, between each other, Colonial officials could agree to proceed as if legally speaking there were "no Indian settlements," then no one needed to represent those interests, neither their political interests nor their interests in land.

Validating or invalidating statements like this is straightforward. Cary was not naïve about this. As Attorney General and as a private lawyer he had prepared countless cases turning on factual assertions. As a serious representation of the conditions on the ground, Cary can only have expected something more to take place between the time when his statement was made and the time when it might be tested.

However that may be, good lawyers come prepared to argue alternatives. Speaking hypothetically, Cary continued,

(E)ven were there [an Indian settlement supposed for the sake of argument]...my clients would be perfectly prepared to settle the Indian claim out of the funds arising from the sale....

This envisions that any lingering indigenous occupants could be paid a small token out of the proceeds to settle the minor interest of their aboriginal title. Then they could be expected or compelled to relocate quietly elsewhere at the convenience of settlers. Douglas would propose something very similar to this in Cowichan territory just a few weeks later. In a legal sense, this proposal was for the residents to sell their aboriginal rights via a "quitclaim" for a token "all-cash reserve." In Cary's presence, at Cowichan, Douglas would proffer a similar take-it-or-leave-it offer of two blankets a head for smallpox survivors, the equivalent of less than one week's labor for the purchase of their whole communal aboriginal title and for that of their community's children forever.[239]

(O)r in the event of any difficulty either in arranging this or on account of any wish of the government to keep any portion for the use of the Indians the quantity required might continue unsold.

This was the most costly option. Some land would be unsold. Notice Cary's assumption that whether the native occupants might be moved

---

239. For the Insurrection in Cowichan territory, see *Canada's 'War'* ss. 94-98.

or allowed any land at all was the government's choice. This is another way of implying that the land was unoccupied by anyone whose interests required respect or equitable treatment; that is, just as one might expect to find in a context of ethnic cleansing.

On this last option, the development might be unattractive to purchasers prejudiced against any lingering indigenous presence. The target class of purchasers likely would have regarded indigenous neighbors just as those at New Westminster. One of the first civic actions there had been to prohibit hiring indigenous labor.[240] Then, when a city crew's negligence caused 15 indigenous houses to burn, settlers considered it *a matter of thankfulness that this fire was confined to property of a comparatively worthless character.*[241] Such attitudes seem consistent with a cultural practice of denying the human dignity of indigenous people as lesser "other" beings. This is also a circumstance one might expect in a context of ethnic cleansing.

With resolutions like this next one from New Westminster, some future New Aberdeen Council might even demand that the Ancestors' be removed and their economy or freedom of association limited:

> *As numerous complaints have been made to council respecting the Indians settling and building houses on lots in this city belonging to white parties, the council petitioned the government to lay out a piece of land three miles from the city to be set aside as an Indian reserve, and that the northern Indians (who are now arriving in large numbers) when they visit us have some portion set apart for their residence and that some system be adopted for giving these northern Indians tickets of residence for a limited time, sufficient for them to transact their business and all the while be placed under a superintendence of an officer appointed by the government.*[242]

Settlers commonly found the presence of indigenous neighbors uncomfortable. This discomfort undoubtedly had roots in the Douglas Regime's dishonorable policies toward the host regimes. As an apparent refuge for self-regard, settlers preferred creating out-of-sight out-of-

---

240. *The British Columbian,* July 11, 1861.
241. "Great Conflagration," *The British Columbian,* Aug. 8, 1861.
242. "Municipal Council," *The British Columbian,* July 25, 1861.

mind circumstances. Lt. Palmer would propose just such a resolution at Bentinck Arm.[243]

Successful vendors always anticipate the central desires of their prospective purchasers. This intensified the motive for an ethnic cleansing-like policy at New Aberdeen: to ameliorate the lingering "nuisance" of indigenous neighbors and, thereby, to increase the land's value in the eyes of prospective settler purchasers.

In a 14-point reply to Cary's appearance at New Westminster, Crease only briefly alluded in passing to indigenous occupancy.[244] This issue was not of real concern for New Westminster officials, as would become clear through Lt. Palmer's visit.

Cary's endeavors did not fail over concern about indigenous interests, rights or dignity. Vancouver Island M.L.A. Colonel Foster put the final spike in Cary's dream. After crossing the route with Lt. Palmer, he publicly declared, *The expense is too great in a barren and unproductive country to warrant it.*[245] The political constituency favoring Bentinck Arm then quickly wasted away. By 1863, Victoria had turned its public favor to an alternative road from Bute Inlet.

Foster crossed the road only after the contemplated land sale of early June. Backtracking to early June, then, how did Cary expect his bold affirmation, that "There is no Indian settlement" would be true for all practical purposes when tested by the B.C. government in July to see if his development substantially met its requirements?

---

243. See the discussion in Chapter 14, part i.

244. BCARS. GR-1372. British Columbia. Colonial Correspondence. B01313. F275. No. 68. Attorney General Henry Crease to Colonel Richard Moody, Chief Commissioner for Lands and Works, June 19, 1862, para. 11.

245. "Letter from Fort Alexandria," *The British Colonist*, Sept. 6, 1862, p. 3.

12

The Smallpox War,
June 1862

The 1862 smallpox epidemics severely reduced the Ancestors' number, morale, political presence and *de facto* power. It was only this reduction that eventually allowed every future colonial policy to proceed here with little violent resistance. Beyond initially seizing land and territorial control, this included confining the People to small reserves, residential schools, outlawing the Potlatch system and the unilateral designation of new leadership structures.

The means by which smallpox first arrived among the Ancestors is not an issue. Francis Poole admitted some role in it several times. Moreover, coincident with his arrival at Bella Coola an eyewitness expressly noted the lack of any disease there.[246] Nor did any other previous visitor report it. However, soon after Poole arrived, every eyewitness would note it. In short, it is beyond any reasonable doubt that Poole's party began the first smallpox epidemics here in 1862.

At issue is whether Poole's party committed some criminal act while introducing the disease. Innocent introduction would include unknowingly, accidentally or despite appropriate caution. Criminal acts would be through unlawful lack of caution, with an intention to kill or with deaths resulting from some depraved indifference to life.

Poole commented on this fateful journey several times. In assessing these statements, one must keep in mind that, as a rule, people can be expected to minimize their shameful or criminal acts. People also tend to paint themselves more heroically than the truth would allow. For example, in his memoir, Poole claimed credit for drawing attention to Haida Gwaii for copper and for inspiring the Queen Charlotte Mining

---

246. "From Bentinck Arm, Fort Rupert and Nanaimo," *The British Colonist*, June 20, 1862, p. 3.

Company.[247] Both claims were false. This company began mining copper at Haida Gwaii months before Poole even arrived on the Pacific.[248] Those facts are unimportant to this context. But, when a man is seen so easily to lie in his own case, one must weigh all his accounts with a suitable caution, and in the light of other facts or against all the circumstances.

I

Poole's party at Bella Coola, introduction.

Describing his second visit to Bella Coola in mid-November 1862, Poole's memoir says,

> *I learnt that smallpox had carried off hundreds of Indians since my first visit there* [in early June;] *and, as the party I then headed was the unfortunate means of introducing the disease I began to fear lest the natives should oppose my landing.*[249]

On his own account, then, Poole "headed" the party introducing smallpox at Bella Coola in early June. Then, while the Ancestors clearly blamed someone as culpable, apparently they let Poole land a second time as a mere tool with no personal animus. This raises two questions: who hired Poole to head this party and for what purpose?

Discussing a subsequent epidemic on Haida Gwaii, Poole says,

> *Prior to this* [Haida Gwaii outbreak in December 1862] *it had been my already-mentioned misfortune to carry the plague to the tribes along the North and South Bentinck Arms of the mainland.*[250]

Poole takes responsibility here for having "carried" the disease to affect many "tribes along" both Arms. Did he introduce the disease only once then, after which it spread naturally, or did his party introduce it several times? These two scenarios have very different implications. They reflect on the scale of his party's actions and on the purposefulness or intention driving them.

---

247. Poole, *Queen Charlotte Islands*, pp. 65-66.

248. "News from Queen Charlotte's Island," *The British Colonist*, July 21, 1862, p. 3. And "Queen Charlotte's Island Copper Mines," *The British Colonist*, May 9, 1862, p. 3.

249. Francis Poole, *Queen Charlotte Islands*, p. 179. This memoir was ghostwritten nine years later from his diaries with an eye to it being an adventure tale. The heroes of such tales seldom admit anything dishonorable. The ghostwriter's contribution, however, seems to have been limited to structuring a narrative thread. Poole had the opportunity to read and approve the manuscript before publication. Poole died in Feb. 1874.

250. Poole, *Queen Charlotte Islands*, p. 194.

Then, leaving Bella Coola for Haida Gwaii in Nov. 1862, a storm blew Poole's ship off course but still along his original route. It found shelter at a Heiltsuk community.[251] His memoir says,

> *We heard they had recently deserted their old camping-grounds up the Arm* [perhaps on King Island] *and had come down here in consequence of the fearful gaps and ravages caused by smallpox. Many mournful hours of reflection did it give me when I came face to face with the enormous sacrifice of life I had unwittingly brought about through my unfortunate exploring party...introducing that pest in the neighborhood of the Arm.*[252]

Poole again accepts responsibility from a position of authority. This statement now expands his responsibility from specifically along North and South Bentinck Arms to "the neighborhood." It now also includes both Nuxalk and Heiltsuk communities along his route.

Poole repeatedly describes his own party as victims. He uses "unfortunate" and describes himself as "unwitting." How should one take this? Remember that Poole deliberately painted his role in copper mining on Haida Gwaii as much more heroic than the simple truth allowed. Our prudential assumption, therefore, must be that deceptively shading his own role in events was his usual practice. Moreover, in the narrative context of his memoir, Poole does not necessarily mean to imply that the resulting "enormous sacrifice of life" was accidental. He only wants his readers to believe that, while he and his party were the means, they were innocent actors. Some corroboration of this seems in the Nuxalk blaming someone, yet letting Poole land a second time as a mere tool of someone else.

If Poole's party was not ultimately responsible for its actions, who was? Poole arrived in the Pacific colonies from distant Canada near broke and "without a friend or relative nearer than 6000 miles."[253] He disembarked with about 400 others, many competing for similar work.[254] He was only 26 years old with just 20 months' mining experience. He

---

251. See Poole's map, *Queen Charlotte Islands*, p. 95. His notation "Bella Bella," was nowhere near Bella Bella proper but is near the right place for this one, perhaps Namu.

252. Poole, *Queen Charlotte Islands*, p. 184.

253. Poole, *Queen Charlotte Islands*, p, 65.

254. Poole estimated 1000 or 1400 on the ship, see *Queen Charlotte Islands*, p. 53 and p. 62. The *Colonist* reported that, of those, 600 actually disembarked at Victoria. "The Pacific," *The British Colonist*, May 14, 1862, p. 3.

landed in Victoria on May 13, 1862 and would leave for Bella Coola May 21, just one week later.[255] All this bolsters his claim to have begun as an unwitting player. He had too little time or resources to have organized any endeavor himself.

So who hired Poole to "head" the party admittedly responsible for introducing smallpox to the Nuxalk Ancestors in early June 1862? Poole explained the context of his first employment this way,

> *What an emigrant looks to, on landing, is to be employed in any manner. For although he may have to endure great hardship from the unwonted nature of the employment [first] offered, he knows that if he will but keep steadily at it he is certain to get on. Sometimes no doubt he acts with unwise precipitancy; but the stimulus to active exertion is nonetheless [positive,] even after a disappointment at starting.... A feeling of this kind led me, in the first instance, to join a prospecting enterprise on the mainland.... But for all my eagerness to earn a status in the colony, could I have foreseen one tithe of the privations before me I would have shrunk back appalled...[add] that for five or six days we were in hourly dread of attack from hostile savages...and that we left a sorrowful trail of blood behind us, nay, the body even of one of our companions.... (B)ut [this first employment] served to start me in British Columbia.[256]*

In his memoir, two newspaper interviews and two articles in a missionary journal, all touching on his journey, Poole never discloses who hired him to "head" this party. Given the usual style of his narration, this omission cries out for some explanation. It suggests his employer required a non-disclosure understanding. Why?

Poole does reveal several facts about his first employment. It was of an "unwonted" nature. It was an assignment from which ordinarily he would have "shrunk back appalled" except his circumstances prompted him to accept with an "unwise precipitancy." Eventually it put him "in hourly dread of attack by hostile savages" while leaving behind "a sorrowful trail of blood."

---

255. Poole, *Queen Charlotte Islands*, p. 61. Born in Staffordshire, England during 1836, Poole appears in the 1861 Canada West Census at Leeds, Canada West. He had a connection to Perth, Ontario, where the newspaper interviewed him in 1872. He died Feb. 15, 1874 and is buried in Kingston, Ontario. On his departure, see information on the *Hamley* below.

256. Poole, *Queen Charlotte Islands*, pp. 63-65.

Would anyone describe being an accidental source of disease as "leaving a sorrowful trail of blood?" Do mere accidents cause "many mournful hours of reflection?" Could a "prospecting enterprise" ever seem "unwonted" employment for a professional miner? Being employed primarily to spread disease, on the other hand for example, would be "unwonted" employment.

Poole was not away long enough for any actual prospecting. He simply crossed to the Fraser River and returned to Victoria. He spent less than three weeks in the field, hiking through an area without gold bearing streams. This was no "prospecting enterprise."

Then, despite Poole's various tales of supposed "great hardship," in fact, this hike was not especially demanding. Actual miners did not "shrink back appalled." This was not the Klondike. Many Europeans crossed the summer before.[257] None complained of "privations" or of the terrain. Colonel Foster called such descriptions "ridiculous."[258] Natives travelled it as a matter of course. It cannot have been the route itself that caused Poole to "shrink back appalled." Moreover, Poole had a Nuxalk guide.[259] The route also was quite well populated with natives to help, most less than a day's travel apart.[260] Unless, that is, one was doing something that caused one to be "in hourly dread of attack by hostile savages."[261] No previous traveller had reported anything but civility from the Ancestors or Tsilhqot'in.

Poole's first employment paid off, as he had hoped. Within days, someone introduced him to the Governor.[262] He also found work with the Queen Charlotte Mining Company. Unlike his first employer, Poole disclosed his second immediately.[263] Since he implies that his second employment was a product of his first, one must seek the link.

Vancouver Island M.L.A. Robert Burnaby controlled the Queen Charlotte Company.[264] Burnaby was Victoria's leading Freemason. Poole

257. As noted extensively in the chapter on roads.

258. "Letter from Alexandria," *The British Colonist*, Sept. 6, 1863, p. 3.

259. Poole, *Queen Charlotte Islands*, p. 179.

260. Poole's account of this crossing is preposterous. There is, for example, no 16,000 ft. peak to climb, as his account claims that he did. From his account, one might also conclude that there were no native villages at all.

261. Poole, *Queen Charlotte Islands*, p. 65.

262. Poole, *Queen Charlotte Islands*, p. 66.

263. Poole, *Queen Charlotte Islands*, p. 66.

264. "Queen Charlotte Mining Company" *Daily Chronicle*, Jan. 15, 1863, p. 3.

was an active Freemason.[265] Without friends or relatives, it would have been logical for him to seek a connection this way. Later, Poole would name "Burnaby Island" to honor Robert Burnaby.[266] Burnaby also was a director of the Bentinck Arm Company, along whose route Poole's first employment would take him. Close friends, Burnaby and George Cary had fostered the steamship committee together. They also had the necessary access to have Poole meet the Governor and to help him gain "status in the colony."

That Poole received his second position as a reward for taking his "unwonted" first assignment more than for any other qualification can be shown another way. In 1908, revisiting Poole's Haida Gwaii work from 1862/63, the Provincial Mineralogist said these properties had no mineralization "of any importance" and were interesting only *as showing what Poole spent two years on [with] so many much more promising showings sticking out of the ground within three or four miles.*[267] In other words, Poole had insufficient mining knowledge to recognize the difference between a pile of rocks and some true copper prospects right in front of his nose. By itself, Poole's mining resume seems insufficient as the explanation for his receiving this second opportunity in the management of a mine.

Poole's memoir, then, provides enough information to identify his first employer as George Cary's Bentinck Arm enterprises. Details from his interviews remove any doubt. One newspaper described Poole as among, *Fourty men who left the Big Slide several days behind Pearson....*[268] The Bentinck Arm Company had hired Pearson to guide these 40 men while blazing its trail.[269] The 40 men said to have included Poole, then, were this next group, advertised as travelling under Pearson, "the well-known coast route guide."[270]

> *(T)he Bentinck Arm Company are determined to prove their route...*
> *is the best and only wants travelling over to be well known and*

---

265. Poole died of Kidney disease, Feb. 15, 1875 in Kingston, Ontario. He was buried in the Cataraqui Cemetery in section B, Lot 30 and 31 with others from Cataraqui Lodge 92. Confirmed by email correspondence between the author and Jessica Hood the cemetery Administrator dated May 11, 2015.

266. Poole, *Queen Charlotte Islands*, p. 100.

267. "Mineral Development on Moresby Island," *Daily Colonist*, Feb. 23, 1908, p. 30.

268. "Important from the Coast Route," *The British Colonist*, July 22, 1862, p. 3.

269. Testimony of Edward Green, *Bentinck Arm Company v. Hood*, First Day, Feb. 11, *The British Colonist*, Feb. 12, 1864, p. 3.

270. "From Bentinck Arm.," *The British Colonist*, June 14, 1862.

patronized. They, therefore, offer to take 40 men with 200 pounds of baggage each to the Fraser above the mouth of Quesnel.[271]

Outwardly, the Company assembled these 40 men as a marketing gimmick for its coastal route to the mines. Marketing is still not "unwonted" employment. In any case, the evidence is well beyond a reasonable doubt that George Cary's enterprises hired Poole and initiated his expedition to Nuxalk and Tsilhqot'in territory.

Pearson left Victoria with the first half, 21 men, on May 12.[272] These arrived at Bella Coola May 27 to 29. Ranald McDonald from the Company's board of directors met them. Pearson and McDonald went ahead to mark the Company's route for the 40 men to follow.[273]

With Pearson gone, the second half would need other leadership. This seems where Poole came in. "Headed by" Poole, these left Victoria May 21 with Captain Going on the *Hamley*.[274] Poole said it was "a two-weeks' voyage."[275] With unloading, this puts him on the ground at Bella Coola on June 5/6. Poole said he then "twice" spent "some useful and jolly days under the roof" of Alexander Wallace during his first visit.[276] This implies that Poole arrived at Bella Coola, spent time with Wallace, and then took a short side trip. This provides a window for a visit to South Bentinck or the Dean Channel.

Positioned as harbormaster and then government customs agent, Wallace had come to Bentinck Arm at George Cary's instance.[277] The only other person Poole noted meeting on his first visit here was Jim Taylor, another Cary and Co. associate.[278] All these facts lend further confirmation that Poole was employed by George Cary's enterprises. Confirming a connection between the two groups in still one more way, Captain Going returned June 14 with a letter from Pearson.[279]

271. "Bentinck Arm," *Victoria Daily Press,* May 5, 1862, p. 3.

272. "For Cariboo via Bentinck Arm," *The British Colonist,* May 13, 1862, p. 3.

273. "From Bentinck Arm," *The British Colonist,* June 14, 1862.

274. See, "Off for Cariboo via Bentinck Arm," *The British Colonist,* May 22, 1862, p. 3. And "A Trip to Cariboo via Bentinck Arm," *The British Columbian,* July 23, 1862, p. 3.

275. "A Trip to Cariboo via Bentinck Arm," as above.

276. Francis Poole, *Queen Charlotte Islands,* p. 178.

277. See testimony of George Cary, *Bentinck Arm Company v. Hood,* Third Day, Feb. 15, The British Colonist, Feb. 17, 1864, p. 3.

278. Francis Poole, *Queen Charlotte Islands,* p. 181.

279. "From Bentinck Arm," *The British Colonist,* June 14, 1862, p. 3.

Returning a week behind Going, Captain Osgoode reported, *An Indian had arrived at Bella Coola June 10 from the Cariboo.... Nothing of interest had transpired at Bella Coola. The smallpox had not yet got among the Indians there; but the Bella Bellas* [Heiltsuk] *were dying off very fast.*[280]

This confirms that there was no visible smallpox at Bella Coola as of June 10, up to five days after Poole's party arrived. New victims typically have the disease for several days before it becomes visible. In fact, the highest probability is that the disease did not begin showing until after Poole left Bella Coola June 15. In any case, while "nothing of interest had transpired at Bella Coola" as of June 10, just three weeks later every visitor would report finding dead or dying Ancestors everywhere. All this dramatically corroborates Poole's admission of responsibility for introducing the disease at Bella Coola.

So, Poole's party arrived at Bella Coola in early June to introduce smallpox while under the sponsorship of developers whose plans required that there should be "no Indian settlement" here on the fee simple town lots that they expected to sell as vacant in early June. Apologists for the Douglas Regime would have to say that this was just one more coincidence in a long line of consecutive chance events, beginning with the arrival of smallpox in the colonies with Cary's steamship committee. Yet the odds against mere chance as an adequate explanation are astronomical. Meanwhile, there is evidence supporting all the elements essential to the usual proof of a crime. And there is much more still to come.

II
Poole's party beyond Q'umk'uts.

In his memoir, quoted above, Poole admitted carrying the disease to affect "tribes" along both "Arms" and to some Heiltsuk resident "in the neighborhood." Did his party introduce the disease once, after which it spread naturally? Or did his party introduce it several times? Once might be consistent with accident or a simple lack of caution. Each successive instance is more consistent with a general purpose.

To begin, why did the Poole and Pearson parties take two weeks or more to reach Bella Coola? Hood left Victoria on the *Labouchere*

---

280. "From Bentinck Arm, Fort Rupert and Nanaimo," *The British Colonist*, June 20, 1862, p. 3.

June 25 and was unloaded at Bella Coola by July 2: eight days.[281] Yet the Pearson and Poole parties were said to have taken 17 and 14 days. Different ships do have different capabilities, and different abilities when loaded or unloaded. Yet a human powered canoe made this journey in 15 days.[282] These ships were capable of 24-hour operation. The *Hamley* took only 7 days for its return.[283]

Then, Pearson's party also carried the disease.[284] Like Poole's party, it "left" at least one sick man among an indigenous community, but not among the Nuxalk Ancestors and so its activities are not covered here. However, like Poole's party, several members returned to Victoria without visiting the mining district. Like Poole, five wrote to the newspapers.[285] The bottom line is that both of these Bentinck Arm Company sponsored parties had the opportunity, means and motive for creating epidemics elsewhere on the coastal route.

Poole admits as much. In addition to accepting responsibility "along the Arms" and "in the neighborhood," he also acknowledged leaving two diseased men at Ft. Rupert and a newspaper said his party left still others at Nanaimo.[286] In addition to admissions of introducing the disease: 1) in locations approaching Bella Coola, and 2) at Bella Coola itself, then, Poole also admitted 3) to introducing the disease up the Valley at Nautlieff and 4) at Chilcotin Lake. (See map p. 188.)

Travellers behind Poole soon reported, *[the Bentinck Arm route] is dotted with the bleached corpses of unfortunate victims who succumbed to hardship, starvation and smallpox.*[287] There were no reports of any non-

---

281. See "Marine Intelligence," The *British Colonist*, June 26, 1862, p. 3 And see Henry Spencer Palmer, *Report of a Journey of survey, from Victoria to Fort Alexander via North Bentinck Arm.* (New Westminster: Royal Engineers Press, 1863) p. 3.

282. See, for example: "Four Days Later from Bentinck Arm," The *British Colonist*, August 27, 1862, p. 3.

283. The harbor log has the *Hamley* returning on the 13th and Capt. Going gave an interview published as "From Bentinck Arm," The *British Colonist*, June 14, 1862, p. 3. This estimate allows one day for unloading and taking new cargo onboard. If Capt. Going stopped at other ports on the way down looking for freight, then the actual travel time was even less.

284. For the known activity of Pearson's party see *Canada's War*, s. 60, pp. 165-172.

285. "Coast Route to Cariboo," The *British Colonist*, July 23, 1862, p. 3. And "The Coast Route," The *British Colonist*, July 29, 1862, p. 3.

286. Like the two men left at Ft. Rupert, those at Nanaimo were said to have been, "put ashore for medical treatment." In that case, however, Poole's party then passed up two separate occasions when ordinarily prudent people would have taken advantage of the opportunity to take precautions in the rest of the group. See "From Bentinck Arm, Fort Rupert and Nanaimo," The *British Colonist*, June 21, 1862, p. 3. For example, when one native among a Vancouver Island Exploring Party came down with smallpox, the party returned immediately to Nanaimo and "the party were vaccinated." See the same article.

287. The *British Columbian*, August 16, 1862, p. 3.

indigenous deaths here when the witnesses made these observations. These were the actual "unfortunate victims."

What about Nautlieff, 60 km up the Valley? One newspaper reported Poole as claiming his party *found it necessary to leave two of their number at Fort Rupert, two at Naukuluff and two more at Chilcotin, the smallpox having broken out....*[288] So the disease struck exactly two men at each interval. That's interesting. In Victoria the newspaper said, *two Canadians (brothers) named Linn, fell sick of the smallpox and were left at Noot-lef village to the tender mercies of the savages. At Chilcotin Lake two more Canadians...fell sick of the same complaint and were left with the Chilcotin Indians.*[289]

After Bella Coola, Nautlieff/Nutl'lhiix may have been the next most valuable location in the Valley. Poole and Palmer each noted its arable land. Venables and Kenny analyzed it while investigating Mackenzie's 1793 route.[290] It was at a junction of trails inland: one to Tsilhqot'in, one to Dakelh territory. A facility here would thrive whichever way the road went. So those associated with the Bentinck Arm enterprises knew its strategic value before 1862. And, therefore, had the necessary opportunity to plan for its prior occupation.

Venables noted 12 communal houses at Nautlieff/Nutl'lhiixw's core for a population over 180-200.[291] When Lt. Palmer passed with the first epidemic just underway, he called it *another large village, at present inhabited.*[292] Settlers began a new epidemic in October.[293] In May 1863, an eyewitness estimated only 15 survivors.[294]

Shortly after Poole "left" the diseased Linn brothers here, William Hood's party and Adam Ross staked claims to 800 acres.[295] Since Hood was with Palmer, Nautlieff would have been visibly occupied as they staked land in this Ancestral precinct.

288. "A Trip to Cariboo via Bentinck Arm," *The British Columbian*, July 22, 1862, p. 2.

289. "Important from the Coast Route-Destitution and Suffering," *The British Colonist*, July 22, 1862, p. 3.

290. "From Bella Coola," *The British Colonist*, Oct. 22, 1861, p. 3.

291. "Route from Alexandria to North Bentinck Arm," *The British Colonist*, Oct. 28, 1861, p. 2.

292. Henry Spencer Palmer, *Report of a Journey*, p. 11.

293. See the next chapter on the second epidemics, especially re: Angus McLeod.

294. "Latest from the North Coast," *The British Colonist*, May 19, 1863, p. 3.

295. BCARS. British Columbia Lands and Works. Claims of Ross, Hood, Barron, Shaw and Wilson, Folders 1 and 2, Cariboo, Lytton and Lillooet pre-emption records taken by P. Nind, & T. Elwyn, 1860-1863 and Peter O'Reilly, 1862-1864, Alexandria and other districts.

Later, Venables made this report, *The Indians engaged to build a store for me and Mr. Hood hardly commenced their work, and I was obliged to hire white men in their place. The boards were obtained from a ranch deserted by them since the smallpox broke out.... [So] I was put to great inconvenience and expense....*[296]

Lo, the poor settler! Not only would natives hardly work at slave rates, they soon found dismantling their own occupation for the dispossession of their children as unendurable. Whatever being "left" here implied, neither Linn brother came to harm from "the tender mercies of savages." Hood employed one.[297] The other drowned.[298]

Nor does Poole's responsibility end here. Between Bella Coola and Chilcotin Lake his party had smallpox carriers the whole way. An eyewitness also reported a carrier undisclosed by Poole but a man who had arrived at Victoria on the same ship and who almost certainly had been in Poole's party.[299] Their guide had the disease.[300] This gave them access and exposed each community in turn.

So the available evidence is most consistent with Poole's party having introduced the disease as it went. It would have delayed them for only a few minutes. Three weeks behind Poole, Palmer reported Nookeetz at 16 km from Bella Coola, Asananny at 25 km and Nooskultst/Nusq'ist at 35 km all deserted.[301] In fact, the residents already were dead from smallpox. A diarist with the 1864 Chilcotin expedition said of Nookeetz, *(A)lmost all died of smallpox.*[302] Of Asananny, *All died save one from smallpox.*[303] However, between Poole's passage and Palmer's behind him, there was an insufficient passage of time for a long series of naturally unfolding epidemics. Instead, the timing was perfectly consistent with all these deaths having been the result of successive introductions by Poole's party along the length of the coastal route.[304]

---

296. "The causes of the Bute massacre," *The British Colonist*, June 28, p. 3.

297. Reported by Alexander Fortune in his diary and "The Bentinck Arm route," *The British Colonist*, Jan. 3, 1863, p. 3.

298. "From Bentinck Arm," *Daily Press*, Aug. 16, p. 3.

299. Duncan McKinnon. See Chapter 13, s. iii.

300. Poole, *Queen Charlotte Islands*, p. 179.

301. Palmer, *Report of a Journey*, p. 11.

302. John Brough, *Diary*, June 20, 1864.

303. John Brough, *Diary*, June 21, 1864.

304. At three weeks, epidemics in these others places should have been just in their early stages when Palmer passed them. See s. iii, in the next Chapter.

III

Preliminary assessment of Poole's party.

In sum so far, Attorney General George Cary's Bentinck Arm enterprises hired Francis Poole to lead a party along the proposed coastal route from Victoria via Bella Coola to the Fraser. In this course, Poole's party knowingly introduced smallpox to multiple locations where Cary or his associates were creating rights to land.

At Q'umk'uts, Poole's party introduced smallpox in "early June" virtually to the day that Cary urgently confronted B.C. officials while seeking to have the land registered and while asserting the absence of any "Indian settlement."

Moreover, at first, the disease arrived in the colonies on a boat sponsored by these same developers after they already had made plans to sell town lots here in early June.

Later, Poole would say that the consequences of actions such as his party performed, not once but repeatedly, were certain. Where the consequences of an action are certain, legal systems typically hold the authors as having intended those consequences. This is certainly the case with respect to English law and there is no reason to believe it was any different for indigenous law.

The Douglas Regime had done nothing yet to extend British Columbia's boundaries to the Ancestors' territory or to assert any sovereign control there. Yet private and public concerns ran together in Cary's endeavors. It seems likely, therefore, that Cary, and others in the know, considered introducing smallpox here as a first assertion, on behalf of the Crown, for *de facto* sovereign control. That is, as a tipping point for constitutional change in what Dr. Helmcken would describe as a "survival of the fittest" relationship. [305] But this Regime acted without honor and outside the rule of law as it pretended to a circumstance of war and a necessity of pre-emptive strikes.

In the next chapter, it will emerge that Staltmc Pootlass also saw this as a constitutionally significant event, though not the same one. Each of these views would turn out as correct: artificial epidemics allowed the Colony to begin assuming control but smallpox also fed an anti-colonial culture perceived as essential to indigenous survival.

---

305. Helmcken, *Reminiscences*, p. 331.

In any case, none of the smallpox activity of Poole's party says accident, negligence or the work of depraved minds. It screams premeditation, bureaucratic planning, intent, mass murder and genocide. And there is still more evidence about the introduction of smallpox by Poole's party that reflects on intent and ultimate responsibility.

13

Systematic Distribution

Some Nuxalk traditions have it that settlers spread smallpox systematically and repeatedly to increase the death toll.[306] Such actions would be more consistent with an ethnic cleansing-like social policy than with ordinary mass murder. One dramatic confirmation of these actions seem revealed in the timing of Staltmc Pootlass' first reported use of "Nuxalk" or "Nuxalkmc" for his social entity.[307]

Understanding Pootlass' political reaction and the significance of some additional evidence about the activities of Poole's party, requires more information about smallpox and about the usual course of epidemics. Smallpox has no known cure. Neither indigenous nor non-indigenous doctors could heal individual cases. Therefore, breaking the chain of transmission is always the most crucial thing to reduce human suffering. How is this done?

Smallpox requires direct contact to spread. This can be contact with infected skin or through an exchange of breath with an infected person. New victims typically infect six others.[308] Once infected, new victims become infectious in their turn only as symptoms begin showing several days later. It is for this reason that the World Health Organization says smallpox epidemics develop slowly, typically with two to three weeks between generations. People then either die or begin recovering in another two to three weeks. In a typical epidemic, then, after a first carrier arrives in a community, one should anticipate finding about six

---

306. For example, Devon Webster reports the conversations known to him from potlatches and other contexts in his unpublished paper, "Bella Coola, A Story to be Told." The reference there is to smallpox blankets for which there is confirming evidence in the second wave still to be covered. For Poole's party, there seems no outside evidence of infected blankets, although his party had access to them at Victoria and Ft. Rupert.

307. Nuxalkmc refers to a "gathering of the Peoples," borrowed in part from the way in which fish might gather in a school or be gathered in a net.

308. Comparative statistics on infection and death rates collected from the Center for Disease Control and the World Health Organization can been found in an accessible chart created by "KnowledgeisBeautiful. net" and republished in *The Guardian*, Oct. 15, 2014.

more victims after two weeks and about 36 after four weeks, with the first carrier now dead or recovering. In any case, at four weeks or 28 days, a typical epidemic is still in its early stages.

The lull between first contact on Day One and the second victim becoming a danger to others allows for timely control measures. These measures have always included quarantine for the sick and isolating the healthy from known carriers. Doctors then discovered that inoculating people with small doses of the disease could produce mild cases while gaining protection from full-blown cases. These subjects, however, became infectious in the usual way. So inoculation created a public health risk. It was unlawful to inoculate people without protecting the public from exposure to them.[309]

Doctors next found that vaccination with cowpox gave protection from smallpox while eliminating the public health risk. With vaccine easily produced and widely accepted, Great Britain (1840), Canada (1855) and most European nations outlawed inoculation completely. In 1855, as a matter of British law, Parliament also required doctors to vaccinate children. From a legal and public health standpoint, this was the non-indigenous state of the art in 1862.

In passing, recall how remarkable it seems that men in Poole's party repeatedly came down with smallpox always two at a time. And at what seem convenient intervals. While remarkable as coincidence, one can produce this same effect easily by inoculating subjects on a schedule. Since inoculation was the original means of securing protection, one also can understand the subjects readily agreeing to it. Those so protected, however, can spread the disease in the usual way.

I

A public health duty of control measures knowingly failed.

Once the Douglas Regime had invited non-indigenous activity in territories where it had not yet negotiated treaties, officials had a duty to protect the Crown's honor by ensuring an appropriate standard of public health care wherever its actions put indigenous residents at risk. Since indigenous susceptibility to smallpox and the effectiveness of vaccine were both well known, this duty's minimum requirement seems uncontroversial: to make vaccine available in a timely way.

309. R. v. Burnett 1815. K.B. 4M&S 272-274. Defendant jailed for six months.

Moreover, the Douglas Regime understood the Crown's pubic health duty in case of a smallpox epidemic. It immediately created smallpox wards at its public hospitals in both Victoria and New Westminster. Yet these would sit vacant while natives died *en masse* outside. Notice that withholding medical care from an identifiable ethnic group is evidence of a public policy for creating conditions of life calculated to see them die, i.e. of genocide.

Showing its appreciation that the Crown's public health duty also extended to the indigenous population, the Regime did pay it some small public relations heed. It pointedly staged the application of a medical procedure to a collaborationist family at Victoria that it claimed was vaccination.[310] Yet even this family did not trust the Douglas Regime's sincerity. Soon after, it fled Victoria from a fear of smallpox. It went to an island where it then killed others, again from fear of the disease despite supposedly having been vaccinated.[311]

In a further sign that the Regime's public professions could not be trusted at face value, it advertised the supposed further vaccination of 500 natives at Victoria.[312] Large numbers of these then died. As observers noted at the time, a failure on this scale suggests that the supposed vaccine was defective or negligently applied.[313] Rather than vaccine as advertised, it also may have been the illegal and dangerous inoculation procedure. This better fits the acknowledged fact that this did not stop the disease but preceded an explosion of new cases.

The Douglas Regime's true smallpox policy, as revealed through the footprint of its official activity, was quite different. In fact, the Regime made itself the primary agent causing the disease to spread. Most notably, between April 28 and June 11, it cruelly and repeatedly forced diseased natives to mix with healthy natives at police gunpoint while expelling them from Victoria.[314] One editorialist acknowledged this as an extermination policy.[315] Remember, simply "incautiously exposing others to disease carriers" was a crime under English law. Yet this was

---

310. "Smallpox," *The British Colonist*, March 28, p. 3.

311. The smallpox-related activities of the local Songhees are described and noted in *Canada's 'War,'* s. 83, p. 258.

312. "The Smallpox and the Indians," *The British Colonist*, April 26, 1862, p. 3.

313. "The Ravages of Smallpox," *Victoria Daily Chronicle*, Jan. 11, 1863, p. 3. Dr. Helmcken himself raised the issue of "vaccine" failure, Helmcken, *Reminiscences*, p. 187. See also *Canada's 'War'* pp. 256-57.

314. The Douglas Regime's Victoria activity is covered in *Canada's 'War'* ss. 79-89.

315. "Smallpox," *Victoria Daily Press*, June 19, 1862, p. 2.

the government forcing contact with the threat of violence: even at its best, this was a gross criminal violation of public trust. At worst, this unmistakably created conditions of life calculated to see an identifiable ethnic group die. This is genocide.

The Douglas Regime's expulsion policy as instituted at Victoria from the end of April 1962 put all natives along the coast at risk. This included the Ancestors. As it happened, other diseased natives were not the source of smallpox among the Ancestors. Nevertheless, when one creates a hazard that puts others at risk, an immediate duty of corrective action arises both in honor and law. A duty of protecting the Ancestors from the Douglas Regime's smallpox expulsion policy arose, then, with its first expulsion beginning April 28, 1862.

Whatever else this required, it certainly included forwarding vaccine. Vaccine was readily available on the Pacific shelf. Natives widely accepted it when offered. Missionaries vaccinated thousands in good faith. This kept the death rate below 20 percent in one region[316] or, with other measures, near zero in another.[317] Neither the Douglas Regime nor Attorney General Cary's enterprises showed any similar good faith to the Ancestors. The opportunities were legion. Vaccine forwarded with the Bentinck Arm party of May 12 would have prevented everything that followed. Moreover, the *Tallyho*, *Northern Light* and *Antelope* all went to Bentinck Arm before early June and could have taken vaccine.[318]

What about Poole's party? As Poole first arrived at Victoria, the Douglas Regime was burning native dwellings by the score. Every observer knew that this would put countless disease carriers in motion to create new epidemics along the coast.[319] The Regime also burned native dwellings at Esquimalt.[320] Poole and others in his party would have witnessed all this official destruction first hand. It would have confirmed a sense of social license from the authorities, if asked to produce similar consequences. There seems no qualitative difference between the Regime hiring extra police for this exercise in Victoria and with Cary then hiring

---

316. The circumstances are covered in *Canada's War*, s. 93, pp. 299-301.

317. See *Canada's War*, s. 103, p. 352.

318. See the harbor records as reported in the Victoria newspapers between May 12 and June 6. Sill others advertised their readiness for such a voyage.

319. As described in *Canada's War*, s. 85, pp. 267-271.

320. *The British Colonist*, May 15, 1862, p. 3.

Poole for a similar purpose on behalf of the quasi-public Bentinck Arm enterprises. Once again, such a policy would be all one garment.

Poole's party left diseased men at Nanaimo, just a few hours' journey from Victoria.[321] These men almost certainly already had visible signs of disease before leaving Victoria. And, therefore, it is certain that someone knowingly included smallpox carriers with Poole's party from the first. In the ordinary course, not vaccinating the rest at Nanaimo showed bad faith. By way of contrast, when a party exactly contemporary with Poole's discovered a carrier in their midst near Nanaimo, it immediately had the rest vaccinated.[322] That was the normal reaction of people acting in good faith. In short, those directing Poole's party from the first not only failed to assist control, but showed behavior most consistent with spreading the disease.

John Morris' Bentinck Arm party behind Poole included a French doctor. This doctor was reported to have carried out smallpox related procedures at Ft. Rupert along the way.[323] If he had vaccine with him as he advertised, then it was in his medical bag as he arrived at Bella Coola. Others confirmed that the doctor was among a party on its way "to assist in making or improving" the Bentinck Arm Company's road.[324] Yet, if there had been no prior anticipation of disease, then it is hard to see what role in "improving" the road might have been foreseen for a doctor. Though, if one anticipated using inoculation to produce carriers for creating artificial epidemics, then a doctor would have been most useful. In any case, this doctor included as part of a Bentinck Arm Company party travelled the length of the Bella Coola Valley just as the disease broke out in Poole's footsteps without any observer mentioning his taking part in any prevention measures.[325] If he had instituted only the usual measures called for by the circumstances, the second wave of epidemics beginning in Oct. 1862 would have been much less severe.

Governor Douglas might have sent vaccine with Lt. Palmer's party, arriving here July 2. Moreover, after Poole met Douglas in July on his return[326] and after Colonel Moody received confirmation from

---

321. "From Bentinck Arm..." *The British Colonist*, June 21, 1862, p. 3.

322. See adjacent paragraphs in the *Colonist* article cited above.

323. "From Bentinck Arm, Fort Rupert and Nanaimo," *The British Colonist*, June 21, 1862, p. 3.

324. "From Bentinck Arm..." *The British Colonist*, June 21, 1862, p. 3.

325. Trip to the head of Bentinck Arm..." *The British Colonist*, August 28, 1862, p. 3.

326. Poole, *Queen Charlotte Islands*, p. 66.

Lt. Palmer about the devastation in Poole's wake, his Regime still did nothing.[327] Douglas and Cary simply left them to die.

The Ancestors suffered as much from the failure to act of both private and public agencies pursuing interests in their territory as they did from those knowingly spreading disease. Unless, that is, these were all the same people pursuing a single underlying policy.

II

Circumventing control measures taken by the Ancestors.

What about indigenous control measures? Measures, that is, by which the Ancestors might have reduced the death toll? Anticipating such measures or eliminating the vagaries of chance would be where a plan for systematic distribution would come in.

From knowledge gained through previous experience with European diseases, especially the recent measles epidemics of the late 1840s, most Pacific shelf indigenous communities knew the basics of epidemic disease control by 1862. Eyewitnesses widely reported the following measures.

First, infected individuals went into quarantine on the outskirts. Among the Nuxalk, William Wattie reported a case that was particularly telling about the strict discipline of those communities.

> *As soon as they take it, they are put out of the camp.... [We] went into one of the "ranches" as they are called. It was a large building 150 by 75 feet with an opening in the roof to let the smoke out. The floor would be about five feet raised from the ground.... We went out the opposite end and, on hearing a child crying...we [searched and] found a six-month old baby in a little booth made of brush. It was dreadfully broken out with smallpox and so it had to be put out of the camp...and the wild beasts would carry it away at night.*[328]

327. BCARS. GR-1372. British Columbia. Colonial Correspondence. B01353. F. 1302a. Lt. Henry Palmer to Colonel Moody, July 16, 1862.

328. City of Kamloops Archives. Wade Family Fonds. Box 2, File 12, William Wattie, "Lecture Given at Worcester Mass. in 1913, pp. 9-11.

In other cases, older children with the disease were tied to trees so that they could not return to infect others. One man who freed his child and brought it back into the village was himself executed.[329]

When a disease protocol requires that mothers abandon their babies within reach of wolves or when a community must defend itself by executing those who endanger it only out of parental love, then the probability of a consistent and rigorous application seems high. While effective, this system depends on an early recognition of symptoms. It is certain to reduce the number of people an infected person might touch, especially outside his or her own house.

Notice that one can defeat quarantine controls like this by introducing the disease to several houses all near the same time.

Second, when outbreaks became known in one's own village, or in neighboring communities, the healthy fled to other camps. The sick stayed put and, therefore, did not multiply the opportunities for infection. Although, at Soonochlim, at first so many became diseased at once that the sick left in a group to isolate themselves.[330] This is most consistent with systematic introduction and little consistent with natural development. Taking a rifle, they fired a shot to let those in the village know when another had died. This measure proves again knowledge among the Ancestors about the necessity of quarantine and isolation. Elsewhere, people dug their own graves so that others could bury them without the risks entailed in handling bodies.[331]

This control depends on an accurate early separation of sick and healthy in the lull between infection and infectiousness. It reduces casual transmissions and breaks the chain of infection, especially when a whole house could flee before the disease appeared among its members. It also reduced the risk in tending the sick or of handling bodies. Hood[332] and Palmer[333] each reported instant flight among the Nuxalk. These measures should have decreased the death toll.

Again systematic introduction would defeat this control.

329. From the author's conversations with senior members of the Pootlass family at Bella Coola, Aug. 2 to Aug. 8, 2015.

330. From conversations with Elder Roseanne Andy at Bella Coola, Aug. 2 to 8, 2015.

331. From the author's conversations with senior members of the Pootlass family at Bella Coola, Aug. 2 to Aug. 8, 2015.

332. Testimony of William Hood, *Bentinck Arm Company v. Hood*, Afternoon Session, Sixth Day, Feb. 18, 1864, *The British Colonist*, Feb. 19, 1864, p. 3.

333. Henry Spencer Palmer, *Report of a Journey*, p. 7.

Third, local authorities closed their communities to outsiders. Along the coast, communities fired on or killed several settlers who did not respect this measure. It led to a war between the Colony and the Tsimshian. Among the Nuxalk, Lt. Palmer canceled his visit to the Dean Channel because, *The Bella Coola Indians were afraid that they would not be allowed to land with me at Dean's Canal on account of the smallpox.*[334] If applied in time, this measure prevented the disease completely. Later, it prevented new sources from beginning new disease chains.

However this measure would be too late in the case of any systematic introduction in the initial stage.

III
Poole's artificial epidemics differed from natural cases.

If Poole's party had introduced the disease accidentally, or in some casual way, then its subsequent progress should resemble a natural epidemic. Anything different suggests systematic distribution.

Since we know when Poole's party arrived within a day or two, we can determine the disease's rate of progress with some precision. Its introduction cannot have begun any earlier than June 6-8. Since Poole arrived at Ft. Alexandria late July 4 after 18 or 19 days travel, his party remained in the Bella Coola area until June 15. Then, Poole said he was "twice" under Wallace's roof on this first occasion. This allows opportunity for a visit to South Bentinck Arm before arriving at Bella Coola and then an excursion to the Dean Channel from a base at Bella Coola. And, thereby, the opportunity for disease introduction at all three places where New Aberdeen had land claims.

Lt. Palmer and several others arrived at Bella Coola July 2 only about three weeks after Poole's party began introducing the disease. Using the World Health Organization's figures as a guide, Palmer's party should have discovered less than a dozen dead or dying and perhaps another 30 to 50 out of 2000 or so in various earlier stages. Whatever the actual figures, these witnesses should have found and reported an epidemic in its comparatively early stages.

Nor do we need to rely on a theoretical model alone to picture what Palmer's party should have encountered in the case of a natural

---

334. BCARS. GR-1372. British Columbia. Colonial Correspondence. B01353. F. 1302a. Lt. Henry Palmer to Colonel Moody, July 16, 1862, Postscript 1.

epidemic. Witnesses documented the disease's rate of progress in 1862 among similarly susceptible populations at both Victoria and Fort Simpson. These are exceptionally comparable cases.

At Victoria, the disease arrived March 12 on the same boat as Cary's steamship committee returning from San Francisco. Given the extensive evidence of its subsequent intentional applications by the same agencies as were behind the committee, the probability of its having arrived at Victoria merely by chance in the first place is near zero. The weight of the evidence is that, to use the description of one regime insider, settlers "imported the disease."[335]

Smallpox was not epidemic in San Francisco at this time. The original importation seems the only record of outside cases in the whole disaster. So, between the probable intentional introduction on March 12 and the seven weeks before April 28, when the Douglas Regime began forcing sick and healthy natives to mix at police gunpoint, there seems only natural progression from a single source.

The total native population visiting Victoria was comparable to that of Bella Coola, 2000 to 3000. According to several eyewitnesses, at seven weeks, the disease had not spread beyond the Tsimshian community where it had begun and who may have been 1000.[336] Six weeks from Day One, only 20 to 30 of these Tsimshian were said to be dead or dying.[337] As another sign of an epidemic still only in its early stages at six weeks, several observers believed the disease could have been contained yet.[338] So, at six weeks, the death toll among even the most affected community was still less than five percent. This is well within the range that the World Health Organization's estimates would lead one to expect.

What about at Ft. Simpson in Tsimshian territory? On May 1, the Douglas Regime expelled sick and healthy Tsimshian from Victoria by the hundreds to mix in the close quarters of canoes and make for their home territory.[339] These arrived at Ft. Simpson May 17.[340] Once again, we know the exact day of the disease's arrival. Once these arrived, there is little evidence of other intervention. 2000 to 2500 Tsimshian lived

---

335. John Sheepshanks, *A Bishop in the Rough* (New York: E.P. Dutton, 1909) p. 70.

336. See *Canada's 'War,' s.* 261, p. 261, on the Tsimshian resident at Victoria.

337. "Smallpox," *The British Colonist*, April 28, 1862, p. 3.

338. "The Smallpox and the Indians," *Victoria Daily Press*, May 1, 1862, p. 3.

339. See articles in the *Victoria Daily Press* for April 30 and May 1, 1863, p. 3.

340. BCARS. A/C/20/Si, William Henry McNeil, *Fort Simpson Journal*, 1859 – 1862, May 17.

near Ft. Simpson, a population comparable to Bella Coola. 18 days later, the Ft. Simpson Post Manager wrote, *We do not hear of many deaths from smallpox.*[341] At four weeks, he reported that "several" had died. Most had fled to their more remote hunting grounds or with Rev. William Duncan who led his adherents away to a strictly quarantined refuge at the first notice of disease.

The Post Manager does not say whether these "several" included those carriers who had brought the disease, as opposed to people newly infected on their arrival. Not until June 25, would he report "many" dying.[342] He does not quantify many but the real dying had just begun. They continued dying into September with the vast majority dying after five weeks. As for the final death toll here, out of 2000 to 2500 residents, the H.B.C. Post Manager said 25 percent died; the master of the *Devastation* said 35 percent; the master of the *Plumper* said 30 percent and Rev. William Duncan said 20 percent.[343] This all resembles the World Health Organization's projection.

At Bella Coola, both the rate at which the disease progressed and the final death toll were dramatically different. All the following observations by Lt. Palmer and those who arrived with him on July 2 came absolutely no later than four weeks from Day One and probably at three weeks. Palmer left the area July 9.

Confirming introduction by Poole's party in yet another way, Lt. Palmer believed the disease had been readily apparent here for just one week when he arrived July 2. Poole had been gone for only 18 days. It is a near certainty that his party left the area before the first symptoms would begin showing among its victims.

The importance of this is that there had been enough time for only one generation of disease by the time Palmer's party arrived. In a natural epidemic, even a dozen dead might have been unusual.

> *During my stay there* [at Bella Coola] *this disease, which had only just broken out when I arrived, spread so rapidly that, in a week, nearly all the healthy had scattered from the lodges and gone to camp by families in the woods only, it is to be feared, to carry away the seeds of infection and death in the blankets and other articles they took with*

341. *Fort Simpson Journal.* June 4, 1862.

342. *Fort Simpson Journal,* June 25, 1862.

343. For the Ft. Simpson experience see *Canada's 'War,'* s. 103, p. 339.

them. Numbers were dying each day; sick men and women were taken into the woods and left with a blanket and two or three salmon to die by them selves and rot unburied....[344]

Privately to Colonel Moody, Palmer wrote,

Poor creatures, they are dying and rotting away by the score, and it is no uncommon occurrence to come across dead bodies lying in the bush. They have now dispersed from the villages, but it seems to be spreading through the valley.[345]

Again "seems to be spreading" implies an outbreak in the early stages. Yet Poole's party had only just passed through these villages with the first carriers. Further, when the newspaper correspondent arrived at Stuie past Nautlieff, three weeks behind Poole, he met Duncan McKinnon, a Canadian "convalescent of smallpox."[346] McKinnon had arrived in Victoria on the same ship as Poole.[347] Most probably, he had been in Poole's party. If so, this seems confirmation that Poole's party left behind more diseased men than Poole admitted. His party was 22 at Victoria. Poole acknowledged leaving behind six, but only eight arrived with him at Alexandria, 13 less in all.[348]

Given that Poole's party introduced the disease just three weeks before, Palmer's comment "spread so rapidly" tends to confirm systematic distribution. Rather than the disease spreading "a to b, b to c, c to d," the best explanation for it to have "spread so rapidly" would have been for a common source to have infected many at once: "a to b, a to c, a to d and so on" all in the first generation. That is, instead of one infecting six others, one (or two) spread it to hundreds.

The apparent large death toll after just such a short time also tends to confirm simultaneous introduction. At just three weeks from Day One, bodies already were putrefying, and not just one, two or a few but "by the score." Even if this susceptible population died comparatively

344. Henry Spencer Palmer, *Report of a Journey*, p. 7.

345. BCARS. GR-1372. British Columbia. Colonial Correspondence. B01351. F1302a Lt. Palmer to Colonel Moody, Bella Coola River, July 16, 1872.

346. "A Trip to the Head of Bentinck Arm on the Steamer Labouchere," *The British Colonist*, Aug. 18, 1862, p.3.

347. See "Passengers," *The British Colonist*, May 14, 1862, p. 3.

348. "Important from the Coast Route," *The British Colonist*, July 22, 1862, p. 3.

quickly, all these bodies already putrefying can only have been infected in the first generation, directly by Poole's party.

Then, even though they fled almost instantly in a way that should have interrupted the chain of causation, as it did at Ft. Simpson, Palmer believed they took the disease with them. This is evidence that the disease was introduced in such a way that no one could count on having escaped becoming a carrier in his or her own right.

The newspaper correspondent arriving with Palmer reported,

> *We...arrived before dark [near] McLeod's Wharf.... (F)irst is the whiskey mill of A. Wallace, about three miles [below] the Indian villages. There is another building belonging to Capt. McKay...Mr. Wallace and Mr. Kenny were the only white men [here.] The next house is a little further...then comes a roofless hut put up by Mr. Taylor.... (W)e now reach Capt. Venables' hovel and afterward the house of Barney Johnson.... At the head of navigation, Mr. Morris and [his] party left the day before I arrived there...the feet of the doctor who accompanied Morris [were] in a terrible condition.... We camped near the Bella Coola Lodges where the smallpox was raging fearfully, Indians lying about in all directions dead and dying.*[349]

After three weeks there were not just a few deaths here, as there had been at Victoria or Ft. Simpson. Here the Ancestors already were "lying about in all directions dead and dying." This is not the kind of report one expects from an epidemic that had become apparent only just the week before. It is the kind of report one expects near the end.

Capt. Mountford left Bella Coola Aug. 8, eight weeks after Poole arrived. After the same interval at Victoria, observers still imagined control possible and, at Ft. Simpson, the greater dying had just begun. Mountford said, *At Bella Coola nearly the whole tribe has been swept away by the smallpox and at Deane's Canal but one Indian was seen.*[350] After just eight weeks, this epidemic was more near its end.

Travelling with Palmer, and therefore with observations made no later than four weeks after introduction, Colonel Foster quantified the death toll. Arriving at Ft. Alexandria in August, he spoke to Bishop George Hills. In his diary, Hills noted Foster as saying, *Dead and*

---

349. Viator, "A Trip to the Head of Bentinck Arm on the Steamer Labouchere," serialized in *The British Colonist*, August 18, 19 and 20, 1862.

350. "Four days later from Bentinck Arm," *The British Colonist*, August 27, 1862, p. 3.

putrefying bodies were lying about in all directions. Out of 2000 Indians he thought from what he saw not 500 would be left.[351]

Not just dead bodies, bodies dead long enough to have begun putrefying. Compare this with Ft. Simpson. There, after six or seven months, the death toll was only 25 percent. While still a significant number, it was of a completely different order than where an observer at the four-week interval could estimate the dead might exceed 75 percent.

Corroborating Foster's estimate, Poole also quantified the death toll. Before the additional toll from the second epidemic could have been known, walking to Q'umk'uts and Soonochlim, he noted, *We passed two Indian settlements…they were almost deserted, the smallpox reduced the tribes there from 4000 to a few dozens.*[352]

The disease's rapid progression and the extremely high death toll, combined with an urgent motive and the knowing introduction, are most consistent with the disease having been distributed here in a methodical or systematic way. How was it done?

Other B.C. Elders also report settlers using systematic methods while creating artificial epidemics in 1862. At Lytton, they describe a diseased man being sent to every house in a village.[353] This would produce two effects: a sudden explosion of cases as the disease would break out in each house at once and an increase in the death toll as residents could not escape, as they might from a natural outbreak in one house only. These seem telltale signs of systematic distribution. It is very likely that this same method was used wherever Poole went.

IV
Nuxalk: a new social entity rises from the catastrophe.

Dramatic evidence about the disease's unnatural rate of progress at Bella Coola seems contained in the very use of the term "Nuxalk." Nuxalk refers to the political project of drawing survivors together for strength in number. Under this policy, Staltmc Pootlass would marry several high rank women from other Ancestral communities. These unions created the necessary rights of citizenship so others could follow these relations

---

351. Anglican Archives of B.C. B8/S1, George Hills, *Journal*, 1862, Aug, 28, p.135.

352. Poole, *Queen Charlotte Islands*, p. 181.

353. See *Canada's 'War'* s. 108 for Fraser Canyon and page 377 for Lytton.

to Q'umk'uts.[354] After the epidemics, several other Peoples took similar actions. What is especially notable here, though, is the speed with which this necessity became recognized.

Before Poole arrived, no one reported the term Nuxalk ever used for those living here. Alexander Mackenzie did not report it in 1793. Fur traders used "Bilwhoola,"[355] "Bellwhoola," "Billechoola" or other variations.[356] No one interacting with Staltmc Pootlass during 1861, Kenny, McKay, Barnston or Venables, reported it. Venables and Kenny had an extended interaction with Pootlass in 1861, with the assistance of Jim Taylor who had lived there for several months. Yet Venables' map still refers to "Bill Whoalla" and the "Bill Whoalla River." If Pootlass ever had referred to his community as Nuxalk, Venables was certain to have referenced it.

Anthropologists also confirm that, prior to Poole's arrival, the People here had names only for particular communities with no prior identification of a wider political cohesion or entity, except for a common language and culture.[357] The overwhelming weight of the evidence is that the term was not in use before Poole's party arrived.

Less than four weeks after Poole's party arrived, however, Lt. Palmer's report shows that Staltmc Pootlass was now suddenly applying the term to his people and the river already as of July 3.[358] Governor Seymour's 1864 expedition also reported it.[359]

The implication is this: however Poole's party introduced the disease, its first phase was so devastating as to be recognizable within mere days as an epochal event for an entire population. Less than four weeks from Day One, and with Palmer reporting that the disease became visible just the week before, Pootlass already understood the necessity of "Nuxalk" as a political policy! The Biblical flood or the advent of Mohammed would be comparable events.

---

354. Expressed here as refined in correspondence with Clyde Tallio, July 10, 2015.

355. William Fraser Tolmie, *Physician and Fur Trader*. (Vancouver: Mitchell Press, 1963) p. 261.

356. See selections quoted in Richard Somerset Mackie, *Trading Beyond the Mountains*. (Vancouver: UBC Press, 1997) pp. 132-33.

357. The seminal work is Thomas McIlwraith, *The Bella Coola Indians*. (Toronto: University of Toronto Press, 1948, reprinted 1993.) See Vol. 1, Chapter One.

358. Henry Spencer Palmer, *Report of a Journey of survey, from Victoria to Fort Alexander via North Bentinck Arm*. (B.C. Royal Engineers Press, 1863) pp. 3-6.

359. The Governor does not report it but see John Brough, *Diary*, June 17, 1864.

V
Conclusion concerning Poole's party.

Poole's admissions alone prove culpable behavior. "Incautiously exposing people with contagious diseases to the public" was a crime under English law.[360] Beyond this, the overwhelming evidence is that his party distributed smallpox with murderous intent, and that it did so especially in places where his employers had both private and public motives to remove the resident population.

Leading settlers knew something of this at the time. Speaking of the Bentinck Arm enterprises, Major William Downie wrote,

(I)n the year 1862 small-pox was carried by the whites to Bella Coola.... The manner in which unscrupulous adventurers repeatedly broke faith with natives had done much harm and reflected even on those with honesty of purpose and good intent.[361]

Proof of systematic distribution on this scale, however, is most consistent with genocidal intent. Central to the activity of these "unscrupulous adventurers" was Governor Douglas' formal legal adviser and the first minister in the Vancouver Island Assembly, Attorney General George Cary. It is this official involvement that raises the probability that the events in Nuxalk and Tsilhqot'in territory were only one part of a much larger *de facto* social policy, one intentionally instituted and licensed by the Douglas Regime.

---

360. R. v. Burnett (1815) 4 Maule and Selwyn 75; 105 ER 762. R. v. Henson (1852) 1 Dears 24; 169 ER 621; cited in R. V. Rimmington [2005] UKHL 63. [2006] 1 AC 459.

361. Major William Downie, *Hunting for Gold.* (Palo Alto: American West Publishing Company, reprint 1971) pp. 267-8.

Staltmc Pootlass bears the Crown's First Request for Permission to Access Nuxalk Territory, July 3d, 1862 — Artwork by Shawn Swanky.

14

First Approach by the Colony

During the Poole epidemics, Lt. Henry Spencer Palmer of the Royal Engineers arrived at Bella Coola. He made the Colony's first official contact with the sovereign authorities of this still autonomous and separate territory. This visit became the first attempt by a British official to assert sovereign rights in Nuxalk territory.

In his final report, Palmer identified two representatives of the local authorities, Staltmcs Pootlass and Annokeetsum.[362] While he did not initiate contact as the "Honor of the Crown" required, and while Governor Douglas' instructions for such an eventuality were never disclosed, Lt. Palmer and Staltmc Pootlass eventually did meet as the official representatives of their respective social entities.

I
The Douglas Regime's Bentinck Arm policies.

What we already know: Colonel Moody dispatched Palmer here following George Cary's face-to-face meetings at New Westminster in early June. Cary still expected New Aberdeen to sell town lots and for the Bentinck Arm Co. to open a road. British Columbia officials were not keen on either project, but they could not be seen as unaccountably slowing the advance of non-indigenous settlement. In a transparent move to protect its interest, the Colony of Vancouver Island sent M.L.A. Colonel George Foster, head of its militia, to accompany Palmer. Public and private motives ran together again.

Moody ordered Palmer *to proceed...to North Bentinck Arm and after laying out a town site and Indian reserve, and mapping the location of buildings, to travel along...the proposed Bentinck Arm Road.*[363] At Victoria,

---

362. Henry Spencer Palmer, *Report of a Journey*, p. 5.

363. Moody's order to Palmer is republished at www.royalengineers.ca/Palmer.html.

Palmer received "verbal instructions" directly from Governor Douglas.[364] Since Palmer was otherwise an exemplary officer, the assumption must be that Douglas explicitly authorized any deviations from his written orders and that he coached Palmer on interacting with the local sovereign authorities.

In particular, Palmer did not "lay out" any "Indian reserve."[365] More revealing, he also did not make even a token attempt to implement Douglas' explicitly expressed policy for North Bentinck Arm as contained in a directive to Colonel Moody written just four months before. In March 1862, Douglas had instructed Moody,

> *[At] North Bentinck Arm, the land about the Indian villages, which is in no case open to pre-emption, should be marked upon official maps and distinctively reserved to the extent of 300 acres or more around each village.... The foregoing remarks [on buffer zones around places of higher density indigenous usage] being applicable to the whole Colony.*[366]

In theory, then, Douglas had instructed Colonel Moody as B.C. Commissioner of Lands and Works to create 300 acre buffer zones around places of indigenous occupation throughout the Colony. This seemingly was to secure these under Colonial laws, following an example to be set at North Bentinck Arm. It should go without saying that, since the Colony had not approached the Ancestors yet for any reason let alone for jurisdiction over land, Douglas had no constitutional authority for any such policy. None. This proposal was still another provocation of war in The Settlers' Insurrection.

The difference between Douglas' policy pretense as written in March and the Colony's actual performance at North Bentinck Arm illustrates well the contrast between the illusions of good faith Douglas spawned for the record and the Regime's true policies. The Ancestors had many villages, fishing weirs, gardens, hunting grounds and fruit harvesting locations the entire length of this valley. To have reserved all this so

---

364. In a letter referring to Douglas' verbal instructions, Palmer mentions only a budget and a need to cross on the Bentinck Arm Road to the Fraser. BCARS. GR–1371. British Columbia. Colonial Correspondence. B01351. F1302/9. Lt. Palmer to the Colonial Secretary, June 25, 1862.

365. Palmer Map, Bentinck Arm, British Columbia Surveyor General's Branch, Vault, Roads and Trails Drawer.

366. BCARS. G.R. 1372. F.327/25, Douglas to Colonel Moody, Chief Commissioner for Lands, March 4, 1862.

as to leave them in control with self-determination was completely incompatible with the advent of settler farms, villages and roads. Each location properly "reserved" under the policy of March 1862 would have been a roadblock to settlement.

So the written policy was inherently incompatible with the goals of colonization. Douglas could only ever have committed such a proposal to paper if he knew that it would not be implemented. It was for show only. His apparent oral instructions to Palmer reflect this.

Douglas' supposed good faith policy also already contemplated a dramatically reduced indigenous presence. His land policies allotted 160 acres to each settler, plus services, towns and roads. Meanwhile, the 2000 or so residents of Q'umk'uts were to be allotted 300 acres in total. The best land, the land chiefly required to supply livelihoods to these same villagers, was to be reallocated for settler usage. An equal allotment as that for settlers would have seen, say, upwards of (McKay's estimated 2000 warriors x 160 acres each) 300,000 acres reserved. There's the rub: equity left no fertile ground for settlers.

So Douglas' formal policies contemplated an insurrection and a massive reduction in the indigenous population equally as much as did Cary's plan for Q'umk'uts. Remember that, just as Douglas was creating these 300 acre reserves on paper in early March 1862, sitting across his desk as it were, Cary was planning Q'umk'uts' destruction. Precisely as Douglas wrote these instructions in March, two smallpox carriers were boarding a ship arranged by the steamship committee. If the presence of these carriers was known to Cary as part of his already conceived plan to sell vacant lots at New Aberdeen in early June, then it is just as certain that Douglas already knew he could anticipate the disease and its probable destruction as he wrote these fanciful instructions. Assuming anything else seems willful denial.

Then, Palmer's report concerning Bella Coola is filled with deception, minimization and denial.[367] While Venables had noted areas under cultivation in Sept. 1861, Palmer noted none. Where Q'umk'uts had its community garden, Palmer indicated only space suitable for a town. The simple truth was that the Nuxalk fully occupied all the land wanted by settlers. None was suited to European agriculture in 160-acre homesteads. Protecting the "Honor of the Crown," and considering

367. Henry Spencer Palmer, *Report of a Journey, especially in the Bella Coola Valley. But he also notes almost no Tsilhqot'in centers.*

Nuxalk interests as Palmer heard them from Pootlass, the only appropriate course was to close this area for non-indigenous settlement pending Nuxalk representations.[368]

Instead, with a typical cruelty and lack of respect for the dignity of indigenous citizens, Palmer proposed the final dispossession of Q'umk'uts. As he confirmed, its southern precinct occupied the only ground "suitable for a town site."[369] So Palmer proposed relocating survivors onto the north bank, *singularly dotted with low marshes and damp streaming ground...unadapted to white settlement, though the natives... probably value it highly, and retaining this, be content to abandon to the whites the drier land on the south side....*[370] In other words, he proposed forcibly removing survivors from their homes on the best ground and relocating them in a salt-water marsh.

This confirms Palmer's foreknowledge that, actually, survivors were to be dispossessed and not protected by 300 acre buffer zones. Palmer's activities and his report expose the truth that Douglas never contemplated action on his elaborate March instructions. The fraud seems even more apparent as Douglas himself was the last official to brief Palmer before he went to Bentinck Arm.

By speculating about what they "probably valued" Palmer implicitly confirms yet one more way that he did not discuss Douglas' policy with Pootlass. If he had, the Nuxalk certainly would have "reserved" their own homes, fishing sites, hunting grounds, agricultural land and trails or rights of way while perhaps providing marginal land for "settler reserves" under Nuxalk jurisdiction.

Palmer's proposed alternative also came to nothing. After Fraser Canyon opened in 1863 and the 1864 Chilcotin War, settler interest here languished. The H.B.C. assumed the New Aberdeen claim for a small trading post. The Nuxalk regrouped on Venables' abandoned claim and at Soonochlim, where they remain to this day.

---

368. In 1872, Canada reserved the entire Chilcotin River Valley to protect Tsilhqot'in interests, removing it from the operation of the Pre-emption policy. However, within months the B.C. Legislature broke the agreement made with the Tsilhqot'in.

369. Palmer, *Report of a Journey*, p. 5.

370. Palmer, *Report of a Journey*, p. 5.

II
An oral treaty confirming Nuxalk sovereignty?

Nevertheless, while at Bella Coola, Palmer may have made an oral treaty with Pootlass and the *de jure* authorities.

Arriving on July 2, 1862, Palmer set up camp on Cary's claim. He was just above high tide on the river's south bank, a few hundred meters below Q'umk'uts. His party included sappers Edwards and Breckenridge, a packer named George Wilson, along with M.L.A. Colonel George Foster. On arrival, Palmer tried hiring Nuxalk help to move his party's baggage from the harbor. But they refused him.[371]

The following day, Palmer cut a flat surface into a large tree and carved "Palmer Camp 8."[372] This memorialized the eighth day from his start in Victoria, and his final report would begin, *The voyage from Victoria....* All this underlines that, to Palmer as well as to Cary and Co., the coastal route to Canada began and ended in Victoria.

By 1862, to the Nuxalk, Palmer's carving likely resembled the blazes settlers made while claiming land. For that matter, as the first official Colonial representative here, Palmer's visit was the first step in a political claiming process. Just as the settler blazes had been harbingers of the coming Insurrection, Palmer's carving would be the first symbol of the coming paramilitary occupation and subjugation.

A Nuxalk contingent soon began paying attention to his camp. These observed Palmer confirm his location with a sextant. In a private letter to Colonel Moody, he wrote, *(T)hey think, when I am observing with the sextant, I am having "cloche nanitsh"* [a careful look] *at the "Sockally tribe"* [spirits of the air] *to find out whether the smallpox is going to be bad.*[373] It would have been understandable by now for the Nuxalk to connect the "claiming" activity involving blazes cut in trees with waves of disease. Under these apprehensions, the Nuxalk would have been justified in simply killing Palmer's party in self-defense. They only relieved him of some tin cups.

---

371. That's the implication of the quote below from "An Incident amongst the Indians at Bentinck Arm," *The British Columbian*, Sept. 1862.

372. A subsequent surveyor cut the blaze from the tree. It is preserved at the B.C. Museum. See BCARS. Visual Records Catalogue. D-08482, I-59581, and I-59583.

373. BCARS. GR-1372. British Columbia. Colonial Correspondence. B01351. F1302a Lt. Palmer to Colonel Moody, Bella Coola River, July 16, 1872.

In any case, Palmer ordered them to leave. Meanwhile, as the party's cook, Edwards had purchased salmon from a son of Pootlass. The young warrior gave Edwards notice about the law of the land as it concerned the connection between the Nuxalk, the salmon and the river. This was common practice. In 1793, Alexander Mackenzie repeatedly noted the Ancestors' respect for salmon and their customs in this connection. They had prevented him from cooking salmon in an iron pot after his fashion.[374] Poole also noted that the Nuxalk had specials rules about interactions with the river, catching and cooking salmon.[375] The notice given by the young warrior was the natural expression of a civic desire for guests to have information and for them to respond with a willingness to embrace the laws of the land.

Instead, a political crisis ensued. An eyewitness said,

> *[The Nuxalk] will not allow salmon to be cut with a* [steel] *knife, or cooked by any means of frying. They will not permit smoking on or near the water; nor will they allow washing in the river, or throwing anything fowl into it, believing that a breach of these rules would cause the salmon to leave them...famine and starvation would be the result.... The cook purchased a salmon...with the distinct condition that it was to be boiled. Disregarding this condition, he went about preparing the fish in the usual manner, whereupon an Indian stepped up and kicked over the pan in which it was being fried. The indignant cook dealt the redskin a blow, which brought him to the ground. The Indians flew to arms and, presenting their muskets at the lieutenant as the Tyhee* [leader] *threatened him with instant destruction.*[376]

With typical settler colonial disrespect for the law of the land, Palmer's party knowingly created a flagrant provocation. His party made an agreement and then deliberately breached it. It was as if they thought promises to indigenous Peoples did not create obligations. Moreover, apparently as a matter of routine, they intended to make it a point that the law of the land did not apply to them. Palmer then downplayed the

---

374. Alexander Mackenzie *Voyages from Montreal through North America to the Frozen and Pacific Oceans in 1789 and 1793*. Vol. II, Chapter 9, July 1793, p. 256.

375. Francis Poole, "Two Years Amongst the Indians of the Queen Charlotte's Island," *Mission Life*, Feb. 1, 1868, p. 103.

376. "We have just had an interesting conversation with an intelligent gentleman who went up via Bentinck Arm and travelled over a greater portion of it with Lt. Palmer's party." See "An Incident amongst the Indians at Bentinck Arm," *The British Columbian*, Sept. 1862.

subsequent assaults by his men. Instead, he blamed the chief's son as "impertinent" merely for doing his duty to the law.

> *I had a row...on sending them away from my camp. They refused to go. Meanwhile, Edwards had given an impertinent young savage a black eye and Breckenridge had stoned two or three more. I pushed one. He raised his knife. I got my revolver and aimed at him. Edwards ditto.... Half a dozen rushed for firearms. I put the revolver away. They came back with muskets cocked and were going to shoot me. Unarmed, I walked into the middle of them and told them my patience was very good but I could not stand being threatened with a knife. They wanted to know why I would send them away: did I suspect them of stealing?* [I.e. taking more than their due.] *I told them that I would not suspect them of such a thing...the beggars had stolen two small tin cups that morning...but that I feared the smallpox.*[377]

In other words, he claimed that he feared catching the disease from them. This was a lie. It was meant to play dishonorably on their natural empathy for fellow humans. Notice that he did not then do the obvious honorable thing: send for vaccine. A request for vaccine sent then would have saved hundreds of Nuxalk lives in November.

> *This knocked them down for their chiefs are always telling them to keep away from the whites* [confirming once again that the Nuxalk knew how the disease had arrived.] *Down went their muskets, "capit wa wa"* [talks between the heads of delegations] *was the word and peace was declared. All this amidst the most horrible howling and yelling I have ever heard.... An old fatigue jacket was given to the boy with the black eye and the young gentleman...offered Edwards and Breckenridge some of his relatives as sweethearts pro tem, favours which were declined.*[378]

As told in the local tradition, it seems the party of Nuxalk present at first surrounded the visiting delegation. Then,

> *The People from the main village* [a delegation from Q'umk'uts headed by an authority] *were summoned to come down and greet*

---

377. BCARS. GR-1372. British Columbia. Colonial Correspondence. B01351. F1302a Lt. Palmer to Colonel Moody, Bella Coola River, July 16, 1872.

378. BCARS. GR-1372. British Columbia. Colonial Correspondence. B01351. F1302a Lt. Palmer to Colonel Moody, Bella Coola River, July 16, 1872.

them [formally.] *Two canoes were put in the water behind them to prevent their escape. It was how we protected our community while we found out if the visitors wanted a war. We treated guests like relatives until our People determined their intentions.*[379]

In other words, the Nuxalk honored these strangers as family despite the smallpox horrors surrounding them and for which others among the non-indigenous community were responsible. Treating strangers as family or friends is a true sign of civility the world over.

The first eyewitness reported this resolution, *After this fracas, [Palmer's party] found no difficulty in getting the Indians to work at $2.50 a day* [i.e. probably one blanket,] *a thing they could not be persuaded to do previously.*[380] This confirms a change of behavior. At first, they had refused Palmer. Now they seemed to have a mutual understanding. If this included a public aspect, then they considered Palmer as having made a treaty.

For his part, Palmer wrote to Moody, *As for the row, I was glad when it was over as they would have murdered us all, had I not been able to pacify them. Discretion, in this case, was the word.*[381] Yet he does not supply any details about the promises or assurances that he gave to secure this pacification. His oral treaty went unreported.

Palmer uses "discretion" here to invoke Shakespeare's *Henry IV, The better part of valour is discretion....*[382] There a soldier deceived the enemy by pretending to be dead. Palmer played dead, too. He did this by not asserting openly to the Nuxalk that he, not Pootlass, now represented the sovereign authority here. In the same scenario on Jan. 2, 1865, a subsequent agent for the Crown would explicitly state the new reality.[383] Unlike the second agent, Palmer also did not assert that Nuxalk citizenship now contained a duty to obey the Crown as directed. His perceived need for "discretion" reflected the reality that no regime change had taken place on the ground as of his visit in July 1862. This territory still had not yet become part of B.C.

---

379. As conveyed orally to the author by Peter Snow following a public meeting at Bella Coola in September 2014, confirmed later by correspondence.

380. "An Incident amongst the Indians at Bentinck Arm," *The Columbian*, as above.

381. BCARS. GR-1372. British Columbia. Colonial Correspondence. B01351. F1302a Lt. Palmer to Colonel Moody, Bella Coola River, July 16, 1872.

382. *Henry IV, Part 1.* Act 5, Scene 4, 115-121.

383. See Chapter 17.

So, how did Palmer "pacify them?" Palmer's letter notes that what began as a confrontation evolved into a "heads of delegation" conference. Since Palmer refers to the "Nuxalk," Pootlass apparently began by inviting the Crown's support as his community recovered. Both Palmer's accounts about this meeting include Pootlass offering traditional marriage alliances. Finding some innovative way to have accepted this, say, by seating Pootlass and other Staltmc "like family" in discussions affecting their ancestral families, probably, would have given the Crown some color of legitimacy in Nuxalk territory.

Palmer eventually gave his future wife a larger account of this meeting. Her retelling included these elements,

> *Lieutenant Palmer shouted out in Chinook, asking the chiefs what they wanted.*
>
> *"We've come to kill you," was the head chief's answer.*
>
> *"Why?" demanded Palmer, "I don't mind being killed, but I would like to know the reason."*
>
> *"You cut the backbone of a salmon. That will make the Salmon God angry and he won't send any more fish."*
>
> *"What?" demanded the Lieutenant, "Have you only one God who controls the salmon?"*
>
> *The old chief nodded.*
>
> *"I have two," asserted the Lieutenant. "I have the Saghalie Tyee, up above. He knows everything. Then there is another, but it takes six months to go to her [Queen Victoria.] I am sorry if I offended by cutting the backbone of the salmon, but I'll go and make it right with the god whom I am telling you about. She will arrange it so that you will have twice as many salmon as before. I'll fix that for you."*
>
> *The Indians...retreated in good humour.*

Only nominally was this about fish. It was about different views of the world. On the indigenous view, if one treated nature with the respect due to sacred things, or with the humility appropriate where one does not know everything, one would receive her normal benefits in one's own turn. The British view, instead, was that nature could be commanded to produce, dependent only on the right policy and sufficient effort. Each system has its virtue. Reconciling them for the greatest ongoing social benefit has always been more art than science.

Generally, Palmer was promising that, in exchange for his safe passage and his community's continued access to Nuxalk territory, the Crown would stand in nature's stead as the guarantor of Nuxalk well-being. More particularly, in exchange for access, he promised that the Crown would: a) make reparations if its officials interfered with the law of the land under the precedent set here; b) respect the Nuxalk perspective on the human condition; and c) work with the local authorities to ensure Nuxalk prosperity.

This seems the oral treaty negotiated during the Crown's first approach to the Nuxalk as a People. These promises are what pacified them. This agreement also would have protected the Crown's honor.

> *Presently Edwards called out. "They are coming back sir, but this time they have their women and they are all decorated."*
>
> *The whole of the village appeared to be in the procession, led by the head chief, who had on ceremonial robes, and was accompanied by two young women.*
>
> *When he came up to Lieutenant Palmer, he delivered a long address in Chinook, the purport of which was that they wanted him to come and live with them and become one of their chiefs.*
>
> *The chief concluded his talk by presenting his two daughters to Lieutenant Palmer to become his wives.... [He]...exclaimed at her beauty and evident charms. Such a wife, he declared, was fitting of the highest rank. Then he...spoke most flatteringly of her sister also.*
>
> *The old chief was pleased. Then the Lieutenant went on to explain that he would have first to obtain the permission of his second goddess [Queen Victoria.] If she disapproved, it would mean that he would not have the [wealth and position] so necessary for a chief who was to acquire two beautiful wives.*
>
> *Then again, if he married without permission, it might mean that, in her anger, the goddess would not send any salmon at all. And his first duty was to see that the salmon runs were preserved.*[384]

---

384. "Mrs. Henry Spencer Palmer," *The Daily Colonist*, Nov. 9, 1930.

While confiding the details to his wife, who retold the story with an admittedly romantic flare but with what seem authentic elements of ceremony, Palmer mentioned nothing of the substance in writing to his superiors.[385] Just as he acknowledged his deception to Moody, the oral tradition also associates Palmer with dishonor.[386]

The Crown's first attempt to assert sovereign rights in Nuxalk territory had produced an armed stand-off. The Nuxalk still had more *de facto* power than Palmer's party of five. While self-admittedly only pretending to honorable intentions, Palmer declined Pootlass' genuine offer of some association. To secure his party's safe passage, however, Palmer seemingly made a counter-offer promising that the Crown would increase Nuxalk prosperity while leaving the citizens with control. This insincere proffer contradicted the colonial ideology that necessitated a Setters' Insurrection, except in its deception.

Truly, Palmer's second promise had no more weight or share of honor than his party's first promise concerning respect for a sense of sacred connection between the People, the fish and their river.

---

385. Palmer's wife could little have known the details of such ceremonial processions from her own experience as she was the fifteen-year old daughter of an English minster when Palmer married her the following year and they left the Colonies within 18 months.

386. As conveyed to the author via Clyde Tallio in the course of a public meeting at Bella Coola September 2014, concerning associations with the name "Spencer."

15

The Smallpox War,
October 1862

Poole's party was not the only source of artificial epidemics in Nuxalk territory during 1862. While analyzing the causes behind the Chilcotin War in 1864, Alfred Waddington confirmed non-indigenous knowledge that the June epidemics here were artificial creations.[387] He then went on to note a second wave.

I

A second wave of artificial epidemics in Nuxalk territory.

This new wave coincided with the October 1862 epidemics in Tsilhqot'in territory. There, John McLain would admit using infected blankets at Tatla Lake.[388] From Tatla, McLain went to Bella Coola. Nuxalk traditions include him as among those distributing infected blankets in the Bella Coola Valley.[389] McLain also was a disease carrier.[390] This is consistent with his having been inoculated for protection while spreading the disease. But it made him a lethal disease source for any Nuxalk near enough for an exchange of breath.

Referring to this second wave, Waddington wrote,

> *And did not...one Angus McLeod and another named Taylor go and collect...infested blankets in the bushes [at Bella Coola], which the Indians had deposited with the bodies of three men dead of smallpox and put them up carefully as new and sell them again to the Indians*

---

387. "The Bute Inlet Massacre and its Causes," *The British Colonist*, June 13, 1864.
388. Franklin memoir as reported in Maurine Goodenough, *Only in Nazko*, 2008, p. 19.
389. From a conversation with Arthur Pootlass at Bella Coola, Aug. 2 to 8, 2015.
390. *Canada's 'War,'* s. 63, pp. 176-77.

which brought on a second contagion, carrying off another third, and Angus McLeod, [one of the] perpetrators....[391]

Nuxalk traditions have it that the perpetrators made these blankets infectious by bringing them into contact with dead skin, rather than that they were grave-robbed blankets.[392] This account of infected blankets being manufactured is more consistent with evidence from other territories and it better explains the large number of blankets reported in October. It makes no difference to culpability.

Waddington's allegations provoked an immediate response from an anonymous newspaper correspondent. This correspondent claimed that some Heiltsuk expelled from Victoria had brought the disease to Bella Coola in June.[393] This was false. However, if this writer had the advantage of local knowledge as he implied, then he was not simply mistaken. He had a motive for deception. He continued,

> *There is a colour of truth [in Waddington's claim about the second epidemics being artificial] but he has mistaken the names, Angus McLeod and Wallace...the government's Collector of Customs...were the perpetrators of this most gross crime of appropriating the blankets of the dead Indians.... Mr. Taylor has been resident at Bella Coola for over two years and has always been respected by the Indians and is on the best terms with them....[394]*

As Cary's agent, Taylor had a unique motive both for deception concerning the June epidemics and for exonerating himself in setting a second wave. Was Taylor, himself, the anonymous author?

In any case, these two sources agreed that settlers intentionally created more epidemics in Nuxalk territory during the fall of 1862. They agreed that these were criminal acts and on the method used: diseased blankets. Neither specifies whether the accused worked in concert or if these were separate attacks. There is disagreement over the identification of only one party.

These accounts agree about Angus McLeod. Who was McLeod? Edward Green told *Bentinck Arm v. Hood* that he engaged two agents

---

391. "The Bute Inlet Massacre and its Causes," *The British Colonist,* June 13, 1864.
392. From a conversation with Arthur Pootlass at Bella Coola, Aug. 2 to 8, 2015.
393. "To the Editor," *The British Columbian,* June 22, 1864.
394. "To the Editor," *The British Columbian,* June 22, 1864.

at Bella Coola. The first settlers reported two men who threatened them while protecting prior claimants.[395] A newspaper correspondent reported, *At the upper village...are two white men, Mr. Taylor and Mr. McLeod holding claims I am told for some Victoria folk.*[396] So Angus McLeod arrived with Taylor as an agent for George Cary's enterprises. McLeod staked land in the Soonochlim precinct.[397] This gave him, in addition, a personal motive for creating vacant land.

During winter 1862/63, only three settlers were said to have died from smallpox in the Bella Coola Valley.[398] Two crossed Tsilhqot'in territory from Ft. Alexandria in the same cohort as John McLain and died waiting for passage home. Angus McLeod was the third.

Behind McLain were three Canadian tourists, James Wattie, William Wattie and Alexander Fortune. In the Upper Valley, these noted a man with smallpox at what they called "Barron's store." On the available evidence, this seems Angus McLeod. One called him a "siwash." If McLeod had H.B.C. origins, as seems likely, he probably had a native mother qualifying him for this term in Canadian eyes.

Referring to his journal, James Wattie later wrote,

> *[At] the ferry there was Alex McDonald from whom we received provisions. We were still 40 miles from Bentinck Arm. [At Bella Coola] met Taylor...we lodged with him for about three weeks.*[399]

Referring to his journal, William Wattie later wrote,

> *[At] the Indian camp we found one white man* [McDonald.]... *He warned us that his siwash was sick with smallpox in the house.... They informed us that it was about 50 miles [to the coast.]... At Bella Coola, we found three men trading whiskey with the Indians. One invited us to stay in his shack* [Taylor,] *which we gladly did.*[400]

Referring to his Journal, Alexander Fortune later wrote,

395. "Threatening Settlers," *The British Colonist*, Mar. 31, 1862, p. 3.

396. "A Trip to the Head of Bentinck Arm..." *The British Colonist*, Aug. 19, 1862, p.3.

397. Venables' map, BCARS CM/B91.

398. "Latest From Bentinck Arm," *The British Colonist*, Jan. 15, 1863, p. 5. See also the discussion in *Canada's 'War'* p. 180.

399. Kamloops Archives, Wade Family Fonds, Box 2, File 12, "Narrative of James Wattie," p. 6.

400. Kamloops Archives, Wade Family Fonds, Box 2, File 12, "Lecture Given at Worcester, Mass," p. 9.

Hungry, tired and very wet reached Mr. Barron's store. The man in charge was down with smallpox. A traveller [McDonald] *was engaged to nurse him and attend the store. Indians had been camped around the place and many [had] died of the plague. We found two canoes ready to run the 30 miles to salt water. We soon landed at Mr. Taylor's cabin near an Indian village. We waited here 21 days.*[401]

William Barron of Quesnel had encouraged these travellers to take the Bentinck Arm route. His seeming relation, M.D. Barron, had claimed land here adjoining others associated with William Hood above Adam Ross' ferry.[402] In a newspaper interview, Fortune said,

Fourteenth day [Oct. 19]*...we reached Newcliff. Mr. Hood has a trading post or storehouse at this point* [Barron's store, probably in the building reported by Venables as in partnership with Hood. Barron came with Hood in June.] *We here engaged Indians who brought us to the salmon dam near the mouth of the river.... The trail crosses the river ten miles below Newcliff. Mr. Adam Ross has built a house and keeps the ferry.*[403]

If McLeod was manning "Mr. Barron's store," then there was the same motive to make this land vacant as at other locations and by the same interests. If McLeod died distributing infected blankets here, this was done, at a minimum, to kill those "dead around the place" at Nautliff, renamed Newcliff, who had escaped the first epidemic.

What about Wallace? Wallace arrived here in connection with the service arranged by Cary's steamship committee.[404] He eventually became the government Customs Agent. Venables had staked the land where Wallace lived.[405] Wallace probably expected to receive title when New Aberdeen went ahead. He called it "my property."

401. Kamloops Archives, Wade Family Fonds, Box 2, File 12, "Alexander Fortune sketch," pp. 5-6.

402. Claim of M.D. Barron, 160 acres, junction of Bella Coola River and Newcliff Creek. BCARS. GR-1182, B.C. Dept. of Lands and Works, Cariboo, Lytton and Lillooet pre-emption records, Folder 2, Records taken by Peter O'Reilly, 1862-1864.

403. "The Bentinck Arm Route," *The British Colonist*, Jan. 3, 1963, p. 3.

404. Testimony of George Cary, *Bentinck Arm v. Hood*, Third Day, Feb. 15, *The British Colonist*, Feb. 17, 1864, p. 3.

405. Venables' map, BCARS CM/B91.

I intend to remain here and take the fortune which Heaven may send me; I cannot leave my property on which I have expended so much hard labor without seeing what will become of it.[406]

If Wallace distributed infested blankets in fall 1862, he would have had the private motives of securing land for himself and for the vacancy required for Cary's development, along with the usual public motive of settlers for overthrowing indigenous rule. The urgent need for this will be a theme of Wallace's statements reported in later chapters.

What about Jim Taylor? Taylor relocated here in mid-1861 as an agent for George Cary's enterprises. According to Venables' map, Taylor then made his own claim at a spectacular site overlooking the bay. From descriptions by Poole and others, though, it seems he lived near Q'umk'uts or Soonochlim, perhaps on McLeod's claim.

William Wattie described a macabre scene at Taylor's residence. Despite the devastation of June, "many" Nuxalk were again now sick and dying as these tourists paused here in late Oct./Nov. 1862.

We arrived at the main camp of the Bella Coola Indians about 6:00 p.m. [Oct. 19.]... This had been a large camp, but smallpox had reduced them about one-half that season and about 400 had died.... We found three men trading...whiskey. One [Taylor] invited us to stay in his shack.... (M)any of this tribe were sick with smallpox at [this] time. As soon as they take it, they are put out of the camp. They try to get where there is a white man and...die in the bushes near his house. They have the idea that if they can die near a white man it would be good for them. As a result there are a great many Indians in the bush around our camp [Taylor's house.] Large grey wolves would come...at night and carry them off...so any who died during the day would be gone by morning except some bones.[407]

Wattie had no personal knowledge of the pre-smallpox numbers. However, he implies that there were about 400 survivors in early November with the second epidemic still to run its course. Given the location of Taylor's cabin, this reference may be to the death toll at Soonochlim rather than Q'umk'uts.

406. "Bentinck Arm Tragedy," *The British Colonist*, July 15, 1864, p. 3.

407. Kamloops Archives. Wade Family Fonds. Box 2, File 12, William Wattie, "Lecture Given at Worcester Mass. in 1913," pp. 9-11.

"A great many" crawled to die near Taylor's doorstep. Wattie generalizes his explanation for this, one he was sure to have received from Taylor. Yet this behavior seems unique to Taylor's doorstep. The local tradition also recalls a place just here where people went to die if they could.[408] So all this might be better explained as evidence that Taylor played some role attracting it. Poole said Taylor had, *tremendous risk of life and [only] the distant hope of profit*.[409] Taylor was not at risk from nature. So the risk to which Poole refers can only have had to do with his human relationships. Within two years, Taylor had disappeared from the record to an unknown fate.[410]

These Canadian travellers lived with Taylor "about a month."[411] Within only a few days of their leaving, Francis Poole returned to Bella Coola.[412] Poole makes a point of his then having sought out Jim Taylor at this location.[413] He remains silent about the "great many" Nuxalk seeking to die on Taylor's doorstep. Afterwards, a smallpox carrier would accompany him to Haida Gwaii.[414] Left under Poole's supervision, this carrier began a new epidemic there to benefit his second employer. If Poole might have begun his involvement with smallpox as an "unwitting" participant, by October he seems witting.

Poole now describes Taylor as "an educated man." Taylor gave him a pup. Poole named it "Cato."[415] In context, this seems revealing. The Roman Consul Cato gave the most famous call to genocide in the history learned in a typical British education. At Cato's urging, Rome so destroyed the Carthaginians that they became lost even to memory.

Picture the scene at Taylor's cabin as these two visited. Nuxalk victims of an epidemic Taylor was said to have helped create were outside

---

408. As conveyed to the author following a public meeting at Bella Coola, Sept. 2014.

409. Poole, *Queen Charlotte Islands*, p. 181.

410. In his romanticized history of Bella Coola, written with access to local traditions, Cliff Kopas has it that the Tsilhqot'in executed Taylor in the context of the Chilcotin War. See Cliff Kopas, *Bella Coola*. (Surrey: Heritage House, 2002) pp. 134-35. The credibility of that account is undermined by its reference to McLeod as still alive at that time.

411. See Wattie's lecture notes, p.10. Above, Fortune specifies 21 days. They missed Poole by about a week.

412. Poole says the *Leonede* stayed only a short time, suggesting no more than, say, two days to unload its cargo destined for here, take on passengers or new cargo and return to sea. The captain reported leaving Bella Coola Nov. 18. See, "Bentinck Arm," *The British Colonist*, Dec. 15, 1862. Poole's memoir implies that it was Nov. 23.

413. Poole, *Queen Charlotte Islands*, pp. 180-181.

414. For detail on Poole's second smallpox journey, now to Haida Gwaii, see *Canada's 'War'* s. 102, pp. 331-338.

415. Poole, *Queen Charlotte Islands*, p. 182.

seeking to die on his doorstep. Thus, it seems a very unlikely coincidence that Cato came to Poole's mind by chance. It seems more creditable that Poole found Taylor supportive in recalling Cato's Carthage policy to justify another genocidal policy closer at hand.

II
The October epidemics, conclusion.

Four men are each said to have used smallpox blankets to create new artificial epidemics among the Nuxalk in October 1862. Two were accused by multiple sources. At least two were carriers who could multiply their contacts easily. Multiple sources among the non-indigenous community publicly acknowledged these as criminal acts.

Given the perpetrators' common connections with speculators or George Cary's enterprises, this second activity in October seems as little a convergence of random crimes as did the activity of Poole's party. And just as purposeful for all the same motives.

In the final analysis, the Douglas Regime failed to protect the "Honor of the Crown" by piercing the perpetrators' sense of immunity. This is apart even from the role played by Attorney General George Cary as the central figure here. All this is consistent evidence of the Regime's licensing or ratification of these killings as a "survival of the fittest" *de facto* social policy or an ethnic cleansing-like genocide.

The dying ended by spring. The final toll, though, would include those who suffered diminished lives under many headings. Most probably experienced some post-traumatic shock. Among the Nuxalk, this event was of an order equal to or greater than the Holocaust, the Holodomor or the atomic bombing in Japan.

16

Spring 1863 to June 1864

After the dying stopped in spring 1863, the Nuxalk authorities remained the only legitimate government in their territory. This was through *de facto* inertia. While administering the law of the land in this context, the indigenous regimes killed at least five settlers along the Bentinck Arm Road. Settlers reported three dead at Tsilhqot'in hands.[416] Two deaths were from Nuxalk actions.

On a community-to-community level, when the dying stopped, the Nuxalk began withdrawing consent for a settler presence. By 1864, an actual expulsion of settlers was under consideration. Then the colonial Governor visited Nuxalk territory in June 1864 and the *status quo* with respect to *de facto* sovereign control began shifting.

I
The James Fisher case.

In the very midst of the fall 1862 epidemics, Assalslick and his son, Irin, of Q'umk'uts killed James Fisher. Who was Fisher? At Ft. Alexandria on Aug. 31, 1862, Bentinck Arm Co. director Ranald McDonald had contractor William Hood hire Fisher, who had come to B.C. with the Boundary Commission locating the 49th parallel, to make surveys and maps along the road.[417] So, as a discharged soldier down on his luck, Fisher had relocated to Bella Coola as an associate of the George Cary enterprises.

---

416. One reported by Poole outside Chilcotin Lake and two by William Wattie, "Lecture Given at Worcester Mass. in 1913," p. 8. Without corroboration, it is difficult to confirm the accuracy of these reports. This does not include the three additional settlers killed by the Tsilhqot'in, also in a smallpox related action, on May 30, 1864.

417. Testimony of Ranald McDonald, *Bentinck Arm Co. v. Hood,* Fourth Day, Feb. 16, 1864, *The British Colonist,* Feb. 17, 1864, p. 3.

In the third week of November, Fisher left Bella Coola for a visit to Nautlieff.[418] He may have been surveying, mapping or joining Alex McDonald, then at Nautlieff nursing Angus McLeod. According to Pootlass, like McLeod, Assalslick also had smallpox.[419] It seems a plausible explanation that this family blamed Fisher for it. Since they had more convenient targets and considerable opportunity, this attack was not random. They targeted Fisher. It seems certain, therefore, that Fisher had committed some capital harm to prompt this attack.

The news of Fisher's death arrived at Bella Coola just in time for Francis Poole's departure in mid-November. Poole's memoir says,

> *[Fisher] had been barbarously murdered by the Chilcoaten Indians... he strayed from his camp...no sooner was he out of sight of his own men than some Indians, who had been tracking his party for several days, pounced on him, stabbed him to death with their knives and then stripped the body naked.*[420]

In his memoir, Poole said that he sent a notice of Fisher's death to the *British Colonist*. As conveyed to Poole, this story implicitly appealed for the Crown to defend settlers from "barbarous" natives. Since Poole and Fisher each were Cary and Co. associates, it would have been natural for this notice to pass through their superiors before delivery to the newspaper. As subsequently published in the *Colonist*, the story became: *It is supposed that [Fisher] drowned.*[421] This astonishing misdirection told of an unfortunate death from natural causes. Fisher's employers apparently saw a need to obscure what he may have been doing to provoke his death.

Settlers at Bella Coola knew Fisher had not drowned. They kept pressing Douglas for a response. Every account referred to Fisher as having been "murdered." None disclosed the prior events leading to his death. In March 1863, Alex McDonald supplied two different accounts of Fisher's death.[422] He included these details,

---

418. "From Bella Coola," *Daily Chronicle*, May 5, 1863.

419. See "From Bella Coola," *Daily Chronicle*, May 5, 1863.

420. Poole, *Queen Charlotte Islands*, p. 183.

421. "Bentinck Arm," *The British Colonist*, Dec. 15, 1862, p. 3.

422. Bute Inlet a Success," *Victoria Daily Chronicle*, Mar. 31, 1863, p.3. "Murder at Bella Coola," *British Colonist*, Mar. 31, 1863. p. 3.

[Fisher] was murdered by the Bella Coola Indians...neighboring tribes [i.e. the Tsilhqot'in denying responsibility] gave information to a party who found the poor fellow's body with his pistol lying a short distance...where he fell from the bullet of the assassin.... (B)y his death has been lost the surveys and maps of the country....

This demanded the Crown's attention. It implied that the Nuxalk were killing settlers without cause and to the detriment of settlement. On McDonald's account, Fisher was "assassinated." Assassinations resemble executions except the speaker does not believe a legitimate authority approved the killing. That was the crux of it: settlers denied indigenous *de jure* authority. Therefore, they demanded that even lawful indigenous violence be treated as lawlessness.

A Bella Coola settler eventually reported these details,

Fisher was killed by a boy...who shot him through the back, killing him instantly. As soon as he saw the man was dead, the boy fetched some relatives and they immediately made a large fire and burned the body, scattering the ashes afterward in every direction.[423]

Burning suggests a perceived need for this particular remedy. It is also the only sure way to neutralize a source of smallpox. Letting the wolves do the work would have been easier. Still later, another settler with Nuxalk sources confirmed,

James Fisher was murdered on the trail six miles from Bella Coola by an Indian named Assalslick and a boy of 14 named Irin.[424]

There is little chance that Assalslick and Irin took this action without their Staltmc's authorization or ratification. So what they did seems not a crime. Pootlass' initial refusal to surrender Irin for trial under the colonial system tends to confirm this conclusion.

Twenty settlers then petitioned Douglas, *to dispatch a gunboat armed with sufficient force and authority to intimidate and compel the natives to surrender the assassins.*[425] Notice that the "assassins" label appeared

---

423. "Latest from the North Coast," *British Colonist,* May 19, 1863, p.3.

424. *Daily Chronicle,* June 2, 1864, p.3.

425. "From Bella Coola," *Daily Chronicle,* May 5, 1863, p. 3.

again. They said, *Pootlass, the old chief, promised to discover and give up the murderer but has since informed us that he, the murderer, died from smallpox. Many here think otherwise.* In fact, Assalslick and his son were living just "one hundred yards" away under Pootlass' protection.[426] But, *the Indians are [still] too strong for the whites to interfere.*[427]

This last comment proves the *status quo*. This small settler outpost, by itself, was helpless against a host community with a moral conviction of its sovereign rights. This petition was an appeal for the Governor to invade a foreign territory and assert British authority so that settlers could live outside the law of the land.

II
The Bob McLeod case.

In early March 1863, War Chief Solyman killed Bob McLeod in what seems a clear case of execution. Solyman and his son visited McLeod where he was wintering along the trail overlooking Anahim Lake, a little less than two kilometers from Nagwentlun. They stayed for supper. Later, Solyman shot McLeod as he slept.[428] Bob's cousin Malcolm said Nagwentlun Nits'il?in Anaham, *told us the names of the murderers...who are well known to us.*[429] Indeed, they had a history of conflict over the customary tax for access to resources.

Consistent with someone who had acted lawfully, and unlike someone who might have committed a criminal or shameful act, Solyman made no secret of his action. He described it to acclaim and the event was well covered in the Victoria papers.[430]

The Governor still did nothing. Capt. McKay then reported,

> *The late murders have greatly exasperated the settlers, and they openly threaten that if Government does not speedily avenge the deaths of the victims that they will follow the example of the Texas rangers on Fraser River in 1858, and kill every Indian whom they meet. The*

426. "Letter from Bentinck Arm," *Daily Chronicle*, May 30, 1863, p.3.

427. "Letter from Bella Coola," *Daily Chronicle*, May 20, 1863, p. 3.

428. Latest from the North Coast," *The British Colonist*, May 19, 1863, p.3.

429. "From Bella Coola," *Daily Chronicle*, May 5, 1863, p. 3.

430. "Latest from the North Coast," *The British Colonist*, May 19, 1863, p.3.

whites say they are determined to travel the road, and if interfered with to retaliate terribly.[431]

This statement explicitly addressed the issue of a right to do business along the road: this was the precise issue that McLeod had with Solyman. It raised the prospect of violence if the Nuxalk authorities withheld any license for settlers to do as they pleased.

Little of this concerned justice for supposed "murders." Though, again, these seem lawful killings, not murders at all. The talk here is about overthrowing what settlers could feel as the true source of law. The implicit message that the Bella Coola settlers wanted to send was this: if these incidents were insufficient as pretexts, then they would provoke an assertion of sovereignty by escalating the means.

Notice, too, how dramatically their tone now contrasts with that of the pre-smallpox visitors just two years before. With indigenous numbers dramatically reduced and their *de facto* control weakened, settlers no longer needed to pretend good faith. This case ended when Solyman died in a dispute with another indigenous community.[432]

III
The George Wilson case.

George Wilson was among five miners who became lost 15 km down South Bentinck Arm while looking for Bella Coola in summer 1863.[433] Seeing a Nuxalk settlement, they approached it. Some Nuxalk came out to help bring their canoe ashore. Wilson's party panicked and pulled away. By this time the village headman had appeared. He called out in English that his community was friendly to British and American citizens. He invited them to "come ashore." Instead, Wilson's party began to run. Suspicions aroused, a Nuxalk canoe gave chase. The superior Nuxalk paddlers began overtaking the settlers. Wilson's canoe put ashore and prepared to repel an assault.

As the war canoe approached, the settlers called to the headman. He *waved a red handkerchief in one hand and what appeared to be a revolver*

---

431. "Later from Bentinck Arm," *Daily Chronicle,* May 19, 1863, p. 3.

432. "Bentinck Arm Route," *Daily Chronicle,* July 2, 1863, p. 3.

433. "Latest from Stekin," *The British Colonist,* July 23, 1863, p. 3. This seems the same George Wilson who accompanied Lt. Palmer here in 1862 as a packer. He may have misrepresented his knowledge of the area to the others, getting them lost in the first place.

in the other.[434] Calling for the intervention of good spirits using the medium of red cloth was common during the epidemics.[435] By custom, harming a messenger presenting red was shameful. The settlers opened fire anyway. Wilson gave one Nuxalk a flesh wound then ran to the woods. The Nuxalk withdrew to await reinforcements. Wilson's party used this opening to escape, leaving him for dead.

Two days later some passing Nuxalk rescued Wilson and made him "a prisoner."[436] However, instead of returning him for justice to the precinct from which the injured man had originated, they took him to Bella Coola as he asked. At Bella Coola, *He was freed on payment of ten dollars and his rifle.*[437] The Nuxalk then provided a guide and safe passage to Nautlieff. This seems a measured result.

This summer 1863 incident showed the local authorities still controlling access to their territory, greeting visitors cautiously with the fear of smallpox still in mind and dealing fairly with a settler who unlawfully wounded a community member.

IV
Withdrawing consent, discouraging settlers.

After the epidemics had run their course and as the Nuxalk began regrouping, they also began withdrawing consent for non-indigenous activity. While delivering the settlers' May 1863 request for military intervention "to intimidate" the indigenous authorities, Wallace said,

> *[There are now gathered in the Lower Valley] 2,000 [Nuxalk] or upwards. They are very insolent and unruly, and it is not uncommon for some to enter the settler's dwellings and endeavor to provoke the latter to resistance by spitting upon them and insulting them.... The cause assigned for this hostile feeling...is, that since the introduction of the smallpox, some 2,000 have perished, and they charge the white men with having introduced the disease.... The settlers only number 34 and they consequently feel insecure as long as the Indians are permitted to have their own sway....*[438]

---

434. "Latest from Stekin," *British Colonist*, July 23, 1863, p. 3.

435. For example, see *Canada's 'War,'* s. 103.

436. "Curious case" *Daily Chronicle*, July 29, 1863, p.3.

437. "Curious case," *Daily Chronicle*, July 29, 1863, p. 3.

438. "Intelligence from Bentinck Arm," *The British Colonist*, May 4, 1863, p. 3.

This confirms that Nuxalk survivors, based on direct observation, "charged" settlers with having introduced the disease to kill them. Wallace uses the word "charge" here in its ordinary sense: a formal allegation of culpable behavior. It is this first hand assessment that informs the oral tradition. Notice, also, that it was the intentional distribution of smallpox that led to the original breakdown in trust.

The death toll of 2000 as given by Wallace seems only of those who died in the Bella Coola precinct. Meanwhile, the 2000 survivors would have been some of those to whom Pootlass had reached out. If such a population was ever here post-smallpox, it did not remain. The Governor's 1864 expedition did not find anything like this.

Why, exactly, should Nuxalk citizens not be "permitted to have their own sway" within their own territory? This was an explicit expression of insurrectionist thinking.

Those settlers who "felt insecure" under indigenous rule understood perfectly well that their own intentions were treasonous rather than of good faith. As for Wallace, if he had participated in distributing smallpox blankets, he had a special reason to be concerned about native justice. Wallace would disappear from notice in the record after the Chilcotin War.

Once the Nuxalk had determined under their law that settlers had spread smallpox intentionally, it may have been legal to kill them all. That they instituted only this apparent rudeness or "unwelcoming" shows either great restraint or great fear.

Notice that the Nuxalk had begun this incipient expulsion policy already by spring 1863, a year before the Chilcotin War. It was Nov. 3, 1863 that they "pulled down" Venables' house, rolling back the settler occupancy when and where it seemed safe to do so.[439]

V

The 1864 expulsion of settlers to June 18.

In spring 1864 settlers threatened a new artificial epidemic in neighboring Tsilhqot'in territory. The Tsilhqot'in then asserted their *de facto* sovereign control. At the end of April, a Tsilhqot'in war party killed 14 settlers from a Bute Inlet road crew. On May 30, while executing two settlers believed responsible for smallpox at Puntzi, the Tsilhqot'in killed

439. "News From Bentinck Arm," *The British Colonist*, Nov. 20, 1863.

a Bella Coola settler, Clifford Higgins, and injured two others resident there, Malcolm McLeod and Barney Johnston. The Tsilhqot'in allowed those two and three others to escape. A war party followed behind as all settlers evacuated to Bella Coola.

In early June 1864, a Bella Coola settler wrote,

> *The Indians* [Nuxalk] *here have been very saucy ever since they heard of the Bute Inlet massacre and that so many white men fell at the hands of their redskin friends and so few of the latter hurt. The [Tsilhqot'in] are coming down here among the Bella Coolas to try and persuade them to follow their example with the white men on this route. Some Bella Coolas are willing and some not. We are in great danger of losing our lives at present. We number 16 souls all told.*[440]

That is, the Tsilhqot'in sought to enlist Nuxalk support in closing the Bentinck Arm Road as they had closed the Bute Inlet Road.

Notice that this settler outpost in Nuxalk territory had been squeezed from 34 in May 1863 to 16 by May 1864. It would now become further reduced to two. British Columbia's boundaries still cannot have included Nuxalk or Tsilhqot'in territory as of this time. On the other hand, Nuxalk citizens seem divided now about their *de facto* ability to assert control in the face of so few as 16 settlers.

The Colony then mobilized several militias to invade Tsilhqot'in territory. It deployed one through Nuxalk territory. When this militia arrived at Bella Coola, it found settler establishments deserted, except Wallace's and one other. Two settlers joined the militia. Most left for Victoria. In essence, the settler community had been expelled from both Nuxalk and Tsilhqot'in territories as of June 18, 1864.

---

440. "The State of Affairs at Bentinck Arm," *The British Colonist*, June 27, 1864, p. 3.

17

Second Approach by the Colony

It is in the usual nature of a legitimate sovereign power for *de jure* authority and *de facto* control to be unified. Once deprived of its *de facto* abilities, an authority's legitimacy also comes into question. Taking advantage of this effect, successful insurrections will find pretexts to demonstrate the prior regime's powerlessness. After reducing the indigenous political presence by spreading smallpox, the insurrectionists still needed to displace the original authorities out on the ground.

I
Dishonorable intimidation of the weaker power: defense.

A colonial gunboat visited Nuxalk territory as a first menace in November 1863. Its officers seemingly made no formal approaches to the Nuxalk and left little impression, not even with settlers.[441]

The second official approach here began when the Governor of B.C. came with a foreign militia bound for Tsilhqot'in territory June 18, 1864. This event closed Sept 30 with the militia's departure. The last settlers but two went with it. This left the Nuxalk with their first respite since March 1862. In the meantime, everything had changed.

The Governor and the Colonial Chief of Police, Chartres Brew, arrived in Nuxalk territory on the British warship *Sutlej*. One militia volunteer kept a detailed diary. Boarding the *Sutlej*, he wrote,

> *June 14: H.M.S. Sutlej carries the flag of Admiral Kingcome, who is in charge of the Pacific Squadron. The Sutlej is said to be the largest ship and the finest Frigate on the Pacific.... The Sutlej carried 500 men beside officers. Her complement was 800.*[442]

---

441. "News From Bentinck Arm," *The British Colonist*, Nov. 20, 1863, p. 3.

442. BCARS. Add MSS. 2796. John Brough, Ed. Sheila MacIntosh, "Diaries of John Brough in British Columbia." Quotes preceded by a date are from Brough's *Diary*.

The *Sutlej* also had 50 cannon. The Admiral fired them in the Bella Coola harbor. It was an intimidating display of readiness for the use of organized violence. An officer reported, *The appearance of the Sutlej excited considerable awe among the natives, and her shell practice astounded them beyond measure.*[443] The *Sutlej* anchored at Bella Coola carrying out its usual drills for 20 days. Its 500 men-at-arms outnumbered the whole surviving resident population.

> *June 18: Arrived at the head of Bentinck Arm.... A large river called Nookhalt or Bella Coola flows into the Arm.... Lots of the Bella Coola Indians came off in canoes to see the big ship. Old Pootlass, the Chief, and his family were taken on board and seemed quite bewildered at the size...and number of men. The Governor made him and his followers presents of blankets and other things. The Admiral gave him a suit of clothes, which he put on and cut quite a figure.*

Taking advantage, the Governor attempted to appropriate some color of Nuxalk authority for his campaign against the Tsilhqot'in by securing a contingent of Nuxalk warriors. This exercise did not have any real military purpose. The Crown had 500 professional soldiers in reserve, should the militia have fared badly. The only purpose for a Nuxalk detachment was to foster bad feelings between adjoining peoples and, thereby, to hinder possible future joint actions.

The Governor reported the interaction this way,

> *Feeling that the presence of a powerful ship like the Sutlej would overawe the Coast Indians, Mr. Brew, with my concurrence, took thirty, under a young [War Chief,] into his pay. With 38 volunteers from New Westminster, our Indian band [of 30 Nuxalk] and 19 packhorses, we started [for Tsilhqot'in Territory.]*[444]

The colonists so desired this indigenous validation that, when *H.M.S. Sutlej* returned to Victoria, its officers publicly claimed,

> *Some of the Bella Coola Indians refused to accompany the expedition unless they were allowed a carte blanche to shoot any Chilcotin they*

443. "Return of H.M.S, Sutlej," *The British Colonist*, July 13, 1864, p. 3.

444. Great Britain Public Records Office, Colonial Office Records, CO 60/19 p. 149, 10601, Frederick Seymour, letter to Cardwell, vo. 37, Sept. 9, para. 13.

came across. One man is already believed to have killed two or three on his own account.[445]

However, this supposed disposition of these new allies came as something of a "too good to be true" surprise to the resident settlers.

Those well acquainted with [these] Indians express much surprise at the course adopted by Governor Seymour in arming and taking with the expedition 30 or 40 Bella Coola Indians. Setting aside the well known treachery of these savages, it is a notorious fact that this tribe is closely connected by blood and marriage with the very rascals whom the volunteers are in search of...some of them at least were prepared to join the Chilcoatens in cutting off every white man on the coast routes...it is not at all unlikely that that the Bella Coolas may lead the expedition into an ambush...or with their habitual treachery, they may, in the first skirmish, turn suddenly around and attack the very party they have been engaged to assist.[446]

In reality, Colonial officials had merely extorted an unwilling participation by intimidating a community fearing extermination. The truth of this assessment can be confirmed through observing the Bella Coola contingent's contribution to the Chilcotin War.

Diarist John Brough logged the expedition's advance as follows:

June 19: On getting all to land, we walked across a muddy flat three miles to Koomkrotz.... The fronts of the buildings are painted with strange hieroglyphics; the red hand of spirits and powers being predominant. Most of the white men...have left. All the stores closed but one, Ellice and Robertson.... At 10:00 a.m. Mr. Brew gave orders for us to march to Soonachlim, three miles up the Bella Coola River. At Soonachlim there is a large fishing dam across the river.... A life size figure of the Chief cut out of a tree is set up on a pole; he has his bow and arrow in hand as a warning to intruders to keep off.

Can any person passing these structures ever have been unaware of the political authority behind them? Again, given that Colonial officials had no plans for treaties, this underscores the motive for killing sufficient numbers as the only real certainty of displacing it.

---

445. "Return of H.M.S. Sutlej," *The British Colonist*, July 13, 1864, p. 3.
446. "The Bella Coola Auxiliaries," *The British Colonist*, June 27, 1864, p. 3.

June 20: Camped at 5:30 p.m. on the bank of the river above Nookeetz, [a Nuxalk village,] *where almost all died of smallpox.*

June 21: Around Assananny [a Nuxalk village] *good feed for horses. The Assananny Indians all died save one from smallpox.*

June 22: Arrived opposite Noothulott [a Nuxalk village] *Rancheria at noon. Here the trail crosses the Bella Coola River.... There is a small Indian Rancheria belonging to the Ansinis* [the people of Solyman from] *Dean Channel but who come here...to fish and trade. Mr. Hamilton had to fly with his wife and daughter as the Chilcotin were expected to loot and plunder all before them.*

In fact, the Tsilhqot'in war party had revealed its presence and then waited patiently for the settlers to evacuate. Despite widespread non-indigenous' fears, the Tsilhqot'in accomplished their policy with almost the least harm possible.

June 23: An Indian from the Upper Country [Dakelh] *met us and stated that the Chilcotin had gathered in great numbers and had plenty of powder and ball, and he advised us to return and get more men.... Passed a deserted Indian Rancheria* [probably Nautliff] *with large wall posts still standing on which were carved life-size figures.*

June 24: Arrived Shrooiht [Stuie, a Nuxalk village] *at 3 p.m. It is considered the head of navigation.... There are large fishing dams in this quarter to which* [Dakelh and Tsilhqot'in] *come. Mr. Brew [has] engaged 16 Bella Coola Indians to accompany us in case their services might be required in packing or otherwise.*

In six days, the Nuxalk contingent had declined from 30 to 16.

June 25: Arrived Tapontwoot [a Nuxalk village.]

June 27: As we lay on the bank a party of Indians came along. They were upon us before they noticed and fled into the woods. Our Indians went after them and explained matters. When they returned they said they were Ansinis and were going down to fish.... Started again and arrived at Cokelin [a Nuxalk village,] *foot of Big Slide six miles. The Chilcotin Territory commences at the top of the Slide.*

Notice this long list of Nuxalk villages. Remember that Poole's party passed through each one with smallpox carriers in its midst.

The Governor reached the Chilcotin plateau on June 30. By then, 20 of the 30 Bella Coola warriors had "deserted."[447] That is, their number had declined again from 16 to 10. Three more left July 19.[448] The remaining seven did nothing to merit notice.

In September, the Governor reported to the Colonial Office that the Police Chief, *has nearly completed that which he believed to be impossible* [demonstrating Tsilhqot'in powerlessness,] *and which-to give all their due-would have been impossible without the assistance of the Bella Coola Chief in tracking the Chilcotin.*[449]

Like much else in the Governor's reports, all this was untrue. The Colony had not taken the Tsilhqot'in War Leader's party through the Police Chief's agency in any sense. It took them only through new threats of genocide, deceit and a dishonorable ambush.

When the Governor wrote this note in early September 1864, the militia still had made no contact with Nits'il?in Anaham. Did the Bella Coola warriors, then, perhaps help in tracking him?

August 6, a warrior identified as "Bella Coola Tom," was sent to locate Anaham.[450] He returned a few days later after receiving death threats from the Nimpo Lake Tsilhqot'in whose homes the militia had burned.[451] A more diligent messenger might have by-passed them. By his failure, Anaham did not receive timely notice to attend the Aug. 15 peace conference, there to be ambushed and hanged.

On Sept. 9, after receiving notice of the Tsilhqot'in War Leader's capture, Brew sent the Bella Coola contingent for canoes to return the expedition downstream.[452] These would have come across Anaham camped at Stuie. If he did not already know, they would have advised him of Brew's progress and plans.[453] Anaham then moved his camp so

---

447. Seymour to Cardwell, No. 37, Letter of Sept. 9, para. 14.

448. John Brough, *Diary*, July 19.

449. Seymour to Cardwell, No. 37, Letter of Sept. 9, para. 38.

450. John Brough, *Diary*, August 6.

451. BCARS. Colonial Correspondence. GR-1372, B1310, Chartres Brew to the Governor of British Columbia, August 18, 1864.

452. John Brough, *Diary*, Sept. 9.

453. Morris Moss, "Mr. Waddington's Charges," *The British Colonist*, Oct. 29, 1864.

that the expedition would run into him.[454] So, in all cases, it was the Tsilhqot'in that tracked down the Colonial forces.

The Nuxalk contingent lent the Colonial invasion no discernable assistance. They showed the best possible grace in the face of this humiliating exercise calculated to divide these neighbors.

John Brough described the expedition's return to Bella Coola.

Sept. 16: On emerging from the woods at Nagwentlun saw smoke a little way ahead. Marching rapidly towards it, we found two Indians, three squaws and two boys. The elder Indian rose. He held out a paper written by Mr. Moss to say the bearer was Anaham....

Sept. 18: (W)ent around to Nancootlem lodge [Anaham's home.]... *It is an old building with a loop-holed palisade...deserted now on account of the smallpox.... A number of graves around, some in enclosures and others in boxes above ground, some were burnt and the bones put in small boxes fixed to high poles....*

Sept. 22: Bella Coola Tom and three more of his tribe arrived from Bentinck Arm with a note from Mr. Moss announcing that the gunboat was there lying awaiting us and that canoes would be at Stuie to carry us down which he hoped would be soon as there are scarcely any provisions on board and none at Bentinck Arm....

Sept. 25: Passed the Precipice to the bottom of the Big Slide. Met a whole drove of Anaham's tribe, men and women laden with fish...most of the young men fled...probably afraid that they might be taken, and like enough some deserved hanging. The old men...gazed at us in silence and like enough cursing in their hearts....

Sept. 26 (B)elow Stuie.... There were 3 canoes and 16 [Bella Coola] Indians waiting for us.

Sept. 28: Arrived at Bella Coola at 11:00 a.m. found Mr. Moss and the men with him all well. We went to see an Indian dance at the village. [Likely, they had been invited as a ceremonial send off.] *We got salmon from them but they would not sell one without cutting off a piece as it would displease the Salmon God to sell one whole.*

---

454. John Brough, *Diary*, Sept. 16.

Sept. 30: All up at daybreak.... We got underway at 7:00 a.m. Mr. Moss, Major Robertson and two others are going down with us as they are all going to leave Bentinck Arm....

A Bella Coola Indian is on board [in police custody] to be tried for murdering a white man eighteen months ago.

Pootlass must have turned and sent his delegation to honor the "Chilcotin Chiefs" in late October at Quesnel almost as soon as his community watched the gunboat's departure.

The Chilcotin War revisited Nuxalk Territory during May 1865. Morris Moss returned here that spring. In due course, he became the second colonial "Indian agent" in Nuxalk territory. While travelling downriver from Stuie with the Tsilhqot'in leader Ahan, who was bearing a peace offering in good faith under a customary protocol for reconciliation and with a promise of immunity, Moss ambushed Ahan near Nautliff. The Colony put him and another of his party through show trials at New Westminster. It hanged Ahan in July 1865.

II
Dishonorable humiliation: the administration of justice.

The "Bella Coola Indian" taken into custody was Assalslick's son Irin over the death of James Fisher. Yet, at the time and place of Fisher's death, the Crown had no jurisdiction over the administration of justice. Moreover, the *de jure* authorities already had refused to surrender him. Either this case was *res judicata* (finally disposed) or the *de jure* authorities had refused to extradite him on the ground that he could not receive fair treatment in the Colonial system.

In any case, having displayed its readiness for violence to control territory, the Colony would now interfere with the administration of justice. If he had been alive still, the Colony also would have arrested Solyman for McLeod's death in Tsilhqot'in territory. Yet arrests in either territory were the same form of sovereign injustice as that for which B.C. has now apologized regarding the "Chilcotin Chiefs."

Elsewhere when indigenous officials refused to surrender their citizens, the Douglas Regime would send a military force to seize and hang them in public. Pootlass now surrendered his without further incident. The Police Chief interviewed Irin. Irin surely explained why he had killed Fisher. The Policeman then broadcast that Irin "was crazy."[455] If this had been true, settlers would have said it before now. With the trial of a crazy person not in the public interest, but also one where Irin's description of Fisher's activity might have made the newspapers, the Police Chief released him. So the seeming cover up of this Bentinck Arm Co. agent's activity continued.

As it punished the Tsilhqot'in for the example of their resistance, the Crown rewarded the Nuxalk for their co-operation.[456] Still, this case set a precedent for jurisdiction in the administration of justice. Settler behavior now was off-limits. Rather than justice, the more powerful community's perception of its interests would become the standard against which every concern would have to be measured. A Staltmc's new duties included managing the Nuxalk relationship vis-a-vis the occupiers for survival. They would need to master "fighting like a woman." That is, to use the art of securing the benefits of *de facto* power through persuading, or even honorably deceiving, a more powerful entity to see its interests as coinciding with theirs.

III

First "Indian Agent" asserts de facto sovereign control.

Jan. 2, 1865, a Colonial "Indian Agent" arranged to meet the area Staltmc with a third official approach.[457] The paramilitary occupation of Nuxalk territory might be considered as having begun here. This agent asserted openly to "the assembled chiefs" that it was the Crown who had the sovereign right to a monopoly on the official use of violence in their

---

455. "Mr. Waddington on the Chilcoaten Murderers," *The British Colonist*, Oct. 28, 1864, p. 2.

456. See Police Chief Brew's glowing reference to Nuxalk cooperation in Note C, "Remarks on Mr. Waddington's Petition," Great Britain Public Record Office, Colonial Records, 1865, CO 60/22 p. 192.

457. This Indian Agent, J.D.B. Ogilvy, was killed near North Bentinck Arm five months later, May 11, 1865. At the time, Ogilvy was attempting to enforce Colonial customs laws against a smallpox survivor trading between Heiltsuk and Nuxalk territory. Yet anyone who considered his primary political obligation as to an indigenous political entity would have felt little obligation to obey Colonial laws. The best account of his death is "Murder of Mr. Ogilvy," *The British Colonist*, May 24, 1865. The background politics are unclear. The shooter fled to Tsilhqot'in territory. That fall, accompanied by some Nuxalk, he was southbound outside Ft. Rupert when his companions killed him rather than delivering him to colonial officials where he would have told his story as they collected a substantial reward. See, "Death of Antoine Loucanage," *The British Colonist*, Oct. 17, 1865, p. 3. The Nuxalk were said to have killed him because he would not pay for their labor on his boat. But the reward for his capture would have exceeded his obligation by several orders of magnitude, so that story rings false. Moreover, they left the body and his boat in a smuggler's cove where they were sure to be found. This leaves open the interpretation that the Nuxalk preferred to see him dead rather than to see him tell the whole story behind Ogilvy's killing. Perhaps some indigenous authority had encouraged him in this. And was at risk of discovery.

territory.[458] And they did not have the ability to expel him as someone hostile to their legitimate authority or to the rule of the citizen majority. The involuntary accretion of Nuxalk territory to the Colony of British Columbia might be dated from here.

The Nuxalk now were to be governed within their own territory by agents accountable only to a foreign power. The new constitution imposed by this unilateral declaration arrogated all sovereign power to a foreign government. It had little *de jure* root to support any willing sense of political obligation. It lacked all foundation in an extension of the *Smayusta* or in consent from the governed. Its imposition relied on: 1) fear in a citizenry terrorized by a weapon of mass destruction; 2) the threat of British violence; 3) the false hope raised by insincere promises of care; and 4) the recognition of their own smallpox-degraded *de facto* capabilities. Every exercise of legitimate indigenous power involving coercion now would violate Colonial law and incur the risk of punishment as common criminals.

In future, the Staltmc would have no reliable influence on law or policy in their own territory, except as supplicants through the Indian Agent. Published with a flourish in an extraordinary issue of the *Government Gazette*, the Indian Agent's report included these notes,

> *Pootlass [returning from a Heiltsuk feast] arrived.... I went up to his camp* [that is, the Staltmc's longhouse, a large cedar building surrounded by others and not a collection of moveable or temporary structures for nomads as "camp" might be taken[459]] *where I found all the chiefs assembled, Anaham among the number. Many complaints were made of the manner in which they had been treated by some of the whites who resided here. Not only have debts been incurred to a considerable amount of labor, but blankets have been borrowed...and payments made in notes not worth the paper.... All these men have now left* [Nuxalk territory. Likely, though, these pioneer settlers were still elsewhere within the Colony. Officials issued no warrants.]

> *The Indians also complained of the property left at the graves of the dead having been taken away by the whites, I explained to them that all this would be put a stop to; and that Your Excellency took the same interest in their happiness and welfare as that of the whites; impressing upon*

458. J.D.B. Ogilvy, "News From Bentinck Arm," *The Government Gazette Extraordinary*, Feb. 27, 1865.
459. William Wattie, "Lecture," p. 10.

them at the same time that the Government would severely punish any white man who injured them, while they would be equally strictly dealt with should they molest any of the whites....

I also warned them that they must not take the law into their own hands but represent their grievances to the proper authorities and that Your Excellency would see them addressed.

I found some laboring under the impression that the whites were going to cause the smallpox to come among them again in the spring...some of the whites [from] Victoria threatened them with it.[460]

Before this, no one would have thought to question that it was the assembled Staltmc who were "the proper authorities" here. Notice the reference to "causing" smallpox "again." That is, like before. This was yet another admission of guilt that went unprosecuted by the Crown, proving again that settlers had a social license for it.

The Staltmc dutifully "represented" their grievances: widespread abuses of labor, fraud or abuse of credit, grave robbing and the terror of renewed artificial epidemics. To little avail. Enduring injustice at non-indigenous hands, being treated as ghosts on their own land and seeing officials disrespect the "Honor of the Crown" to take advantage of their political weakness became features of the occupation.

---

460. J.D.B. Ogilvy, "News From Bentinck Arm," *The Government Gazette Extraordinary*, Feb. 27, 1865.

18

Conclusion

The Smallpox War transformed Nuxalk territory. The knowing introduction of smallpox by Poole's party in June 1862 marked the outbreak of violence as settlers began the process of colonizing this territory. Within just nine months, most of the Ancestors were dead. It was this action that effectively removed any real concern that some future Nuxalk counter-insurgency might threaten the non-indigenous community's freedom to exploit the resources of this territory.

The process through which the Crown asserted control over the Nuxalk and their territory was dishonorable. This process included an intentional mass killing of innocents, the crime of genocide. This left the Staltmc with moral authority despite their new *de facto* weakness and despite their dishonorable and impolitic lack of recognition under the new constitution. Meanwhile, the Crown's agents, who would come in many guises, had *de facto* power but little of the moral authority required for the legitimate exercise of power. Little changed after the Crown's initial assertion of control and Canada inherited this dishonorable legacy at Confederation in 1871.

Continuing the original colonial attitude of disrespect for indigenous institutions, settler apologists today typically still deny the Nuxalk perspective on this political transition. Yet, when read with attention to detail, even the documentary record shows beyond a reasonable doubt that agents for Attorney General George Cary intentionally created multiple artificial epidemics in Nuxalk territory during June and October 1862.

The facts admitted by Francis Poole alone for the period when he was in the employ of Cary's enterprises show that his party knowingly distributed the disease repeatedly and systematically along Cary's coastal route. The true nature of this as intentional activity is especially revealing at Q'umk'uts in early June. That is, just when Cary's plan called for the delivery of vacant lots and just as he formally asserted that there was no "Indian settlement" on his claim.

For that matter, the written record also supports a conclusion that Cary's steamship committee imported the disease to Victoria in the first place to begin the whole series of epidemics that then swept the Pacific shelf. This action coincided with the final policy choice of the Colonial authorities not to purchase "Indian title" and where, in place of funds for purchases, the Imperial government supplied arms in apparent anticipation of "Indian wars." So these first carriers began the chain of infection leading to Bella Coola exactly coincident with a recognized need for anticipating "Indian wars" as settlers arrived to take land occupied by indigenous residents: as at Q'umk'uts.

Apart from the way that settlers created artificial epidemics in Nuxalk territory with impunity, many circumstances point to this as just one part of a larger colonial policy. Foremost among these is the fact that it was the Douglas Regime's highest officer of the law and the leading minister of the Vancouver Island Assembly, Attorney General George Cary, who employed those distributing smallpox in Nuxalk territory. While it is true that the Governor controlled the usual day-to-day administration of policy, given the Regime's other smallpox-related actions, it would be naïve or bad faith to view the actions of Cary's agents here in isolation. As detailed at length in *The True Story of Canada's 'War' of Extermination on the Pacific*, through its actions at Victoria and elsewhere, the Douglas Regime itself was the most egregious violator of the ordinary legal norms and practices concerning contagious diseases.

Then, when perpetrators admitted, or if others reported acts ordinarily held as culpable behavior in spreading contagious diseases, the Colonial authorities took no action against the killers. In Poole's case, after broadcasting in newspaper interviews that he had sent disease carriers into healthy communities in an obvious breach of English law, his employers introduced him to the Governor and he imagined himself as having gained status in the colonies. Failing to prosecute the acknowledged perpetrators of mass killings targeting identifiable groups seems a reliable sign of a social license for it.

All this shattered the sense of trust and common purpose with which, at first, the Ancestors had invited a non-indigenous presence. The historical fact of this genocide has affected relations with the non-indigenous community since. On one side, this has become part of the

Smayusta concerning recent Nualk origins. Yet, to Canadian officials or educators raised in colonial mythologies and who have not yet transcended their origins by meeting the "duty to learn," it is either an unknown fact or one consistently denied and dismissed.

In the result, having failed to protect the "Honor of the Crown" in Nuxalk territory by formally negotiating an appropriate constitutional recognition for the *Smayusta*, officials of the Crown still today follow the colonial tradition that saw the "Chilcotin Chiefs" martyred in 1864/65. Canada quickly criminalizes any Staltmc moved to *de facto* actions that might be seen as rooted in the *Smayusta* and that might challenge public policies developed without Nuxalk consent.

In 1999, for example, Canada sentenced Staltmc *Qwatsinas* to 45 days in prison as leader of one such action.[461] Five other Nuxalk received sentences of 21 days and two years' probation. Each was forced to sign an undertaking to "keep the peace" under Canada's paramilitary occupation. Yet these Nuxalk had done nothing more than institute a non-violent action that they believed, in good faith, was designed to protect the peace. An action under what they believe remains the *de jure* or legitimate law of the land, a constitutional institution displaced through the genocide described here.

Can one regime lose its constitutional legitimacy to another, the Crown, whose claim to rule is rooted in a genocide carried out by its own agents? Who holds the high moral ground? It seems contrary to justice and equity to let circumstances such as these stand. Without healing, without the Crown finding a path back to the high moral ground, the wound festers and new harms continuously arise.

To advance reconciliation here, Canadians should honor the Nuxalk perspective with grace and honor. Then advance the work, out on the ground, of creating a new regime: one with a renewal story that can celebrate overcoming this original harmful transition, now to the benefit of both communities.

---

461. Nuxalk.net/htm/ista_court.htm. The sentences, for the "crime" of contempt of court for refusing to honor a Canadian injunction, were suspended by the judge from a clear sense of an injustice that it was not otherwise within his jurisdiction to remedy.

MAPS AND ILLUSTRATIONS
by Shawn Swanky

Nuxalk and Surrounding First Nations

Note: First Nation boundaries are approximate.

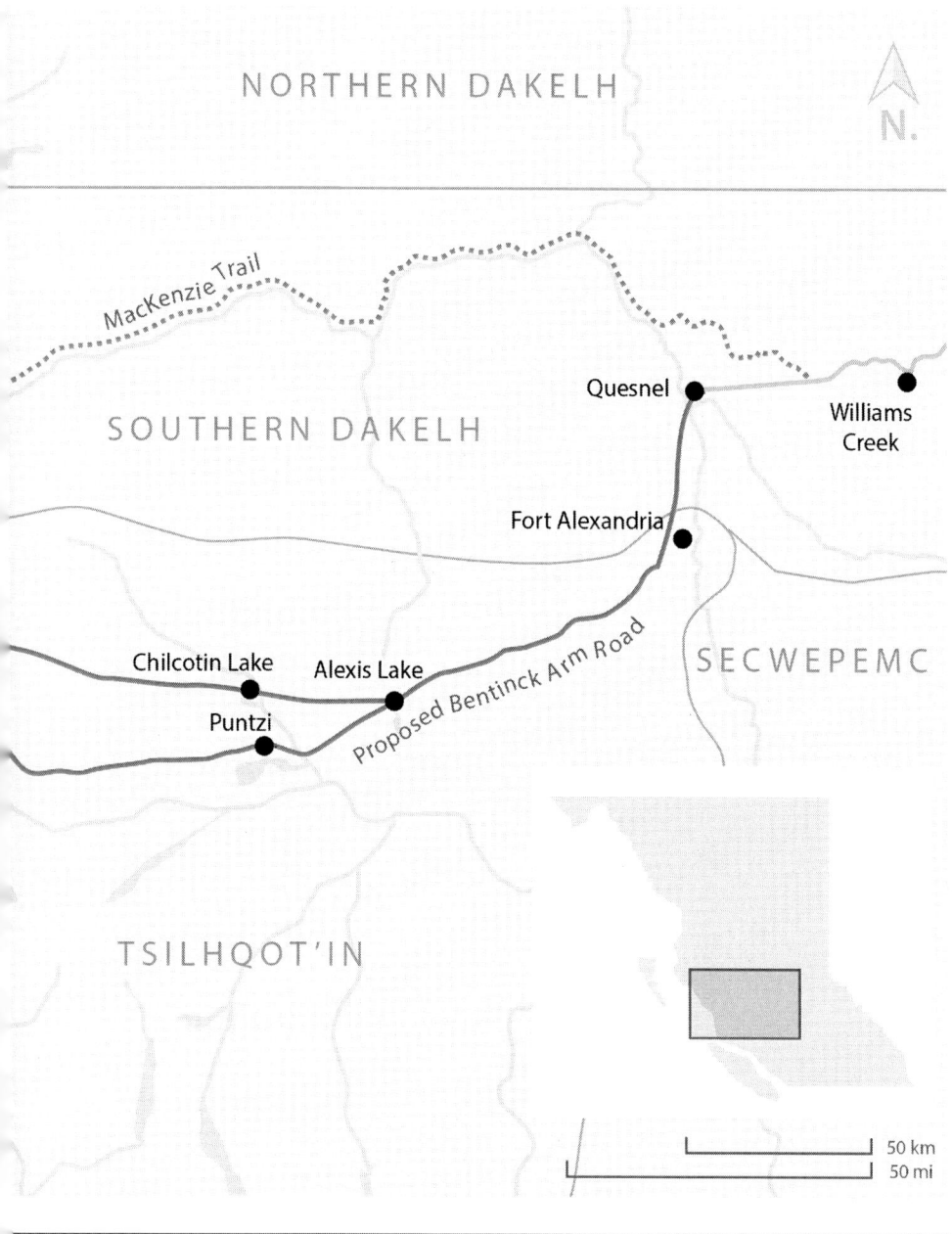

NORTHERN DAKELH

N.

MacKenzie Trail

SOUTHERN DAKELH

Quesnel

Williams Creek

Fort Alexandria

Chilcotin Lake

Alexis Lake

Puntzi

Proposed Bentinck Arm Road

SECWEPEMC

TSILHQOT'IN

50 km
50 mi

The Nuxalk Ancestors Before 1862

Before the artificial epidemics of 1862, the Nuxalk Ancestors, a unique autonomous People sharing a language and a common oral literature, occupied their territory in long-standing population clusters situated to capitalize on the rivers emptying into their inlets.

From the first hand estimates of settlers for the lower Bella Coola valley alone, and from the 45 or so villages identified by anthropologists, their number most probably exceeded 12,000.

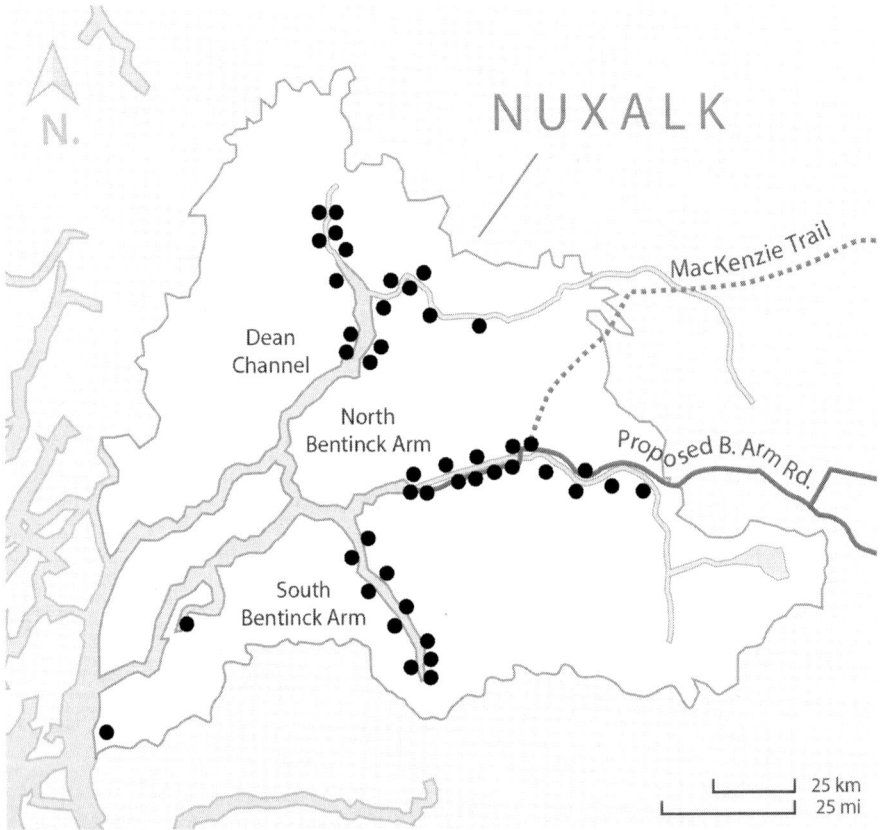

Note: Locations are approximate based on local traditions and F. McIlwraith, The Bella Coola Indians. 2 Vols. University of Toronto Press, 1948.

Staltmc Pootlass, High Chief at Q'umk'uts

Staltmc Pootlass was the widely-respected hereditary leader of Q'umk'uts. Pootlass received prospective road builders and those showing an intention of taking up residence with honor as guests. Initially, Pootlass supervised the provision of native packers and other services for miners arriving at Bella Coola. From the scale of the sudden catastrophe due to the artificial epidemics created by Poole's party, Pootlass immediately recognized the need for pulling together people from previously distinct communities for strength.

Pootlass met Lt. Henry Spencer Palmer in the first official approach made by the Colony to the sovereign authorities in Nuxalk territory. He also met Governor Frederick Seymour onboard a British warship carrying more men-at-arms than there were survivors in the Lower Valley. The lesson was not lost on Pootlass. He supplied a small force of warriors for the Governor's invasion of Tsilhqot'in territory, though these soon melted away to leave only a token force. Pootlass eventually undertook a series of marriage alliances with other communities to aid in the preservation, survival and eventual re-establishment of the Nuxalk throughout their traditional territory.

A Coastal Route to the Interior and Canada

In 1860, Attorney General George Cary led a colonial syndicate seeking a coastal route to connect Victoria with the Interior and Canada via the Nuxalk and Tsilhqot'in territories, bypassing the "Fraser River settlements." At that time, no Colonial official had visited these territories yet to negotiate some understanding with the Crown or for access to land.

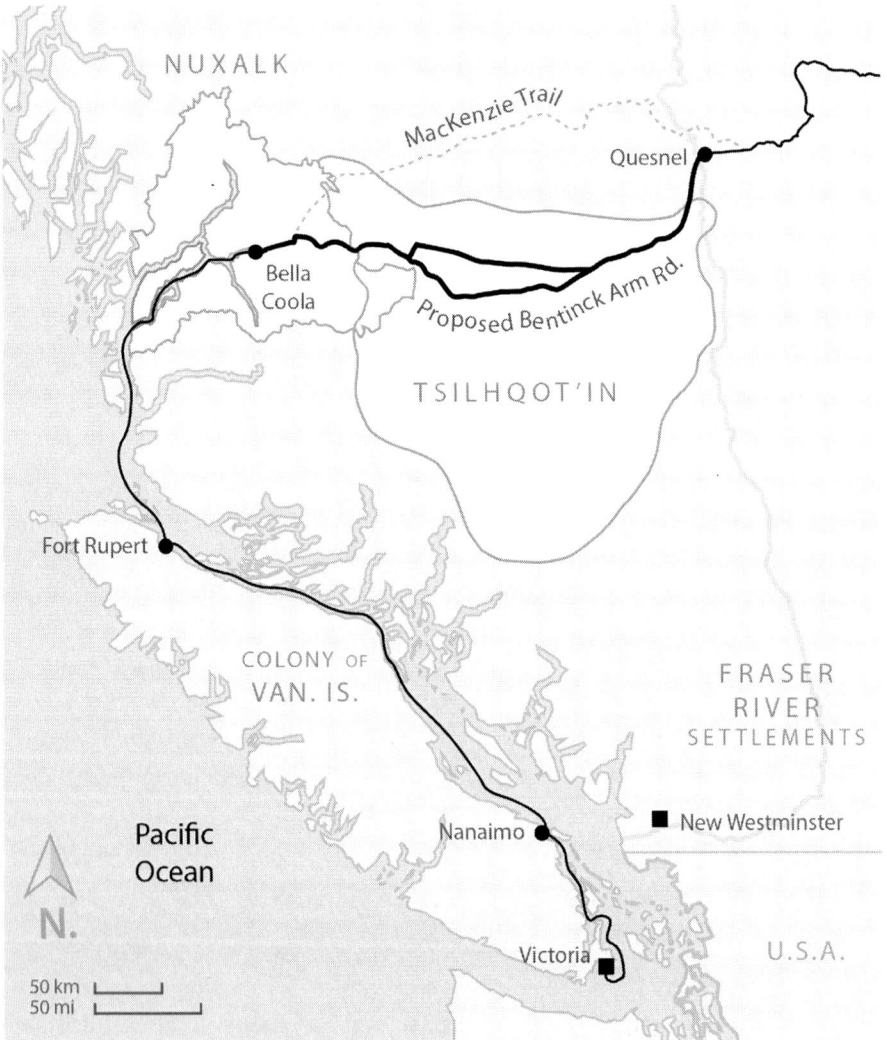

Attorney General George Hunter Cary

An M.L.A. for Victoria, Attorney General George Cary was first minister in the Vancouver Island Assembly and the Douglas Regime's highest legal officer. Cary led the New Aberdeen syndicate as it staked the land under Q'umk'uts, oversaw a steamship subsidy committee designed to increase traffic on Cary's coastal route, and created the Bentinck Arm Road Company.

Smallpox arrived in the colonies on the first sailing arranged by Cary's steamship committee. Asserting that there was "no Indian settlement," Cary sought registration of New Aberdeen's claim to allow the sale of lots at Bella Coola in early June 1862. In what seems improbable as coincidence, also in early June 1862, Bentinck Arm Road Company agents knowingly introduced smallpox along Cary's proposed coastal route and at Bella Coola. Cary's claim of "no Indian settlement" almost literally came true as, after just one month, an eyewitness estimated the Bella Coola death toll already at 75 percent. Suffering a brain disorder, Cary was certified insane in 1865 and died in 1866.

Nuxalk Villages at North Bentinck Arm

Nuxalk traditions and Cavendish Venables' Sept. 1861 map agree on the notable features found at the mouth of the Bella Coola River before June 1862 and the smallpox epidemics.

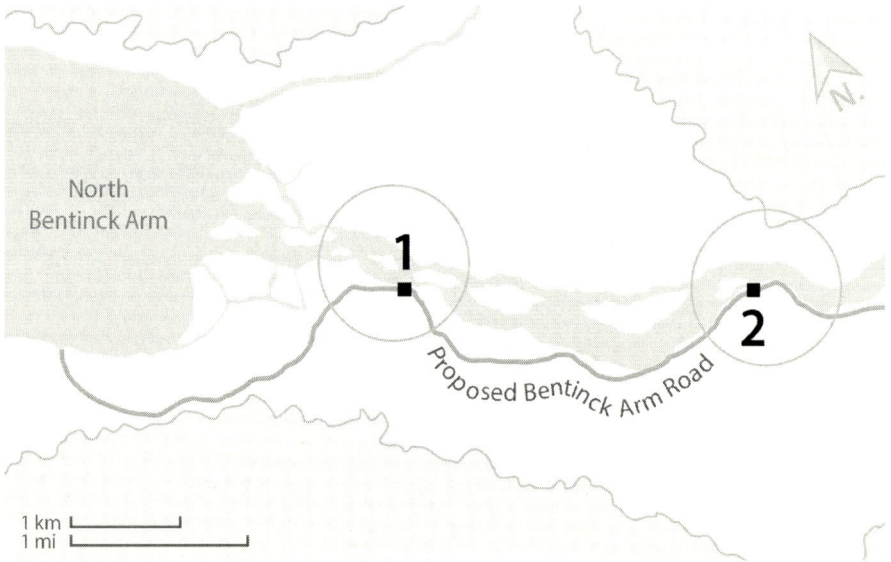

North
Bentinck Arm

1

2

Proposed Bentinck Arm Road

1 km
1 mi

1
Q'umk'uts

2
Soonochlim (Snxlhh)

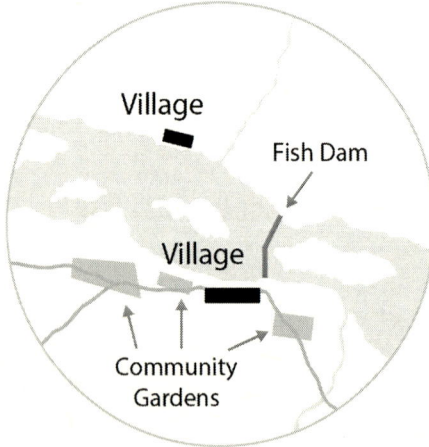

Village

Fish Dam

Village

Community
Gardens

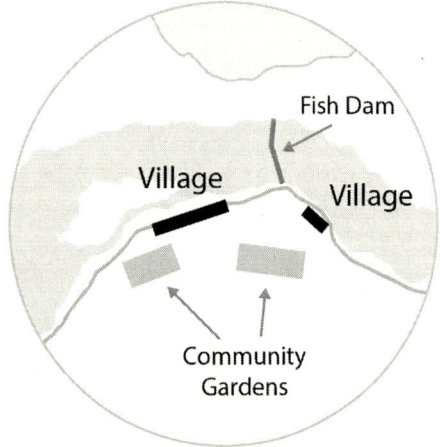

Fish Dam

Village

Village

Community
Gardens

Source: BCARS Map of Cavendish Venables, Sept. 30, 1861, CM-B91.

Cary: There is no Indian Settlement

In early June 1862, Attorney General George Cary claimed that his clients, through a crown grant, had a fee simple title to all the land at the mouth of the Bella Coola River. Fee simple titles imply a right to vacant possession and exclusive enjoyment.

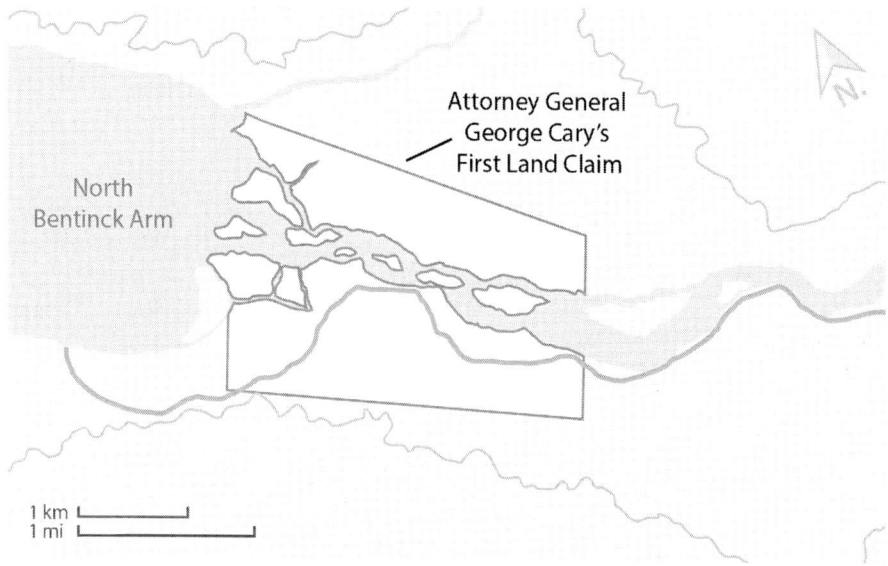

Cary's claim that Q'umk'uts was vacant in his own hand.

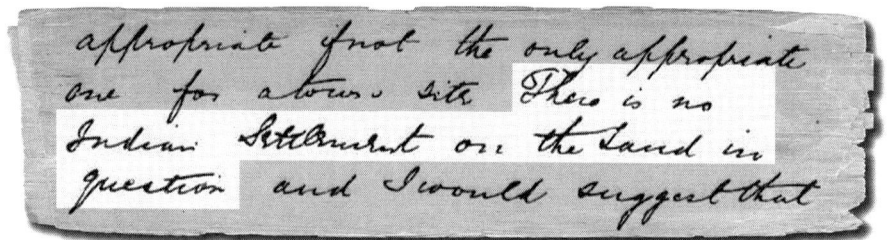

In early June 1862, agents of Cary's Bentinck Arm Co. began knowingly introducing smallpox here. By November, the 2000 to 4000 residents had become a few dozen. Survivors could be forced onto reserves easily, creating vacant land.

Source: BCARS. GR-1372 B.C. Colonial Correspondence. F275 George Hunter Cary to Henry Crease, June 4, 1862, delivered at New Westminster June 11.

Claims Staked at Bella Coola Before Smallpox

1. Barney Johnson
2. Jim Taylor
3. Cavendish Venables
4. John Miles*

5. Robert Miles*
6. Duncan Mackay*
7. Herbert Lewis*
8. Pat Mackay*

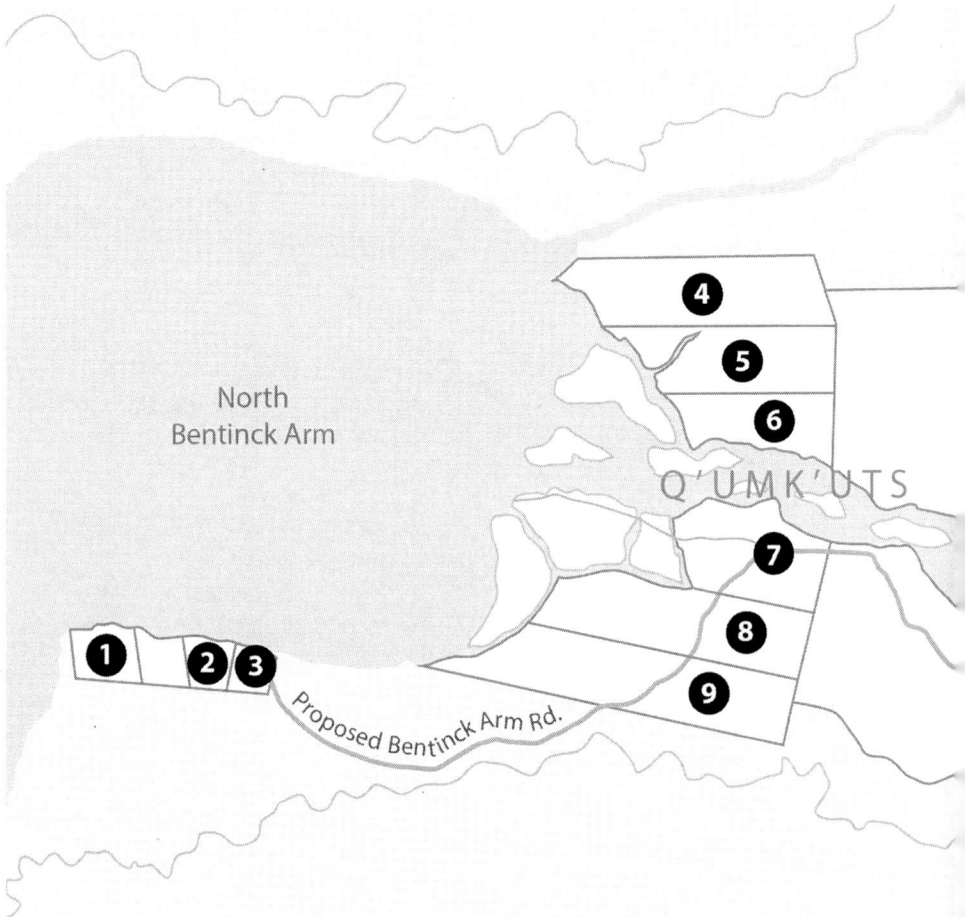

Source: BCARS B.C. Dept. of Lands and Works, Cariboo, Lytton and Lillooet, Preemption Records, taken by P. Nind & T. Elwyn, Alexandria Dist., 1860 to 1863, Folder 1.

 9. William Murray*
10. Cavendish Venables
11. McLeod[†]
12. Dennis Cain

13. McDonald[†]

* Nos. 4-9 the second claim by
  George Cary's syndicate.

[†] Given name unknown.

SOONOCHILM
(SNXLHH)

1 km
1 mi

Source: BCARS Map of Cavendish Venables, Sept. 30, 1861, CM-B91.

Passage of Poole's Party Carrying Smallpox

Before Nuxalk territory, the documentary record has Poole's party leaving smallpox carriers at Nanaimo and Fort Rupert, and, afterward, at Chilcotin Lake. The evidence is that Poole's party spread smallpox to all these villages on these dates.

1. **Tallyu** June 4/5, 1862
2. **Q'umk'uts** June 5/6 and 9-15
3. **Kimsquit** June 7-9
4. **Soonochlim (Snxlhh)** June 15
5. **Nookeetz** June 15

6. **Asananny** June 15/16
7. **Nooskult (Nusq'ist)** June 16/17
8. **Nautlieff (Nutl'lhiixw's)** June 17
9. **Stuie** June 18

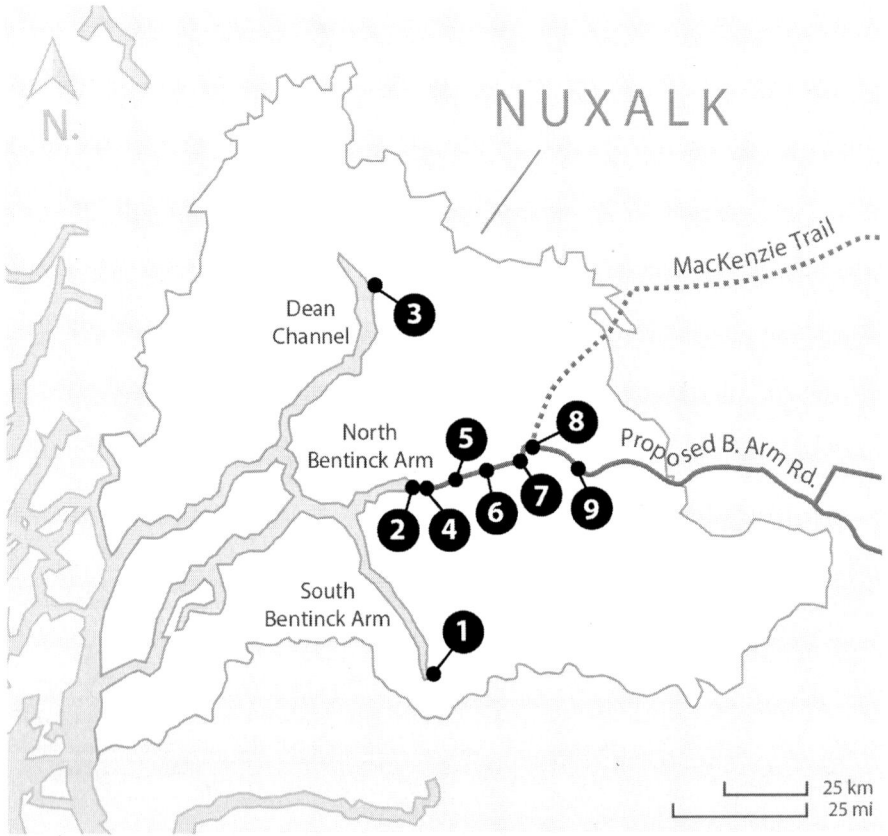

Sources: See Chapter 12.

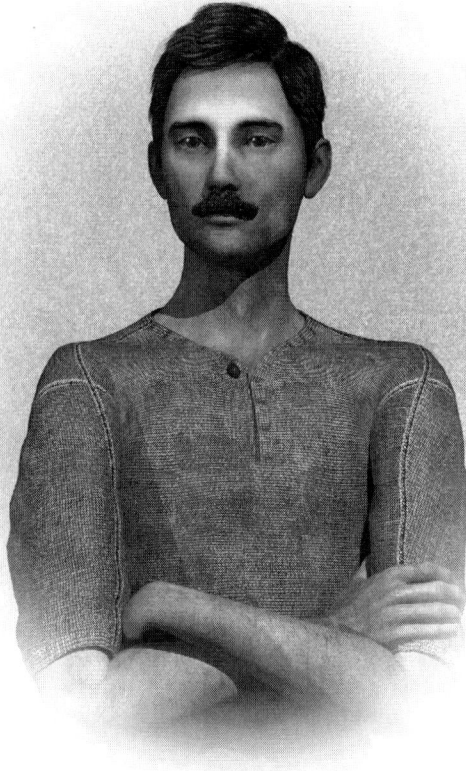

Francis Poole, Expedition Leader

Francis Poole, 26, arrived in the Pacific Colonies on May 13, 1862 with little experience, nearly broke, without friends or relatives and desperate for work. As the Douglas Regime expelled healthy and smallpox-infected natives alike by the hundreds to spread the disease up and down the coast, Poole found employment that he would describe later as of an "unwonted" nature and from which he would have "shrunk back appalled" except for an "unwise precipitancy" due to his circumstances.

Poole would "head" a party that admittedly and knowingly introduced smallpox at strategic locations along the Bentinck Arm Company's proposed coastal route and at Bella Coola where the same interests needed to remove natives from land to which they had staked claims. Thousands died in these artificial epidemics. Poole then found new employment with the Queen Charlotte Copper Mining Company. After a second trip to Bella Coola, a smallpox carrier would accompany Poole to southern Haida Gwaii and become the source of epidemics that would devastate the native population now to the benefit of his second employer.

Colonel Moody's Land Freeze

Before the 1862 smallpox epidemics, Ancestral families, the *Smayusta* and the Staltmc were the legitimate sovereign authority in this autonomous territory.

Coincident with Attorney General Cary's planning, Governor James Douglas and Colonel Richard Moody also began disposing of land at Q'umk'uts without treaties or consulting the true legitimate authorities.

Colonel Moody's objective in freezing private land development on the Ancestor's land at Bella Coola and Kimsquit was to preserve strategic land for the colonial government's use and for orderly urbanization in the most suitable locations.

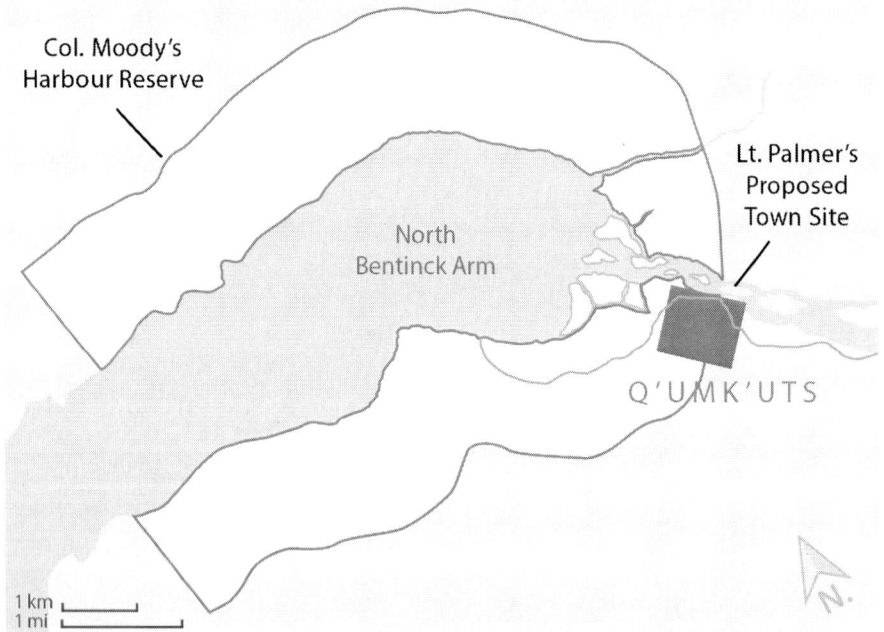

Source: As advertised in "Public Notice" *The British Colonist*, April 8, 1862, p.4.

Governor Douglas' Policy, Theory and Practice

In March 1862, Governor Douglas instructed Colonel Moody to create 300 acre buffer zones around all indigenous villages in the Colony on a model to be instituted at North Bentinck Arm.

Four months later, after the introduction of smallpox, Douglas gave oral instructions to Lt. Palmer before his visit to North Bentinck Arm. Rather than 300 acre reserves, Palmer proposed Q'umk'uts' final dispossession and the relocation of survivors.

All these Colonial actions were provocations of war. Settlers well-understood the need to anticipate violence over dispossessing native communities. The unlawful, knowing and convenient introduction of smallpox by agents for Cary's enterprises left the legitimate authorities here incapable of using official violence in self-defence against colonial encroachment.

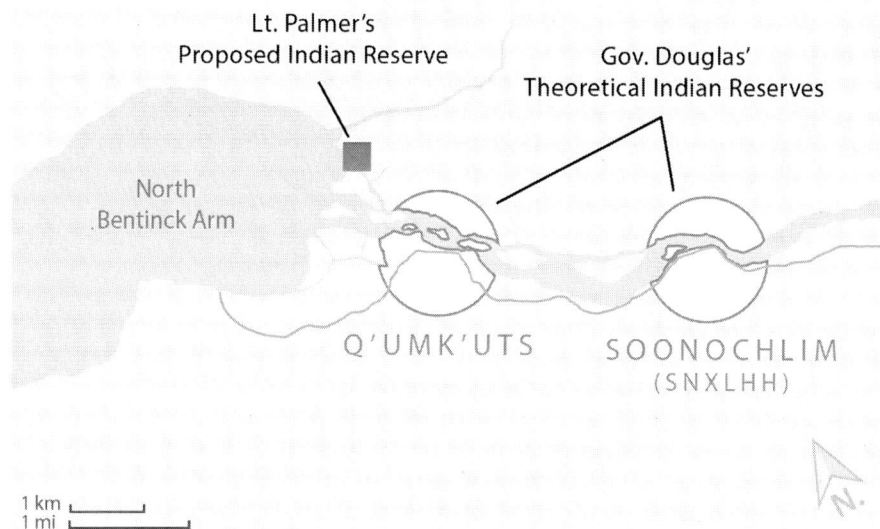

Lt. Palmer's
Proposed Indian Reserve
Gov. Douglas'
Theoretical Indian Reserves
North
Bentinck Arm
Q'UMK'UTS
SOONOCHLIM
(SNXLHH)

1 km
1 mi

Sources: See Chapter 14.

TIMELINE

Date	Non-indigenous community	Indigenous community or territory
June 14, 1846	Nuxalk territory has been continuously occupied for several thousand years. On June 14, 1846, the Ancestors of today's Nuxalk were the sovereign authority here. The governing regime drew on the *Smayusta* for its constitutional form and to channel official authority. The citizens delegated the legitimate exercise of power to ancestral families. The public duties of leadership were carried out, or were directed by, the Staltmc, who also served as spokesman for their ancestral families in diplomatic relations with other political entities.	
June 15, 1846	Great Britain and the United States sign the Oregon Treaty. As of 2016, Supreme Court of Canada decisions date Canada's sovereign interest in Nuxalk territory from here. Since the Ancestors were not a party to this treaty, it can only have indicated the Crown's desire to approach them later for some sort of relationship.	After June 15, 1846, the Nuxalk Ancestors remained the sovereign power in Nuxalk territory. The *Smayusta* remained the constitutional source of law. The Staltmc continued with their constitutional role. Nothing had changed.
Jan. 13, 1849	Great Britain creates the Colony of Vancouver Island as the medium through which the Crown will approach the indigenous People there. With its regional headquarters at Victoria, the H.B.C. will dominate this Colony.	The Colony of Vancouver Island does not touch Nuxalk territory. The Ancestors travel to trade with the H.B.C. in Heiltsuk territory, or receive boat-based door-to-door salesmen.
Aug. 2, 1858	Great Britain creates the Colony of British Columbia. This was done to protect the national status of its subjects with commercial operations in the "Fraser River settlements" vis-a-vis the United States.	There were no British subjects in Nuxalk territory. Without notice or consultation with the resident citizenry, B.C.'s mere creation in London cannot have created any constitutional change in this separate and autonomous territory.

Date	Non-indigenous community	Indigenous community or territory
Nov. 17, 1858	James Douglas becomes Governor of British Columbia. The Douglas Regime begins a no treaty policy. This Regime will begin asserting control over indigenous territories one by one without consent from those to be governed. It will begin asserting control over their resources by considering everything as, suddenly somehow, the Crown's land to do as it will. Fictional "waste land" will be made available for redistribution to settlers without compensation to the indigenous title holders and the prior residents will become confined on small reserves.	The Ancestors remained the sovereign power in Nuxalk territory. The Staltmc remained as the head of government. Douglas had no official status in Nuxalk territory, except as the Crown's representative appointed to approach the Nuxalk through the Staltmc for some relationship and access to resources. The Nuxalk lived in permanent villages with land under cultivation in community gardens. They had other forms of organized harvesting and exported manufactured goods, like fish oil. There was no vacant land anywhere here.
Jan. 4, 1860	Douglas Regime issues a Land Proclamation concerning the Colony of British Columbia. This Proclamation will be used as authority by the Attorney General of B.C., as he then was, George Cary, in claiming land at Q'umk'uts and the mouth of the Bella Coola River. Cary was also the first minister, or Premier, in the Vancouver Island Assembly. His activities in Nuxalk territory will be quasi-public initiatives to further Vancouver Island public policy.	Douglas neither consulted, gained the consent of the citizens nor gave the Nuxalk any notice of this Proclamation. Without a treaty, he had no jurisdiction through the rule of law to apply his Proclamations in this territory: not to the citizens and not to the land.

Date	Non-indigenous community	Indigenous community or territory
Apr. 4, 1860	Concerned about New Westminster diminishing Victoria's dominance in the British Pacific Northwest, important interests in the Colony of Vancouver Island begin considering alternatives to the Fraser River for access to the B.C. hinterland and for a transcontinental road to distant Canada. This included river valleys in the Ancestors' territory.	April 4, 1860 is the earliest date referred to by a colonial court as marking creation of the New Aberdeen syndicate or for the Crown deeding to it 1600 acres at Q'umk'uts, a prospective harbor for a road inland via the Bella Coola valley. Attorney General George Cary controls the New Aberdeen syndicate.
Sept. 2, 1860	Edward Green leads a New Aberdeen party from Victoria to stake land at Q'umk'uts at the mouth of the Bella Coola River on North Bentinck Arm. His party will also stake prospective harbors at Tallyu on South Bentinck Arm and at Kimsquit on the Dean River.	
Jan. 29, 1861	Concerned about an "Indian war" when settlers arrive onsite to take up land sold to them by colonial governments, the Vancouver Island Assembly petitions the Imperial government to purchase "Indian title" in the Pacific Northwest.	Whatever the English legal theory about "Indian title" might be, it is only the law of the land that matters as long as the established system of goverance retains its *de facto* power.
Mar. 17, 1861	Attorney General Cary and M.L.A. Robert Burnaby oversee creation of a "Steamship Committee" to lobby the Governor for a public subsidy to drive traffic from San Francisco to Victoria and then along a coastal route inland via Nuxalk territory.	
Apr. 19, 1861	New Aberdeen files alternative pre-emption claims in the Colony of British Columbia to land in the Q'umk'uts and Kimsquit precincts.	

Date	Non-indigenous community	Indigenous community or territory
Apr. 1861		New Aberdeen agents James Kenny and Colin Mackenzie leave Ft. Alexandria to negotiate the Ancestors' and Tsilhqot'in permission for a Bentinck Arm road along one of the several "Indian trails" from Nuxalk territory through Tsilhqot'in territory to the Fraser River.
May 7, 1861		With Tsilhqot'in permission seemingly granted in meetings overseen by Nits'il?in Anaham at Nagwentlun, a party of nine Tsilhqot'in accompanies Kenny and Mackenzie to Q'umk'uts.
May 13, 1861		Staltmc Pootlass provides "a grand feast" for the Tsilhqot'in and New Aberdeen agents at Q'umk'uts. Every visitor reports the Ancestors as inviting the establishment of a road and the ancilliary services. Kenny and Mackenzie leave by boat. Ansini War Chief Solyman accompanies them and remains in Victoria until the start of the 1862 season. He will become "fluent" in English.
May 24, 1861		Ranald McDonald and George Barnston leave Ft. Alexandria for Tsilhqot'in and Nuxalk territories, also investigating the possibilities for a road.

Date	Non-indigenous community	Indigenous community or territory
June 10, 1861		After two days of meetings with Anaham at Nagwentlun, where they report finding the Tsilhqot'in as cautious, McDonald and Barnston receive a guide for the trail to Q'umk'uts where Pootlass will provide another feast.
Jul. 12, 1861		McDonald and Barnston return to Ft. Alexandria accompanied by Nits'il?in Alexis and Lhats'as?in.
Jul. 18, 1861		Alexis and Lhats'as?in meet with representatives from Klus Kus and other southern Dakelh communities. This conference is certain to have concerned the advent of a road from Bentinck Arm. Whatever issues may have been canvassed here, in 1862 miners receive safe passage and were offered other services.
Jul. 31, 1861	Without consulting the Ancestors, the Tsilhqot'in or the Commissioner for Lands and Works, or considering other proposals, Governor Douglas grants a Charter to Ranald McDonald to collect tolls in Nuxalk territory on a mule trail from Bentinck Arm to the Fraser, later to be upgraded as a road. McDonald has one year to meet its conditions.	
Jul. 1861	The New Aberdeen syndicate sends Jim Taylor and Angus McLeod to take up residence at Bella Coola and protect its interests from claim jumpers. Taylor is also captain of the *Petrel*, a ship engaged in the illegal furs-for-liquor trade.	

Date	Non-indigenous community	Indigenous community or territory
Sept. 1861		A New Aberdeen party including Kenny and Cavendish Venables crosses from Ft. Alexandria to North Bentinck Arm. Merchant Denis Cain stakes the first settler's land claim in Tsilhqot'in territory at Chilcotin Lake. At Bella Coola, Cain stakes the land under Soonochlim, the village next upriver, about the same size as Q'umk'uts, as many as 2000 people. The "fee simple" titles promised by the Colonial land statute contemplate that the land will be vacant when title is issued.
Sept. 1861		Cavendish Venables stakes land at Q'umk'uts and the Dean River. He prepares a map showing all claims for several kilometers up the Bella Coola valley. Venables and Kenny remain in Nuxalk territory scouting locations until January.
Nov. 1861		Dr. J.B. Wilkinson files claim to land in the Tallyu community's precinct at South Bentinck Arm. Tallyu is a separate ancestral area and another large population center.
Nov. 1861	George Cary and Edward Green buy McDonald's Charter. They promise him a substantial minority interest in a Bentinck Arm Company and a directorship.	

Date	Non-indigenous community	Indigenous community or territory
Jan. 1862	George Cary, the steamship committee and Ranald McDonald visit San Francisco to arrange for a shipping line to provide a ship and collect the subsidy for a direct sailing. Cary also arranges for a direct sailing from Victoria to Bella Coola. Alexander Wallace is to become Bella Coola agent. Cary returns Jan. 12 but most of the committee remains to promote the road. Cary is positioned as the greatest personal beneficiary of this public subsidy.	
Mar. 5, 1862	Governor Douglas writes elaborate instructions for 300 acre buffer zones around all places of indigenous occupation in British Columbia on a model at North Bentinck Arm.	
Mar. 12, 1862	The steamship committee and Ranald McDonald return from San Francisco on the first subsidized sailing. The ship also brings two smallpox carriers. Smallpox was not epidemic in San Francisco. These will become the only outside source of the disease that will decimate the indigenous population of the colonies over the next 12 months. A man returning to San Francisco on this ship tells a newspaper that Bentinck Arm lots will be all the rage in a few months.	

Date	Non-indigenous community	Indigenous community or territory
Mar. 21, 1862	The public becomes advised that: 1) the Imperial government refused to purchase "Indian title" in the Pacific Northwest as a means of preventing "Indian wars"; 2) the Imperial government was sending 500 rifles for use by Colonial militias; and 3) the smallpox carriers arriving in the steamship committee's presence had begun the disease among the indigenous population at Victoria.	
Mar. 1862		New Aberdeen pays Bob McLeod to create a wharf at Bella Coola. This is the first step in creating a road. McLeod is also set to become the first non-indigenous packer on the Bentinck Arm route. McLeod refuses to pay the tax for access to territorial benefits. It was reported later that he came to blows with Ansini War Chief Solyman over the tax, which settlers sometimes refer to as "blackmail."
Mar. 27, 1862	Colonel Moody unilaterally reserves land at the mouth of the Bella Coola and Dean Rivers, effectively freezing New Aberdeen's progress. This action was taken without official contact, consultation or consent from the sovereign authorities in Nuxalk territory. As such, it was a provocation of war.	
Apr. 5, 1862	George Cary publishes the Bentinck Arm and Fraser River Road Company *Prospectus*.	

Date	Non-indigenous community	Indigenous community or territory
Apr. 20, 1862	Inconvenienced by Moody's action of March 27, Cary advises the B.C. government at New Westminster of New Aberdeen's intention to sell town lots at Q'umk'uts in "the early part of June." The fee simple titles that will be promised to purchasers imply vacant possession.	
May 12, 1862	Pearson leaves Victoria with the first half of 40 men whose passage the Bentinck Arm Co. will guarantee as a promotional gimmick. The Company pays Pearson to mark its route.	
May 21, 1862	Francis Poole leaves Victoria leading the second half of the Bentinck Arm Company's 40 men. His party will carry smallpox along the length of the coastal route and to Nuxalk territory.	
May 30, 1862		McDonald and Pearson leave Bella Coola marking the Company's proposed road route for the rest of Pearson's party and Poole's party to follow. Pearson will stake 480 acres in the precinct of a large Tsilhqot'in village at Chilcotin Lake along the way.
June 4, 1862	It is now "early June." To advance New Aberdeen's proposed sale of town lots, Cary prepares a letter asserting that there is "no Indian Settlement" of concern regarding its claim at Bella Coola. The purchasers of fee simple titles have a legal right under the Colonial system to vacant possession. Indigenous residents living on land that purchasers expect to be vacant is well known as the usual cause of "Indian wars." The population of Q'umk'uts on this date may have been 2000.	

Date	Non-indigenous community	Indigenous community or territory
June 5/6, 1862	Poole's party arrives at the mouth of the Bella Coola River where it will introduce smallpox at Q'umk'uts, the indigenous village most concerned in New Aberdeen's claim and Cary's endeavors on behalf of Vancouver Island. Poole eventually will take responsibility for the disease among "the tribes" at the mouth of the Bella Coola River, generally along North and South Bentinck Arm and elsewhere along the coastal route. Within a matter of weeks, the indigenous population here will have an insufficient number to provoke any "Indian war."	
June 11/12, 1862	Cary hand delivers his letter of June 4 and confronts B.C. government officials over registration of New Aberdeen's claim at Bella Coola. These officials agree to send Lt. Henry Palmer to assess Bella Coola as a harbor and the Bentinck Arm Company's route.	
June 15, 1862		Poole's party leaves Bella Coola. Passes through Nookeetz where "almost all" then die of smallpox.
June 15-17, 1862		Poole's party passes Asananny and Nooskulst/Nusq'lst, which Palmer reports as deserted and Brough as dead from smallpox.
June 17, 1862		Poole's party leaves two smallpox carriers at Nautlieff/Nutl'lhiix A third carrier who probably originated with his party would be identified later at Stuie/Stuwic. Under English law, it is a crime to "incautiously" expose the public to a contagious disease. By Poole's own admissions, his party engaged in criminal activity here. The issue is which crime: mass murder or genocide?

Date	Non-indigenous community	Indigenous community or territory
June 23, 1862	Palmer receives oral instructions from Douglas. In due course, contrary to his written orders and contrary to Douglas' written policy of March, Palmer will not mark out 300 acre reserves protecting each indigenous settlement in the Ancestors' territory, or any reserves at all. This is a sign that the written record is an unreliable guide to the actual policies of the Douglas Regime. Palmer will leave Victoria with the head of the Vancouver Island Militia, M.L.A. Colonel George Foster and Bentinck Arm Company road contractor William Hood.	
June 27/28, 1862		Poole's party arrives at Chilcotin Lake. Poole would later admit that it then sent two smallpox carriers into the large Tsilhqot'in village here. Simply "incautiously" exposing the public to a contagious disease is a crime by English law. This action is much worse.
July 2, 1862	Palmer, Foster and Hood arrive at Bella Coola. They all remark on the great number of Nuxalk already dying. Palmer says the disease had broken out only the week before. Foster later estimates the dead and dying as 1500 out of 2000. This is the number at Bella Coola alone; that is, without considering the other Ancestral populatons centers also visted by Poole's party.	
July 3, 1862	First ever meeting between officials of the Crown and Nuxalk spokesmen. Palmer meets with Pootlass in a crisis after Palmer's party broke an undertaking to respect the law of the land. The smallpox devastation is so astonishing after mere days that Pootlass already has seen the necessity of "Nuxalk" or drawing together survivors. Outnumbered still by the Nuxalk with weapons, Palmer does not assert the Crown's sovereign control. He pacifies the Nuxalk with promises about the Crown's intentions that he does not report.	

Date	Non-indigenous community	Indigenous community or territory
July 4, 1862		Poole arrives at Ft. Alexandria after being "in hourly dread of attack by hostile savages" for five or six days. As the beginning of settler hostilities, this is the earliest documented reaction leading to the Chilcotin War.
Mid-July 1862		As it begins following the Bentinck Arm route up the Bella Coola Valley, Palmer's party passes deserted villages where the residents already all have died. Later, John Brough will confirm that smallpox was the cause of death.
Mid-July 1862		Bentinck Arm Company road contractor William Hood arrives at Nautlieff. His party stakes claims to hundreds of acres in this ancestral precinct while the residents are still dying.
July 22, 1862	Poole arrives back in the British colonies. Within the next two weeks he will meet with Governor Douglas. And he will be rewarded with employment for which he is little qualified for a company controlled by M.L.A. Robert Burnaby, who was also a director of the Bentinck Arm Company.	

Date	Non-indigenous community	Indigenous community or territory
Oct. 1862		Settlers begin new artificial epidemics in Nuxalk territory. Jim Taylor, Angus McLeod, Alexander Wallace and John McLain each will become variously accused by other settlers of using smallpox blankets. All these came to Nuxalk territory as agents or associates of Attorney General Cary's enterprises. Later, McLain will admit to using a smallpox blanket at Tatla Lake on his way to Bella Coola. The Colonial government takes no action in any of these cases.
Mid-Nov. 1862		A Q'umk'uts family apparently suffering from smallpox, tracks, kills and burns Bentinck Arm Company surveyor James Fisher 10 km along the trail from Bella Coola to Nautlieff.
March 1863		The smallpox epidemics end. From first hand observations made in June and November, Francis Poole said those at the mouth of the Bella Coola River were reduced from 4000 to a few dozens. The indigenous death toll in Nuxalk territory as a whole is difficult to quantify. However, it is a certainty that the political integrity and *de facto* capabilities of the old regime had been crippled. The established constitution and the law of the land remained in effect only from inertia.

Date	Non-indigenous community	Indigenous community or territory
Early March 1863		Ansini War Chief Solyman executes Bob McLeod where he is wintering along the Bentinck Arm Road near Nagwentlun in Tsilhqot'in territory.
April 1863	Staltmc Pootlass refuses to surrender those who killed Fisher for trial in the colonial system.	
May 1863	Settlers complain of the Nuxalk creating provocations that make them feel unwelcome. This seems a sign of withdrawing the consent for a non-indigenous presence granted in 1861.	
May 4, 1863	Settlers in Nuxalk territory petition Governor Douglas to assert Colonial control, citing the deaths of Fisher and McLeod. Douglas eventually sends a gunboat to Bella Coola but to little satisfaction among settlers.	
Nov. 3, 1863		As Venables abandons his claim, the Nuxalk destroy the house that was a token of his occupancy.
April 28-30, 1864	The Tsilhqot'in kill 14 settlers at Bute Inlet to prevent the creation of new artificial smallpox epidemics in their territory.	
May 30, 1864	Along the Bentinck Arm Road, the Tsilhqot'in kill four settlers in connection with the intentional introduction of smallpox at Puntzi in 1862. Five innocent settlers are allowed to return to Bella Coola. All settlers leave the Bella Coola Valley for the harbor. The Tsilhqot'in invite the Nuxalk to join them in closing the Bentinck Arm Road.	
June 18, 1864	On his way to invade Tsilhqot'in territory with a militia, Governor Fredrick Seymour from British Columbia, still a foreign entity vis-a-vis Nuxalk territory, arrives at Bella Coola on the Admiral's flagship. This was the largest warship in the British Pacific fleet. It fires its canon in an intimidating display of readiness for organized violence. Its complement is said to be 800, including 500 men-at-arms. Staltmc Pootlass is taken on board to meet British officials.	

Date	Non-indigenous community	Indigenous community or territory
June 19, 1864	Governor Seymour enrolls 30 Nuxalk warriors in his militia. Twenty will have "deserted" by June 30. The rest provide little material assistance to the Colony in the Chilcotin War, except in helping the militia to leave.	
Sept. 28, 1864		The Nuxalk conduct a dance program at Q'umk'uts, sending the militia away with some ceremony.
Oct. 30, 1864		A Nuxalk contingent visits Ft. Alexandria, apparently on its return from honoring the "Chilcotin Chiefs" martyred Oct. 26 at Quesnel.
Jan. 2, 1865	A Colonial "Indian Agent" meets the Staltmc in council. He asserts a sovereign right in the Crown for a monopoly on the official use of violence in Nuxalk territory. *De facto* public actions by the Staltmc now run the actual risk for prosecution as criminal violations of Colonial law. The imposition of a new constitution and the accretion of Nuxalk territory to become part of British Columbia can be dated from here. If one includes Pootlass' dialogue with Palmer, this was accomplished through fraud, smallpox used as a weapon and the threat of overwhelming conventional violence.	
May 11, 1865	While attempting to enforce Colonial law or collect duties at Bella Coola from a smallpox survivor trading between Heiltsuk and Nuxalk territories, the Colonial Indian Agent is shot and killed on a boat offshore at North Bentinck Arm.	

About the Author

Dr. Tom Swanky, J.D. is a life-long student of political philosophy, history and Canadian government.

Born at the Quesnel hospital beside the burial ground of the "Chilcotin Chiefs," Dr. Swanky first learned that the indigenous Elders' version of B.C.'s founding varies greatly from the authorized version taught in classrooms through hearing traditional knowledge concerning the hanging of the "Chilcotin Chiefs."

Since consistency is the virtue of truth, Dr. Swanky eventually embarked on a decade long odyssey through the non-indigenous documentary record to discover whether the Elders' version of B.C.'s founding could be reconciled with these sources as the foundation for a unified version of this history.

The Smallpox War in Nuxalk Territory continues and expands on the Nuxalk territory part of the account first published in Dr. Swanky's, *Canada's 'War' of Extermination on the Pacific. Plus the Tsilhqot'in and Other First Nations Resistance.*

Canada's 'War' of Extermination also serves as the source of a screenplay for a documentary film in production by Shawn Swanky, *The Great Darkening.*

Dr. Swanky has also explored the great disparity between accounts of B.C.'s founding in *A Missing Genocide and the Demonization of its Heroes*, a review of "Klatsassin and the Chilcotin War," a University of Victoria sponsored work hosted at www.canadianmysteries.ca.

Canada's 'War' of Extermination on the Pacific, A Missing Genocide and a version of *The Great Darkening* screenplay are all available for purchase at www.shawnswanky.com.

Select Bibliography

Behrens, Paul. "The *mens rea* of genocide," in Eds. Paul Behrens and Ralph Henham, *Elements of Genocide*. New York: Routlege, 2013: 70 to 97.

Brough, John. Ed. Sheila MacIntosh, *Diaries of John Brough in British Columbia*. Unpublished manuscript, see BCARS Add MSS 2796.

Cary, George Hunter. *Prospectus of the Bentinck Arm and Fraser River Road Company Ltd.*, Victoria, Printed at the British Colonist, 1862, microfilm identifier cihm 17091.

Doherty, Michael "Recent Developments in Aboriginal Rights and Title cases," Unpublished paper presented at the Aboriginal Law Conference 2009.

Downie, Major William. *Hunting for Gold*. Palo Alto: American West Publishing Company, reprint 1971.

Finch, Lance. *The Duty to Learn: Taking Account of Indigenous Legal Orders in Practice*. Paper presented at the Continuing Legal Education of B.C. Indigenous Legal Orders and the Common Law Conference. Vancouver, Nov. 15, 2012.

Hilland, Andrea. "Extinguishment by Extirpation: The Nuxalk Eulachon Crisis." A thesis submitted in partial fulfillment of the requirements for the degree of Master of Laws in the Faculty of Graduate and Postdoctoral studies (Law), UBC, 2013.

Hopkins, Donald R. *The Greatest Killer: Smallpox in History*. Chicago: University of Chicago Press, 1983.

Helmcken, John Sebastian. *The Reminiscences of Doctor John Sebastian Helmcken*. Ed. Dorothy Blakey Smith. Vancouver: University of British Columbia Press, 1975.

Hyde, Richard. *Regulating Food-borne Illness*. Oxford: Hart Publishing, 2015.

Mack, Jacinda. "Remembering Ista: Nuxalk Perspectives on Sovereignty and Social Change." Project paper in partial fulfillment for the degree of Master of Arts, York, 2006.

McDonald, Ranald. *Ranald MacDonald: the Narrative of his Life 1824-1894*. Portland, Ore: Oregon Historical Press, 1990.

McIlwraith, T.F. *The Bella Coola Indians*. 2 Vol. Toronto: University of Toronto Press, 1948, reissued 1992.

Nuxalk Nation Government, "Nuxalk Nation Position," House of *Smayusta*, Bella Coola, B.C. Sept. 10, 1995.

Palmer, Henry Spencer. *Report of a Journey of Survey, from Victoria to Fort Alexander via North Bentinck Arm*. New Westminster: Royal Engineers Press, 1863.

Poole, Francis. "A year amongst the Indians of Queen Charlotte Island; or, an open field for missionary labour." *Mission Life*, May 1, 1867: 27-35.

Poole, Francis. *Queen Charlotte Islands*. Vancouver: J.J. Douglas reprint, 1972.

Poole, A. F. "Two years amongst the Indians of Queen Charlotte's Island." *Mission Life*, Feb. 1, 1868: 97-107.

Swanky, Tom. *The True Story of Canada's 'War' of Extermination on the Pacific. Plus the Tsilhqot'in and other First Nations Resistance*. www.shawnswanky.com, Dragon Heart, 2012.

Swanky, Tom. *A Missing Genocide and the Demonization of its Heroes*. www.shawnswanky.com. Dragon Heart, 2014.

Webster, Devon. "Bella Coola, A Story to be Told." Unpublished paper circulated by its author.

Whaley, Gray H. *Oregon and the Collapse of Illahee: U.S. Empire and the Transformation of an Indigenous World, 1792-1859*. Chapel Hill: University of North Carolina Press, 2010.